Covering All the Bases

The Ultimate Baseball Handbook

Darren Gurney

ROB,
IT WAS AN INTERESTING EXPERIENCE
COACHING YOU, YOUR TALENT WAS ALWAYS
REMARKABLE, ESPECIALLY THAT PICK-OFF
MOVE AND CURVEBALL.
COACHING WITH YOU IN 2004 WAS
ALSO INTERESTING ... I KNOW THE PLAYERS
LIKED YOU (TOO MUCH OFF THE FIELD)
— COACH Gurney

★ ★ ★ ★ ★
COACHES
≡ **CHOICE**™

ISBN: 978-1-60679-157-8
Library of Congress Control Number: 2011920937
Cover design: Brenden Murphy
Book layout: Bean Creek Studio
Text photos: Daniel Moxey
Copy Editor: Robert Monteleone
Content Editor: Matt La Padula
Cover photo: ©Anthony J. Causi/Icon SMI/ZUMA Press

Coaches Choice
P.O. Box 1828
Monterey, CA 93942
www.coacheschoice.com

For my parents, who provided me with education, opportunities, and exposure to baseball.

Dedication

Acknowledgments

Writing this book required a significant degree of help from the Rising Star Baseball Camp coaching staff. With their patient efforts, thousands of photographs on baseball fundamentals, drills, and mechanics were shot and carefully selected for visual aids. Each year at our various camps and clinics, these coaches work tirelessly to improve the baseball skills among hundreds of adolescent players. Without their work, we would be unable to help place so many aspiring players in high school and college baseball programs around the country.

Daniel Moxey invested dozens of hours of free time in sweltering heat to provide professional, action photographs. His selflessness, sense of humor, and upbeat spirit should be a model for all human beings to emulate.

Rob Monteleone, my close friend and colleague from New Rochelle High School and Iona College, provided a tremendous amount of insight into the writing of this book. With a keen sensitivity to the English language and proper writing mechanics, Rob greatly influenced the final edition.

By analyzing and dissecting hundreds of pages of text, Matt La Padula helped turn this work into a more reader-friendly coaching guide. Blessed with a strong work ethic, passion for baseball, and nose for clean writing, he helped refine this text.

Discussing baseball with Willie McCovey is a joy for me, as it brings back childhood memories of great players from the past. I thank you, Willie, for taking the time and thoughtfulness to write the foreword to this coaching resource.

Coordinating our strength development program with L.I.F.T., Matt Tauber, and Justin Zimmermann has been a fulfilling experience. Thank you for all of your time and efforts in helping our players during the past twelve years.

I thank Coaches Choice and Dr. James Peterson, Megan Comstock, and Angie Perry for working with me on this project and having faith in my work.

Having the opportunity to play for so many different coaches with varied coaching styles and methods helped expose me to developing my own coaching framework. Specifically, Kevin Benzing at Washington University, who delved into the finer nuances of the game, shaped my mindset as a player and coach.

I owe a special thanks to childhood friend John McNiff, who first suggested the notion of writing a book and encouraged me to create a guide for coaches to utilize.

Thanks to my brother Sloan, who is always a source of alternative thinking and innovative ideas.

To all of the enthusiastic players I have been so fortunate to coach, without your love for learning about the great game of baseball and dedicated efforts on the field, I would not have been prompted to write this book.

My wife Toni and son Nolan tolerated the late nights and early mornings that went into producing this book. Like so many great things in my life, I am grateful for Toni and her continual support of my baseball endeavors.

When Coach Gurney called me and mentioned that he was working on an instructional baseball book, I had many thoughts that I wanted to share. Our conversation took me back to some exciting baseball memories and special people on the field. Much of what we spoke about centered on proper fundamentals, effective coaching, player dedication, and just having fun with the game.

Good fundamentals are an extremely important part of all sports, especially the game of baseball. Many players that make it to the big leagues today are physically gifted, but do not have knowledge of the game. I sit at the ballpark and watch young outfielders throw to the wrong base or overthrow the cutoff man. Players today are very talented, but they do not always know the game the way they need to.

There are basics that must be taught early on so players can understand how to play baseball the right way as they move up the line. One of those basics that coaches can help with is hitting fundamentals. This was a great strength of Ted Williams as a teacher. He said that the number-one thing is for players to get a good pitch to hit. Second, players should find a bat that they can handle well. By starting with these two rules, players can give themselves a fighting chance to be an effective hitter.

Coaches should not drastically change baseball mechanics, but instead first look at each player's strengths and weaknesses. I was fortunate to be coached by Hank Sauer, who was a terrific hitting coach. Coach Sauer knew to first evaluate hitters and then focus on their weakest areas. He would sometimes watch my games on TV and then call me at night with pointers so I could fix my swing during batting practice the next day.

Many times, athletes in all sports find out that their weaknesses can later become the strengths of their game once they work on them. Coaches should start off by making observations in each of their players, try to build confidence, and help them pinpoint where they should focus their practice time. You cannot have one system as a coach. You need to be different with every player. Some players may need a boost of confidence or a slight change in their approach, and others may need help in another area. As a coach, don't be a know-it-all. Instead, be open to seeing the whole picture and giving each player what he needs.

Many youth players have a difficult time staying focused on the field. The tough thing about baseball is you never know what is going to happen. You must be alert at all times with the weight on the balls of your feet. You're dead if you are on your heels as a player. You might be standing in the outfield for two days without any balls hit at you when all of a sudden a screaming line drive comes your way. On the infield, players stand closer to the batter and have to be ready. Playing infield and outfield are two different animals, but all players must always be alert. The great players expect the ball to be hit to them on every pitch. All of the spectacular plays that people see on television would not happen if the players did not assume that the ball would be hit in their direction.

I remember one time when I was playing first base, and Joe Morgan of the Cincinnati Reds hit a hard grounder at me with a lot of top spin on the ball. The ball spun out of my glove and ripped my bare hand wide open. In baseball, you never know and must always be ready.

Commitment is such an important factor in sports. Players must dedicate themselves to the game. As with anything in life, you need to have a strong work ethic to become successful. Most of all, my advice to players is to have fun in baseball. And it's up to the coaches to make sure they do. Young players get discouraged very easily. Many times they expect to be a superstar right away. It always troubles me to see talented players give up before reaching their potential. You must work hard and dedicate yourself to improving as a player. Dedication and a strong work ethic will not only lead you to success on the baseball field, but on any path you take in life.

— Willie McCovey
February 2010
Woodside, California

Willie McCovey was inducted into the National Baseball Hall of Fame in 1986. His tremendous career, highlighted by 521 home runs hit mostly for the San Francisco Giants, prompted The Sporting News to rank him number 56 on its list of the 100 Greatest Baseball Players of all time. The inlet of San Francisco Bay over the right-field fence at AT&T Park is known as McCovey Cove in his honor.

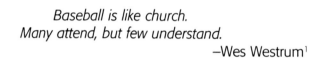

Baseball is like church.
Many attend, but few understand.

—Wes Westrum[1]

contents

10 Principles for Coaching Baseball

Be Passionate

Every time that a coach interacts with his team, whether during practice, games, or just general meetings, he should exude enthusiasm. By modeling this excitement for baseball, players will respond. While some coaches are more mild-mannered or may need to be firm with their players on a given day, every coach must exhibit passion for the game. Players react positively to coaches and teachers who are energized and excited about what they do. In contrast, monotone or apathetic leaders will be a turn-off for adolescents. Therefore, whether it be reviewing the daily practice schedule or giving a pre-game talk, coaches should be fiery and display excitement that their players can feed off.

Organization Is Key

It is imperative that coaches arrive to practice or a game with a clear game plan. Players, regardless of age, can sense when a coach is not prepared. Lack of preparation sends a negative message regarding the effectiveness and competency of the coach. As a result, it is essential for all coaches to be punctual and display a focused demeanor, conveying a sense that certain tasks must get accomplished. One strategy that aids in this process is typing up detailed practice plans, which can be posted for the team to review before practice and/or provided to assistant coaches.

Poor organization can be especially detrimental when scheduling games, practices, transportation, or team meetings/award ceremonies. Furthermore, coaches who are not efficient in this area may struggle managing the paperwork of player medical clearances and academic issues. CPR and first aid certification are safety measures that deal with serious liabilities and must also be part of a coach's organizational system. One way to keep tabs on this tedious minutia is to create "To Do" lists regarding equipment, field maintenance, parent communication, or other administrative issues. Most of all, carefully planning ahead minimizes overlooking administrative responsibilities.

Throughout of this book will be Administrative Time-Out sections provided to help clarify when administrative considerations apply.

 Administrative Time-Out

Teach, Teach, Teach

Many coaches have a false notion that they should not have to teach basic fundamentals to their players. Too often, coaches have an expectation that players' previous coaches covered every baseball mechanic or an unrealistic assumption that players will retain everything they were taught. In reality, players require constant coaching within specific skills and overall game understanding.

Even at the Major League level, players are continually refining or tweaking their mechanics for increased productivity. As a result, coaches should view each new season and incoming group of players as candidates for learning basic baseball fundamentals.

Beyond baseball skills, each coach's unique philosophy should include an emphasis on teaching proper values to their players. Many of the greatest lessons that sports' teams provide include being an ethical person. In the heat of a competitive season, where winning is a focal point, this concept is often overlooked. Coaches may need to bench a player for behavioral reasons, which will affect the team's performance. The disciplined habits and overall work ethic that coaches pass on to their players will serve them throughout their lives.

Baseball has more rules than any other sport. These finer details can be used to help players realize how unique baseball is. By reviewing the multitude of game rules and strange cases that have arisen over the years, coaches play a significant role as teachers. Moreover, if players' baseball participation or skill set does not carry them through high school sports, at least they can become knowledgeable, life-long students of the game.

Within each chapter, this book provides numerous Teaching Tip sections to help coaches communicate specific skills to their players.

 Teaching Tip

It's Not About You

Former Major League manager Bob Lemon said, "Baseball is a kid's game that grown-ups only tend to screw up."[2] It is important for coaches to make an effort to remove their egos and lofty personal aspirations from coaching. Pride and a strong ego can motivate a coach to seek success, but it can also distort his purpose. Many coaches become fixated on winning and lose sense of developing young athletes. Certainly at the college and professional levels, coaches must win to maintain their jobs, yet in youth leagues coaches do not have these pressures. The notion that a game was won or lost because of some brilliant coaching maneuver should not be part of a coach's mindset.

Instead, coaches must be sensitive to personal issues that many players deal with off the field. In addition, players may put pressure on themselves to perform or have unrealistic parental expectations placed on their performance. Parents, especially fathers, frequently take too great a stake in and "live through" the athletic accomplishments of their children. Empowered with an awareness of these issues, coaches should be empathetic toward their players and provide support. In short, while the male ego may be fed through victories or accolades, coaches must not lose sight of their role in helping young people.

Effective Communication

Communication skills are a vital element within a baseball coaching framework. During the course of a season, coaches interact with players, parents, umpires, opposing coaches, and league/school administrators. In all cases, a strategy should be developed to maximize positive outcomes. For example, holding a general parent meeting to review fundraising, playing time issues, proper fan etiquette, and communication guidelines is advisable. Developing an effective rapport with umpires and collegiality with opposing coaches is advantageous. Additionally, a coach must understand the importance of documenting communications with administrators within a school or league association.

Most of all, coaches must establish sound communication skills with players, which includes addressing the entire team and individual conferencing. Coaches should be creative and inspirational in designing pre-game talks as well as day-to-day practice routines. On an individual basis, the player-coach relationship must be fostered with sensitivity to each player's needs, background, and unique psyche. Certain players may need coddling or self-esteem boosting sessions, while others require a more stern approach. Also, coaches must provide clear directives regarding individual player roles and specific areas for improvement.

Given that most batting averages are below .400 (a 40 percent success rate), players frequently deal with failure in baseball. Therefore, coaches must be well-equipped to build player and team morale. Within this book, communication skills and appropriate times for conferencing are highlighted in Conference Time sections.

 Conference Time

Be Consistent

The age-old expression "Practice what you preach" applies to coaches. If a coach stresses the importance of arriving promptly, dressing appropriately, or abiding by team rules, then he must always model these behaviors. Likewise, if coaches mandate that players wear a particular practice outfit or run onto the field in a certain manner, then he should demonstrate these actions as well. It is advantageous for coaches to be fit and look the part of a baseball player. Baseball is the only major sport in which the coach wears the same uniform as his players. As a result, ideally he will be in the proper physical shape to throw batting practice, hit *fungos* (groundball and fly ball repetitions to players), and carry out athletic coaching duties that parallel what he expects from his players.

Furthermore, a coach must follow through on any promises that are made regarding playing time, disciplinary action, or team rules. For instance, if the ace pitcher arrives late or misses practice and is allowed (or not allowed) to play in the next game, then all players must be held to that same standard.

Otherwise, players will understandably question the integrity and word of the coach. Essentially, coaches should view themselves as ethical role models that set the ultimate example for the team's persona.

Keep Learning

A key component of the coaching spirit is a desire for improvement. Coaches can always learn new techniques or strategies for working with players. By attending coaching clinics, reading books, viewing instructional videos, and observing other talented and innovative coaches, they can continually improve their craft. Even successful, veteran coaches who are set in their style and approach need variation. Without it, coaching may become stagnant and players may get complacent following the same basic routine.

The ability to be self-reflective and introspective is crucial for success in any profession. Those coaches who do not get better at what they do are the ones who lack awareness to evaluate their own performance. Whether it is ignorance, arrogance, or some other reason, many professionals simply do not strive to get better at what they do. A desire and willingness to ask questions is essential for improvement as a coach. Throughout this book, frequently asked coaching questions and various instrumental game strategies will be provided in the Question and In-Game Strategy sections to help coaches gain further insight into the game.

 Question

 In-Game Strategy

Find Your Way

Baseball coaches have varied personalities and can be viewed along a wide-ranging spectrum. Lou Piniella and Tony La Russa have been highly successful Major League managers, yet they have two distinctly different styles. Similar to personalities in other fields, some coaches are flamboyant leaders, while others are more introverted and pensive. One style is not necessarily better than another. However, it is important for coaches to be cognizant of their demeanor, strengths, weaknesses, and disposition. Table I-1 outlines four prevalent coaching styles/approaches.

When considering these styles, it is important to understand that a coach's personality generally corresponds to the style that he will find comfortable and effective. A shy intellectual is not likely to fit The Enthusiast model. Similarly, a strong-willed, confident person probably will feel most suited for The Dictator model. Although effective coaches utilize skills and traits from each of the

The Teacher	**The Expert**
• Focuses on fundamentals during practice time	• Knowledge of rules and game strategy is a major focus
• Enjoys "teaching the game" and discussing the finer points	• An intellectual type who likes to study and discuss classic games of the past
• Devises unique drills to foster individual skill development	• Practice time is devoted to in-game strategy and execution of plays
• Provides in-game instruction to players on-field and in the dugout	• Tends to rely heavily on statistics for match-ups and lineups
• Hands out readings/articles to team on proper mechanics	• Devotes time to scouting opponents and video analysis
The Dictator	**The Enthusiast**
• Discipline is a major focus of coaching personality	• Positive, energetic leader type (Tommy Lasorda–like coach)
• Communications with players are not a discussion, but more of "This is the way we do it."	• May be seen as a "players' coach" who keeps his team's feelings and mood in mind
• Often a micro-manager type who relies little on others	• Gives inspirational speeches and is generally an effective motivator
• Tends to be louder than other coaching models and screams at times	• Excels at working one-on-one in providing on-field coaching advice and building individual confidence
• Rarely accepts input from players or parents	• Winning is greatly celebrated; wears his emotions on sleeve

Table I-1

models, many fit into one of the frameworks. More important than asking, "Where do I fit in within these styles?" is asking, "What can I incorporate from each?"

Stay Positive

During the course of a long season, teams experience many ups and downs. Coaches must do their best to both boost team morale and remain positive. After a difficult loss or a season-ending injury for a top player, teams will be dejected. In such times, coaches must step up and provide energy with an upbeat demeanor. In the midst of a grueling season, it is easy to lose sight of what is important. Coaches must remember to keep the atmosphere enjoyable for players arriving at the field. A fun, new competition at practice or a surprise visit to an ice cream parlor are spontaneous and refreshing activities that can bring life back to a team.

As Chris Chambliss observed, "If you're not having fun in baseball, you miss the point of everything."[3] Although winning and losing can become a major focal point of the season, players should be reminded that baseball is just a game. Even Major Leaguers who are struggling need to remember how much fun baseball can be. When playing becomes too much of a job, players lose their zeal and effectiveness on the field. Lastly, coaches can intermittently review team accomplishments and how hard players have worked to get where they are. People yearn to be complimented and teams can be commended for their efforts long before the end of season awards ceremony or dinner celebration.

Cover All the Bases

In developing a comprehensive coaching system, coaches must possess a diverse skill set and be innovative thinkers. By creating a multi-faceted game plan, coaches will make their roles more powerful and fulfilling. This book advocates a four-pronged coaching approach that incorporates elements from administrative, interpersonal, teaching techniques, and in-game strategy to serve as a platform for coaches to build from. By using this book, coaches can develop greater awareness and pinpoint areas of strength/weakness within their coaching framework. Coaches can be empowered to bolster their foundation and overall approach to working with baseball players.

How to Use This Book

Over the past 20 years, many people have communicated to me that they have been unable to find a coaching resource that applies to them. While excellent books exist that discuss specialized skills or aspects of the game, no coaching tool is tailored to meet individual coaching needs.

The goal of this book is to provide a vehicle to improve the areas for your particular coaching methodology. Whether the topic is pitching, hitting, defense, or baserunning, you will find additional content to improve the various aspects of coaching. Within the analysis of a specific baseball skill or activity, references and connections will be made to four basic coaching skill sets. These skill sets will be clearly marked with pictures and labels for easy referencing: administrative, interpersonal, in-game strategy, and teaching skills. Consequently, by conducting self-reflective coaching inventory, you can look to the photographs in each chapter to find elements that may be missing from your current coaching strategy. In addition, pictures will also designate frequently discussed topics of debate and commonly posed coaching questions (with answers) to further enhance the depth of coverage within each skill set.

 Topic of Debate

Three Steps to Success Format

In order to teach the game to your players in a clear and retainable fashion, this coaching guide will break skills into thirds. Players tend to be overwhelmed when coaches throw a great deal of information at them. This resource provides a concrete method for implementing skills and fundamentals with an easy to teach, three-step approach.

The book also features photos illustrating proper form and technique for each major skill. Coaching phrases and teaching terms are in *italic* throughout the book in order to promote the understanding or administering of a particular drill.

Covering All the Bases

A sound philosophy can be established by developing a diverse, all-inclusive coaching game plan. Applying the old proverb "Leave no stone unturned" will ensure that you have done everything in your power to be the best coach possible. Some of the activities and duties of a well-rounded coach may take you out of your comfort zone. Whether it is administrative paperwork, interpersonal contact with disgruntled parents, or other responsibilities that you dislike, this book challenges you to adopt the wide-ranging approach that being a dynamic coach entails. At the conclusion of Chapter 10 is a *self-assessment, diagnostic coaching test*, which you can reference as a checklist for pinpointing the missing components in your orientation to coaching.

The ultimate goal is for you to design a multi-pronged, intuitive system crafted to get the most out of your players and coaches. As a result, coaching will become much more fulfilling as your eyes are opened to new challenges and opportunities both on and off the field.

For additional coaching resources and instructional video footage, log on to www.CoveringAllTheBases.com. When the icon below is present in the margin next to a section of text, there is an instructional video on the website that corresponds to the topic. Videos will be available in Spring 2011.

Comments or questions can be emailed to: CoachGurney@CoveringAllTheBases.com.

Sources

[1]Dickson, P. (1992). *Baseball's Greatest Quotations*. New York: Harper Perennial. P. 467.

[2]Dickson, P. (1992). *Baseball's Greatest Quotations*. New York: Harper Perennial. P. 244.

[3]www.baseball-reference.com. January 14, 2009.

THROWING AND PITCHING

Chapter 1

*The only thing that matters is what happens on that
little hump out in the middle of the field.*
                                        —Earl Weaver[1]

The art of throwing is a learned skill that is often overlooked. It can be the core of a sloppy game or unproductive practice. Baseball fans have all seen innings that turn into what seems like an eternity with errant throws to teammates, who then must scramble after the ball. Conversely, teams and pitchers who execute proper throws are usually the ones who have success. At the outset of practice, throwing is routinely the first activity for players, and, as a result, it sets the tone.

Furthermore, with the increase of arm injuries occurring at all ages, it is imperative that proper throwing mechanics are introduced early. In addition, a growing number of college and professional scouts are now examining a prospect's *arm action* when evaluating player potential. No longer are radar gun readings and player size the sole determinants of throwing ability. Effective arm action may demonstrate potential for movement on pitches, likelihood of injury, and stamina/endurance in a given pitching outing. Certainly, New York Yankee pitcher Mariano Rivera embodies great arm action, as he has been relatively injury-free as the top closer in baseball for 15 years with just one type of pitch.

Throwing on a Knee

Three Steps to Success

1. Lift the throwing elbow above the shoulder.
2. Move the ball and arm straight behind the body.
3. Follow through and finish across the glove-side knee.

A method for isolating proper throwing fundamentals is to have players start their throwing routine on a knee so that players can focus on the elements that will give them a foundation for proper throwing skills. When throwing on a knee, players kneel on the ground and lift their glove-side knee (left leg for right-handed throwers, and right leg for left-handed throwers) (Figure 1-1). Balance and posture are crucial to mastering this skill. *Until players have mastered this skill, it is important for them to pause at each point in the throwing motion.* For three to five minutes, players can start their daily throwing routine with this exercise at a distance of 7 to 10 feet.

Figure 1-1. Step 1—starting position

Players should take the ball back in a circular motion as far back as possible (Figure 1-2). At this point, it is important to monitor that players do not twist or turn their shoulders like an airplane that is turning. Rather, the glove hand should move and point toward the target as the hands separate and ball goes straight back. During the separation, both hands should move in a circular motion.

Figure 1-2. Step 2—separation

 Teaching Tip

A good visual to implement is the "Wax on, wax off" motion from the film, *The Karate Kid*. This technique will reinforce the proper circular arm action of both the throwing arm and the glove hand.

It is important for players to point the ball in the opposite direction to which they are throwing. Once the player's arm is raised in the *flexed bow position* (much like an archer ready to release an arrow from his bow), the player is prepared to release the ball (Figure 1-3). In game situations, reaching the flexed bow position can ensure a pitcher's glove hand blocks the hitter's view of his grip on the ball. As the process occurs, the glove-side arm should pull down toward the chest/biceps area of the glove side of the body.

Figure 1-3. Step 3—flexed bow position

Upon releasing the ball, the thrower will reach out toward his partner and follow through across his glove-side knee (Figure 1-4). Bending the back is a necessary part of the finish. Finishing down and toward the outside of the player's glove-side ankle are teaching points to stress here.

Figure 1-4. Step 4—finish across the knee

After throwing on a knee for several minutes, players should stand up and throw with a partner 10 to 15 feet away from each other. At this point, it is necessary to maintain the proper throwing mechanics from the previous exercise (Table 1-1).

Throwing Fundamentals Checklist	
What to Do	**What *Not* to Do**
• Get the elbow above the shoulder. • Extend the arm back before release. • Stride with the glove side foot. • Point the glove at the target. • Point the glove side shoulder at target. • Maintain circular arm action. • Pull down with the glove arm. • Keep the *shoulders square* (to target). • Maintain effective follow-through.	• Stride away from the target. • Drop the elbow *(flail)* below the shoulder. • *Fly open* with the glove side. • Stop the arm at the release point. • Point the glove to the sky or the ground. • Take the eyes off the target. • Twist the shoulders at the flexed bow. • Collapse the back shoulder under the ball.

Table 1-1. Throwing fundamentals checklist

Administrative Time-Out

Coaches may view partner throwing as an opportunity to get administrative work completed (writing up lineup cards, preparing equipment, talking with coaches, etc.). Nonetheless, it is imperative that player throwing mechanics are monitored very closely and teaching is occurring. Specifically, coaches should make sure players are utilizing the four-seam grip, keeping the elbow above the shoulder, and achieving a proper follow-through. In addition, setting the proper tone for the practice or game occurs at this time.

Long Toss

For many years, players have thrown long toss to increase their arm strength; however, recently discussion has taken place in the college and professional ranks as to the effectiveness of long toss and its proper execution.

Traditionally, when players long toss, they throw the ball high and long to stretch out their arm. At more advanced levels, players are able to throw the ball from the left field foul pole to the right field foul pole. While this exercise certainly allows players to test the limits of their arm, effective throwing mechanics may be sacrificed. Frequently, in attempting to throw high and long, players will fly open (pull off with their glove-side shoulder) to gain power. Some players will release the ball off-balance with poor footwork as they try to muster their strength. Additionally, in this activity, the ball's trajectory of flight is upward. Yet, when pitching off a mound, the angle and flight of the ball is downward. Consequently, *long toss should be utilized if it does not hamper proper throwing mechanics.*

Three Steps to Success ─────────────────────────

1. Throw on a line no higher than player height.
2. Utilize different grips on the ball to gain fluency and comfort with those pitches.
3. Emphasize leg and hip action that will be implemented off the mound.

Proper long toss form starts with the feet (Figure 1-5). Players should bring their throwing-arm-side foot behind the heel of their glove-side foot. During this process, throwers must stay closed with their hips and front shoulder as they *back step* and prepare to throw (Figure 1-6). As an alternative to the back step, coaches can teach players to *shuffle step* by bringing their feet together so that the inside of each foot touches and the throwing-arm-side foot replaces the glove-side foot. The legs and hips provide his power as the thrower gains momentum toward his partner. Players must keep their front shoulder square or in line with their target. As when throwing on a knee, the arms move in a circular motion before coming to the flexed bow position. The throwing elbow must get above the shoulder (Figure 1-7) and release the ball so that it stays at the height of the thrower. By following through properly (Figure 1-8), rainbow or grenade-like throws can be avoided.

Figure 1-5. Starting position

Figure 1-6. Back step

Figure 1-7. Arm extension

Figure 1-8. Follow-through

Players should start with a four-seam grip (see the Pitching/Throwing Grips section in this chapter) and move further away from each other as they get more comfortable. As all team players begin to reach their maximum distance during long toss, coaches can blow a whistle or signal for pitchers only to switch to a two-seam grip. After several minutes, coaches can signal for pitchers to throw with a change-up grip. As players finish the long toss activity, coaches should have all players utilize a four-seam grip on the ball for accuracy and maximum velocity.

Long toss is not only effective at building arm strength, but also in helping pitchers gain comfort throwing a variety of pitches. Accordingly, in a given long toss session, pitchers should throw with several different grips in a rotating sequence. To gain confidence and proficiency, pitchers must throw them during long toss and flat ground workouts, not just off the mound. In particular, many pitchers struggle to master the change-up because they throw it infrequently at practice.

Administrative Time-Out

Coaches can set up their throwing practice so that players throw with a partner who plays his position and has similar arm strength. Some coaches will mandate that infielders throw with infielders, catchers throw with catchers, outfielders throw with outfielders, and so forth. Partners should raise their arms and hold their hands up to provide the thrower a clear target. Players may desire throwing with a friend, which can become more of a social interaction than a productive workout.

 Topic of Debate: Pitch Counts

Decades ago, players pitched daily and pitch counts were not tracked, which is no longer the case. Usually, pitchers below the college level play a secondary position, which is also taxing on the arm. As a result, coaches, players, and parents must communicate about arm fatigue and the planned schedule for throwing in games/practice. A key signal regarding in-game pitch count occurs when a pitcher throws over 30 pitches in one inning or experiences a sudden loss of control. Some youth leagues have tried to set limits on how many innings or pitches are thrown by a pitcher in a four- to seven-day period.

Pitching/Throwing Grips

Four-Seam Grip

The most important grip for all players to master is the four-seam grip because it has the greatest velocity and travels in the straightest fashion among all grips (Figure 1-9). Due to the ball's seams cutting through the air more frequently with this grip, players' throws are most accurate with the four-seam grip. As a result, all position players must only throw with a four-seam grip to make the strongest possible throw. Typically, pitchers will use this grip when needing to throw a strike or maximize their velocity in a particular count. In turn, young pitchers should be throwing this pitch more than any other. A good way to check the proper rotation of seams is to dip half of the ball in paint or color it with a marker across the seams and watch for rotation.

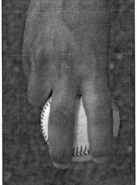

Figure 1-9. Four-seam fastball grip

Conference Time

A difficult issue that coaches encounter with pitchers is agreeing on pitch selection. Pitchers may desire to throw a variety of pitches before mastering the fastball. An effective strategy is to set up a contract or agreement that stipulates how many strikes (the percentage thrown) a pitcher must throw before moving on to throwing a new pitch. Also, conferencing one-on-one can create a sense of trust with your player, and consequently the player may sense that you care about his potential as well as his limits.

Two-Seam Grip

A two-seam fastball is thrown with the fingers across two seams of the ball, not four (Figure 1-10). This pitch tends to dip while spinning sideways. This spin can create *run on the ball*, which enables pitchers to deceive batters while adding another pitch to their arsenal. As a rule, a two-seam fastball thrown from a right-handed pitcher will dive down and in to a right-handed batter. Likewise, the pitch runs down and away from a left-handed batter. The pitch can be used on both sides of the plate to back up (inside pitch) or run away (outside pitch) from a left-handed batter. A left-handed pitcher will achieve opposite results from a two-seam fastball with the pitch running away from right-handed batters and in to lefties. Greg Maddux built a Hall of Fame career by perfecting this pitch.

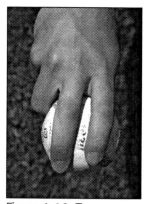

Figure 1-10. Two-seam fastball grip

Change-Up Grip

The change-up is the most underrated pitch in baseball, especially at the youth level (Figure 1-11). Thrown properly, the change-up is a deceptive, devastating tool that can baffle opposing hitters. Perhaps not as glamorous as the curveball, splitter, or slider, an effective change-up will make a pitcher's fastball appear faster than it is. Moreover, if thrown with the same arm speed as the fastball it can fool hitters who struggle to wait for it to cross the hitting zone. Unlike a curveball, which has spinning seams, a change-up can disguise itself as a fastball so the batter prematurely swings before the ball arrives. Perennial all-stars Pedro Martinez and Trevor Hoffman utilized this pitch to dominate major league hitters for many years.

Figure 1-11. Circle change-up grip

The two basic change-up grips accomplish similar results (Figures 1-11 and 1-12). In both cases, the pitch is thrown with less velocity and a side spin. A change-up can dive or sink down, particularly at younger levels when velocity is not as high and gravity takes over. Holding the ball too deep in the hand can cause a choking action on the ball. It is important for pitchers not to choke the pitch, but rather let the grip dictate its movement and change of speed. Pitchers should leave some space in between their hand and the ball to prevent choking from occurring. Other techniques used to throw an effective change-up include dragging the back leg on the ground just before release, slightly lifting a finger off the ball, and putting a knuckle into the ball. Some pitchers will *pronate* the wrist, or turn it so the thumb points down as they release the pitch to create more movement on the ball. This turn can be referred to as *opening the door*, like turning a doorknob.

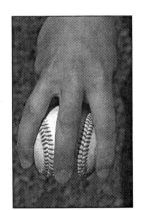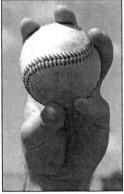

Figure 1-12. Three-finger or "trophy" change-up grip

Teaching Tip

In order to develop proficiency with the change-up, pitchers must long toss and perform other throwing drills with it to gain the necessary comfort level. Habitually, it is important for pitchers to fiddle with different fingertip pressures and grip locations (four-seam and two-seam change-up grips) on the ball to achieve their own personal effectiveness with the pitch. Another method is to flip the ball up in the air and catch it barehanded with a change-up grip and immediately throw it from this loose, three-finger grip position.

Other Grips and Pitches

Inevitably, players will have a yearning to throw pitches other than the fastball and change-up; though, they should be urged to master those pitches before moving on to the curveball, slider, split finger, knuckleball, or other off-speed pitches. Ideally, high school is the appropriate time to begin working on a breaking pitch. It is important to note that if thrown incorrectly, these pitches can cause injury and do not aid in strengthening the throwing arm.

 ### Administrative Time-Out

When creating daily/weekly practice plans, it is necessary to build in time for *position specialization skill work* so that players (pitchers, in particular) can focus on mechanics of their specific defensive area. Coaches can have players report to practice at different times based on their position. If blessed with a talented staff who can teach various positions, then the first 30 minutes of practice is the appropriate time for doing so. College coaches customarily have the luxury of hiring assistant coaches with specialty area(s) of expertise.

Breaking Pitches

Curveball

When directing pitchers to throw breaking balls, it is imperative for coaches to stress the importance of not altering basic pitching mechanics or release point. Quite often, young players will change their arm slot, wrist cock, or pace of delivery when trying to throw an effective curveball (Figure 1-13).

Figure 1-13. Curveball grip

Pitchers keep their middle and index finger next to each other when gripping the curveball. This grip enables them to hold the baseball against a seam and provide pressure against the seam upon release. The goal is to throw the pitch with a tight spin that the batter cannot detect: the tighter the spin, the more the ball will break and deceive the hitter. It is important for pitchers to *get on top* and not drop underneath the ball when throwing this pitch. Pitchers must stay back and not rush this pitch; otherwise the ball will float high with a loose spin.

Three Steps to Success ————————————————————————————

1. Maintain the same mechanics and arm slot as the fastball/change-up.
2. Grip the ball with the index and middle fingers together against the seam.
3. Keep the throwing hand above the ball, and do not rush the delivery.

 Teaching Tip

When trying to throw a curveball, an effective visual for pitchers to utilize is reaching out and pulling down on a window shade. Some prefer to imagine pulling the string/chain to turn on an old lamp. Another helpful tip is for pitchers to imagine they must chop a vertical block of ice in front of them with their throwing hand. These visual techniques will allow pitchers to achieve extension and stay on top of the ball. If a pitcher is below the ball and pushes it toward the plate or rushes the delivery, then the ball will drift high and have limited *bite*. Pitchers can experiment with different grip locations on the ball, although the fingers will ultimately be together and pressing against a seam.

Slider

A faster, complementary pitch to the curveball is the slider (Figure 1-14). The slider, as the name implies, slides or cuts across the plate in a more horizontal manner. The curveball, in contrast, breaks in a more vertical or 12-to-6 trajectory (corresponding to the numbers on a clock). When gripping a slider, pitchers can split their index and middle finger with a seam on the ball. If thrown effectively, the slider will move in a sharp, horizontal, and downward direction.

Figure 1-14. Slider grip

When releasing a curveball, pitchers should let the fingertips lead. Pitchers must extend and feel the fingertips snap off the seam of the ball. Although the first breaking pitch that most adolescent pitchers learn to throw is the curveball, college pitchers usually transition from throwing the curveball to utilizing a slider as their primary breaking pitch. *Hanging curveballs* in the upper part of the strike zone with limited break have a greater likelihood of being hit for extra base hits than poorly thrown sliders.

What mistakes do pitchers typically make when throwing breaking pitches?

Young pitchers are often afraid to commit to throwing a curveball and "baby the pitch," which is caused by a fear of hurting their arm or an uncertainty with the pitch. Other mechanical issues include shortened arm action with limited extension, twisting the wrist upon release, *wrapping the ball* by overcocking the wrist back prior to release, poor follow-through, and not getting on top of the ball. By slowing down the delivery and holding the balance point, pitchers will have a better opportunity to stay on top of the ball and not throw a *spinner* with no break.

 ### Topic of Debate: Curve Balls

Young players may become infatuated with throwing pitches that they see players on television using. Curveballs, knuckleballs, sliders, split-finger pitches, and others can be detrimental to the arm when not thrown properly. Players periodically change their arm slot or throwing mechanics to deliver these pitches. Yet, those and other off-speed pitches do not build arm strength as effectively as fastballs and change-ups. As a result, coaches and parents may debate and struggle to agree on the appropriate age for players to begin throwing curve balls.

 ### In-Game Strategy: Curveball vs. Slider

Pitchers frequently use the slider as a two-strike, out pitch located down and away from the batter. This strategy may cause the batter to *fish* for the pitch down, or in the dirt and induce a weakly batted ball or strike out. The curveball, which is several miles per hour slower than the slider, can be used in any count to provide deception. In particular, an 0-0 count curveball that can be thrown consistently for strikes is highly effective. By using sequences of pitches with the fastball, slider, and curveball to change eye levels of the batter, pitchers can use both of these breaking pitches in tandem.

In a recent study by renowned sports orthopedist Dr. James Andrews, breaking pitches were found to cause a much higher incidence of elbow and shoulder problems. Among 476 pitchers ages 9 to 14, 52 percent experienced more shoulder pain from throwing curveballs. More strikingly, those pitchers who threw sliders were 86 percent more likely to develop elbow pain[2].

 ### Teaching Tip

Coaches can have their position players flip the ball up in the air and catch it in their glove while quickly grabbing the ball with four-seam grip. This *flip drill* can be done at home on the couch as it builds player quickness in getting proper grip on the ball in preparation for game situations. Pitchers can execute the drill with various grips so they can develop confidence finding each grip quickly in their glove as if it were a live game.

Pitching Motion (Windup Delivery)

In teaching players proper pitching mechanics, coaches should break the multifaceted pitching delivery into individual components. Although the pitching motion should be fluid, this important fundamental can be completed in seven, easy-to-teach stages. A coach or partner should call out a number (1 through 7), and the pitcher(s) will go through the mechanics to that point. Many of the other pitching drills presented in this section reinforce the fundamentals emphasized through the seven-step motion of this exercise.

- Step 1: Pitcher starts with his feet shoulder-width apart and hands at the chest (Figure 1-15).
- Step 2: Pitcher takes a deep breath and a small step of two to six inches straight back, or on a diagonal 45-degree angle (Figure 1-16).
- Step 3: Pitcher pivots his throwing-arm-side foot, turning it parallel to the pitching rubber and points his glove-side shoulder/hip at the target (Figure 1-17).
- Step 4: Pitcher lifts his glove-side leg to the balance point so that the knee is waist high as his hands move into the flexed bow position at eye level (Figure 1-18).
- Step 5: Pitcher lands with his glove-side foot and turns the hips in preparation for delivery (Figure 1-19).
- Step 6: Pitcher releases pitch while reaching as far forward as possible toward the target (Figure 1-20).
- Step 7: Pitcher follows through over the glove-side leg while achieving a flat back position and letting the arm decelerate (Figure 1-21).

Figure 1-15. Step 1   Figure 1-16. Step 2   Figure 1-17. Step 3   Figure 1-18. Step 4

Figure 1-19. Step 5   Figure 1-20. Step 6   Figure 1-21. Step 7

When the coach calls out a number and the pitcher acts out the stages of this drill, the motion may appear too robotic or mechanical. However, the purpose of this activity is to familiarize pitchers with the mechanics of the windup, not actually have them deliver a ball as if playing a game. This exercise can be done with no ball several times and in front of a mirror. Once the pitcher is comfortable with the seven steps, he can complete the motion backward and follow steps seven to one, rather than one to seven.

The step back during step two should be short and straight/45 degrees so as to keep the motion compact. Some pitchers prefer to step laterally to the side toward third or first base, but this only takes them out of the pitching lane or *the doorway* without providing any advantage in the process.

During step four, pitchers should focus on staying back and relaxed. This balance point position is crucial as a spot to maintain timing and posture before the release. Also at this stage, pitchers must remember to get their throwing elbow above the shoulder and make sure their glove hand blocks the hitter's view of the ball.

At step five, pitchers must think about their hips. The hips are the engine that provides the power for the delivery (see the Medicine Ball—Exploding Hips Drill in the Pitching Drills section of this chapter). It is important that the stride at this stage is not too long. A long stride will force the pitcher to land on his heel and deliver the ball up in the strike zone. Landing on the heel forces the leg to stiffen, as opposed to remaining flexible. The glove-side leg should not be stiff until the release when the pitcher gets his chest over the stiff front leg and knee. The stride must also be straight and not off to the side. A stride off to the side will force the pitcher to throw across his body or fly open with his front shoulder, which causes wildness.

During the final phase (steps 6 and 7), pitchers should *reach and shake* upon releasing the ball. In reaching toward the target, the pitcher gets over his glove-side foot with the ball. A pitcher's arm should be relaxed and fluid through the completion of the throwing motion. Much like the arm on a pitching machine after release, the pitching arm dangles during this rapid deceleration process.

 Teaching Tip

Several important teaching points should be stressed throughout the windup. Many pitchers start in a pitching stance with their feet together: this position is not a balanced, athletic stance. For this reason, pitchers should begin with their feet shoulder-width apart. Also, the pitcher should not raise his hands above his head during the windup; rather, he should keep his hands at the belt or chin level. Nothing is gained by the glove and pitching hand moving above the head. Even though examples of successful pitchers who bring the hands over their head can be found (Tom Seaver and Nolan Ryan), this motion only prevents the pitcher from keeping his eyes glued on the target or catcher's glove.

Pitching Drills

At the college and professional levels, with so much player specialization, pitchers use an entire practice just to work on their throwing mechanics. At younger ages, teams do not have that luxury as pitchers play other positions and are important offensive players for their team. Nonetheless, pitchers can work on a variety of drills (individually or when team practice time permits) that enhance proper throwing mechanics. Many drills do not require a ball and can be performed *dry*, which reinforces balance, flexibility, arm action, and overall mechanical consistency.

Extension Drill

The extension drill is an effective drill for pitchers to start their workout. Pitchers will spread their feet a bit wider than shoulder-width apart along a line (Figure 1-22). Next, they will *load up the backside* (Figure 1-23) by rocking back on their throwing-side leg. Upon getting their weight back, pitchers will then turn their upper body 45 degrees toward the target (Figure 1-25) and explode the hips as they come toward the finish (Figure 1-26). In this finish, the player must position his chest over the front knee, bend his back, and hold the follow-through (Figure 1-27). This drill can be completed dry, with a ball, or a towel (see the Towel Drill in this section).

Figure 1-22. Step 1   Figure 1-23. Step 2   Figure 1-24. Step 3

Figure 1-25. Step 4   Figure 1-26. Step 5   Figure 1-27. Step 6

In-Game Strategy: Pitcher Control Problems

When a pitcher loses command of the strike zone, fans or coaches repeatedly yell out "Follow through," "Bend," or "Throw strikes." Rarely are these verbal cues helpful. The most common problem for pitchers is staying back. Specifically, their arm lags behind their body during delivery. This problem is evident when players are overly anxious, excited, or pumped up, and they rush their motion. Their pitches will be up and outside of the strike zone. If the pitcher slows down and pauses at the balance point, this issue of hurrying the delivery, and thus causing wildness, can be alleviated.

Spot Drills

In pairs at a distance of 30 to 40 feet, pitchers throw 70 percent of their full speed on flat ground. Players under age 10 can do these drills from 15 to 20 feet apart. Pitchers will throw to their partner, who is squatting like a catcher on the inside or outside of a portable home plate. An effective tool is creating a home plate that is painted different colors on the sides and middle of the plate. The goal of these drills is to *hit* spots (inside or outside) with both types of fastballs and the change-up. Players can rotate between pitcher and catcher after every five pitches, or every pitch. Fluid mechanics and control of each pitch are the focus of these drills. Pitchers can create games with points for accuracy of hitting spots on the corners of the plate. For example, the Game of 21 is a game played with pitchers standing up and alternating pitches, where players receive three points for a throw that lands in the head area, two points for a throw landing in the neck to the chest area, and one point for a throw landing from the chest down to the belt. The first thrower to reach 21 is the winner.

 ### Teaching Tip

On game day, pitchers are allowed eight warm-up pitches in between innings (although some leagues limit this total to five or one minute of time). This warm-up period is an opportunity to get familiar with the mound's firmness, holes/ditches, and slope or angle. Specifically, pitching rubbers in youth leagues usually have a ditch in the front, which creates problems for pitchers' footing. Every mound is different. Pitchers can move to different locations on the rubber to find a starting point and landing area where they are comfortable and can avoid holes. In conjunction, it is advisable to throw several of these warm-up pitches from the stretch position and practice all pitches in the arsenal. It should be noted that pitchers do not have to throw all of their warm-up pitches, especially late in the game after they have thrown many pitches and may be tiring.

Footprint Drill

Players and coaches will need a rake or broom to start this drill. The mound area will be raked smooth of marks on the landing area. The pitcher will go through his delivery and note where his feet land to develop such a repetitive delivery that there are only two footprints or marks on the mound. Pitchers must focus on developing a stride that is straight and consistent in length. Many hitters will do something similar to this to check their front foot stride upon getting into the batter's box for batting practice or in a game. Pitchers can bring a tape measure to check the length of their stride and compare it to their body height. This drill can be done indoors on a portable mound with tape used for marking stride length.

In-Game Strategy: Pitching Rubber

Ideally, a pitcher should throw from the side of the rubber closest to the batter. For instance, with a left-handed batter in the batter's box, a pitcher should throw from the first base side of the rubber. With a right-handed batter in the box, he should pitch from the third base side of the rubber. This positioning makes it difficult for the batter to see the ball and can be especially effective at higher levels, when pitchers throw breaking pitches that start behind or at the batter and break across the plate. Nonetheless, pitchers at all levels do not always follow this guideline, as they may feel more comfortable throwing strikes from a particular side of the rubber.

70-Foot Change-Up Drill

In addition to long tossing with a variety of grips, every day pitchers can throw change-ups to a partner at a distance a bit longer than the pitching rubber to home plate. By doing so, pitchers will learn to throw change-ups with the same arm speed as their fastball. A common flaw with change-ups is that many pitchers choke the ball and struggle to reach the plate. This drill should help solve that problem. As mentioned previously, pitchers should experiment with a variety of fingertip pressures and locations on the ball for grip. Effective communication between partners can determine which specific pitches had excellent movement to determine which grip works best. The key is for pitchers to not drop their elbow while throwing, which leads to them pushing the ball.

Medicine Ball—Exploding Hips Drill

Players should use a medicine ball that is appropriate for their age. This drill centers on the importance of the *lower half* when pitching. Pitchers will hold the medicine ball with two hands in front of their face and get into the balance point position (Figure 1-28). By exploding their hips toward the plate, they will throw the medicine ball down at the ground five to seven feet in front of them.

Figure 1-28. Balance point position

Players can think about *popping the hips* and being explosive. Coaches must stress that this is a two-arm drill, as a player may risk injury holding the weighted medicine ball with one arm.

Should pitchers stand tall or dip and drive during their delivery?

A pitcher's physique should dictate what mechanical approach he uses. A tall pitcher who releases the ball (with his arm raised over his head) at seven feet or higher should not drop down and give away the advantage that his height provides. The greater the downward angle on release, the harder it is for batters to see the ball effectively. Tom Seaver, who is famous for driving with his legs so that his back knee actually touched the dirt on the mound, helped popularize the notion that pitchers should *dip and drive*. Although the legs are crucial in the pitching motion, standing tall, gaining power by twisting/releasing the hips, and not collapsing the backside are also effective mechanics for pitchers to focus on.

Topic of Debate: Pushing vs. Pulling Off the Rubber

Pitching coaches vary in views regarding whether pushing off the rubber actually increases velocity. Proponents of dip and drive mechanics commonly refer to pushing off the pitching rubber. Others claim that the pitcher should technically be pulled off the rubber as the untwisting of the hips pulls the body forward. In making a comparison to hitting, hitters do not push with their back leg or foot. Rather, hitters uncoil their hips in generating torque to drive the baseball.

Ball Up Drill

Pitchers must focus on staying back as they go through their pitching motion in this drill. Players will start in the same position as the extension drill, or get into the balance point position (Figure 1-18) while maintaining balance. Pitchers should raise the *ball up* above their head as they separate the ball from the glove and concentrate on a proper arm slot as they lift the ball above their shoulder. The other goal is to ensure that the body waits for the arm to get back as the motion starts. This drill includes three consecutive, ball-up repetitions before the pitch is released. Ball up is an effective teaching tool for pitchers who struggle keeping the ball down in the strike zone by forcing them to work on a consistent arm angle, pace, and body control through the delivery.

Towel Drill

 This drill emphasizes the follow-through and finish of the pitching delivery (Figure 1-29). Players will hold a towel (12 to 18 inches in length) between the middle and pointer finger of their throwing hand. A partner or coach will extend his glove hand out as a target. The pitcher will execute his delivery and smack the towel down on the partner's glove. If the towel misses the glove and hits the partner's wrist, it will hurt. Therefore, it must be completed in an organized fashion with coaches looking for fluid mechanics and the proper finish. Pitchers can perform this drill while standing or on a knee. When practicing the towel drill independently, players should use a ball bucket as their target. Six repetitions will be enough as the drill is taxing on the throwing arm.

Figure 1-29. Towel drill

Mirror Drills

An invaluable item for mechanical analysis is a vertical, rectangular mirror. Players are able to observe themselves as they go through drills and check for proper positioning. Mirror work can be done at home, especially to reinforce a newly learned fundamental. The mirror is particularly effective at checking proper form in the flexed bow position and ensuring that the hitter cannot see the baseball, or the pitcher's grip on the ball.

 ### Administrative Time-Out

Equipment bags are required for coaching baseball or any sport. Pitchers or coaches should require the following items for drills: towels, therapeutic bands, three-to-five pound dumbbells, medicine balls, balance balls, colored home plates, plastic pitching rubbers, a blindfold, pitching charts, a stopwatch, and colored baseballs. Effective coaches who know where all of their teaching tools are will have more success in running a high-energy, productive practice.

 ### Teaching Tip

During these activities, it is beneficial to emphasize the elimination of tension in the body throughout each drill. In many cases, players will tense up as they hold the balance point position and struggle not to fall over. Fluid, relaxed body language is a key to successful performance in any sport, especially while pitching. For example, Mariano Rivera looks as if he throws the ball effortlessly due to his terrific balance and fluidity.

Blindfold/Closed Eyes Drill

In setting up this drill, coaches should create a lane with cones from the pitcher to the catcher/receiver. This narrow two-foot lane will provide a throwing alley for pitchers to have as a reference point. Pitchers make a visual a snapshot with their eyes and take a deep breath. Next, pitchers should close their eyes and visualize the lane. At this point, pitchers can release a closed-eyes or blindfolded pitch to their catcher. As a precursor to this drill, pitchers can throw several pitches with eyes open using the lane for a target. The blindfolded drill is effective in helping pitchers gain confidence and sharpen their visualization skills. If a player knows he can throw a strike with his eyes closed, he is confident that he can do the same and better with his eyes open. With his eyes closed prior to starting a game, Pedro Martinez was known to throw several pitches in the bullpen.

Conference Time

A major component of success in any endeavor is confidence, especially in baseball. As Yogi Berra said, "Baseball is 90 percent mental; the other half is physical."[3] If coaches can create positive, outcome-based drills or communicate confidence, it will be a tremendous boost to performance of the individual. Simply letting a player know that you believe in him will go a long way in his development, work ethic, and his buying in to your system.

Team Drills

Balance Beam Drills

A narrow team bench or one foot high balance beam can be used to work on pitcher balance (Figure 1-30). Wobble boards, cushion balls, or balance foam pads can also be used in this exercise to test pitcher balance. Pitchers will hold their balance point with hands at the zipper or flexed bow position while maintaining their balance on the beam. Players can have timed contests to see who can hold the balance point for the longest time without falling off the beam/bench.

Figure 1-30. Balance beam drill (on a bench)

Five-Man Bunt Drill

This drill requires five pitchers. Players assume a diamond formation (20 to 30 feet from each other) with one person in the middle of the drill. Each pitcher will rotate in to the middle of the diamond. While in the middle, the player will field bunts rolled out to him by the other players. The players will roll out the ball and yell "One," "Two," "Three," or "Four." The pitcher will field the ball and throw the ball to the appropriate person based on which number was called. The numbers refer to the three bases and home plate that the pitcher will have to throw to in a game situation. The purpose of the drill is to force players to think quickly and throw accurately to the correct base. Players can rotate in the middle of the drill every 20 fielded bunts.

 Teaching Tip

In the five-man bunt drill, coaches should observe that pitchers are not dropping their elbows when throwing to each base. In game situations, it is common for coaches to yell out "step and throw" as a pitcher fields the ball. Ideally, the pitcher will field each bunt with his backside pointed toward the base he is throwing to and simply *drop-step* with his glove-side foot before releasing the ball to the target.

Now Drill

Pitchers will line up and move forward, one at a time, 10 feet away from the next person in the line. Next, the pitcher will turn his back to a coach who hits a ground ball or soft line drive toward the player. As he hits the ball, the coach yells "Now" to alert the pitcher to turn around. Depending on the age of the players, coaches must determine how far away and how hard to hit the ball at the pitcher. As the pitchers become more effective at responding to the balls, the coach can wait longer to yell "Now." This drill can be done off the pitching mound, on the outfield grass, or indoors. Players enjoy this drill as it is fast-paced and requires quick reflexes. For advanced players, coaches can have pitchers start the drill in a kneeling position.

Administrative Time-Out

One of the dangers of pitching, especially when metal bats are used, is the risk of getting hit by a line drive off the bat of a hitter. By practicing the "now" drill, coaches wish to ensure that players react to line drives. This measure may satisfy parents and administrators that their children/students are prepared to properly react to this danger. Younger players can do this drill with soft sock balls or safety balls. The gymnasium or indoor training facilities are venues to practice the "now" drill during pre-season workouts. This drill can also be used to improve infielder reaction time on hard hit balls.

Pitcher Fielding Practice Drills (PFPs)

PFPs are frequently implemented and observed during the first week of spring training. These drills help pitchers rehearse the probable defensive duties they will face in game situations.

Cover First Drill

Pitchers will start by throwing or feigning (going through the motion but not releasing the ball) a pitch toward home plate. Upon release, a coach hits a ground ball to the right side of the field, and the pitcher must *get over* to cover first base. The pitcher will receive a throw from the first baseman or second baseman, step on the base, and turn toward home plate with his throwing arm raised with the ball in hand. It is critical to stress the *banana route* pitchers should take to the base (Figure 1-31). This curved path to first base enables them to touch the base with their right foot and have their body momentum take them out of the baseline. This path is imperative so that the pitcher does not get run over by the base runner running through first base.

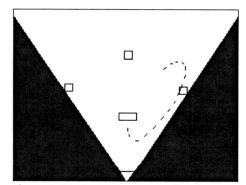

Figure 1-31. Banana route to first base

In addition, the pitcher should reposition himself to quickly turn back to the infield in case another base runner tries to advance a base. Left-handed pitchers must be especially alert in covering first as their delivery will naturally force them to fall off the mound on the third base side. Furthermore, when a left-handed pitcher covers and steps on first base, he has to turn his body at least 180 degrees to throw to third base or home plate to cut down advancing base runners.

Three Steps to Success

1. Quickly run off the mound toward first base in a banana-shaped route.
2. Catch the ball, and step on first base with the right foot.
3. With the ball raised above the head in the bare hand of the throwing arm, turn to face the infield.

Topic of Debate: Covering First Base

For many years, the banana route has been taught as the proper method for pitchers to get over and cover first base on balls hit to the right side. Yet, some teams at higher levels of play instruct pitchers to sprint on a straight line to the base. With speedy base runners at these higher levels, pitchers may not beat the runner to first base if they take a rounded path. Rather, these teams believe pitchers should run on a straight line to get to the base in the fastest way possible.

Cover 4 Drill

Pitchers will feign a pitch to home plate and cover 4 as if a base runner is attempting to score on a wild pitch. As the pitcher feigns the pitch, a coach will throw a wild pitch from behind the pitcher, which the catcher must field. The pitcher will cover home plate, catch the thrown ball from the catcher, and apply a tag to the would-be sliding base runner. Pitchers should be pointing and verbally informing the catcher where the ball is. This drill can be also be done without catchers, as a coach can quickly move in an oval-shaped direction from behind home plate rapidly throwing balls to the incoming pitchers.

Three Steps to Success

1. Quickly run off mound toward home plate while pointing to catcher where wild pitch is located.
2. Bend down low, and present a good target on third base side of home plate.
3. When straddling home plate, carefully position feet to avoid being spiked as the base runner will be sliding in to the frontside corner of the plate.

 Administrative Time-Out

In order to make PFPs or any pitching drills more efficient, coaches can implement *thirds drills*. These drills split the infield into thirds and enable three pitching drills to be running simultaneously. For example, the cover first drill, pickoffs at second base, and fielded bunts on the third baseline can all be done at the same time with players rotating to each drill every five minutes and keeping all 8 to 10 pitchers in constant motion.

Squeeze Bunt Drill

Pitchers will throw or feign a pitch to a catcher at home plate. A coach will roll out a bunt, which the pitcher will field and quickly toss to the catcher. Coaches can run this drill with base runners coming home from third base, especially during the *defensive situations* portion of their practice plan (see Chapter 8: Team Play). However, during PFPs, pitchers need to get a large number of repetitions so that they can learn how to flip underhand, sidearm, or make a backhanded toss in a rushed scenario. Coaches must review with their players when to field the bunt barehanded versus with a glove. In addition, communication skills will be emphasized here as all team members should be yelling "Squeeze" as soon as the batter and base runner reveal that the squeeze bunt is on. This drill is also effective at teaching catchers how to work on their tags and blocking of home plate.

Teaching Tip

Two types of squeeze bunts can be executed. The *safety squeeze* is a sacrifice bunt where the batter shows bunt early, and the base runner at third waits to see if he can advance pending the effectiveness of the bunt. The *suicide squeeze* is different in that the runner breaks from third in the middle of the pitcher's motion, and the batter must *protect the runner* by getting the bunt down regardless of pitch location. Unlike the safety squeeze, where the batter can take the pitch if it is out of the strike zone, the bunter must get his bat on the ball in a suicide squeeze situation.

In-Game Strategy: Squeeze Bunts

The squeeze bunt is one of the most exciting plays in baseball and can quickly change the momentum of a game. The team that executes a successful squeeze play or the team that defends it properly can swing the tide of the game in its favor. Oftentimes, when a squeeze is called, the game is close. The team that executes better gains an emotional edge. Therefore, reviewing how to defend the play is important so players are not surprised when it happens. Coaches can implement squeeze bunts in their daily practice plans within the batting practice routine, thirds drills, or defensive situations.

Conference Time

Coaches need to be able to convey the message to their pitchers that their job is not finished after they have pitched the ball. Many games are won or lost on poorly fielded bunts or errant throws by pitchers. Many times, teams will use the bunt to put pressure on the opposing pitcher if they are struggling to get men on base. Late in games when the score is close, many teams will bunt runners over to make the pitcher field the ball, expecting him to be nervous and throw the ball away.

What is the best way to defend the squeeze bunt?

If a coach senses that the offense may be putting on a squeeze, then his pitcher should be throwing from the stretch position to limit the jump the runner at third gets off the base. In addition, the pitcher should throw a high, inside fastball, which will make it difficult for the batter to bunt the ball on the ground. A *pitchout* is not recommended because the catcher will be forced to vacate the home plate area. Instead, coaches can call for a *pitch-up*, which is a high fastball that does not move the catcher too far from the catcher's box, yet makes it difficult for the batter to make contact with the ball.

Double Plays (1-6-3, 1-4-3, 3-6-1, 1-2-3)

The double play is known as the pitcher's best friend. Yet, many pitchers struggle to help themselves by effectively turning a double play. The most common way a pitcher can be involved in a double play is on a ball hit back to the mound (*come backer*) that he throws to the shortstop, who then throws to the first baseman. This, using the numbers that correspond to specific fielders on the infield, is a 1-6-3 double play. A 1-4-3, in which the second baseman covers the second base bag and throws to first, is a less common double play started by the pitcher. The most difficult double play for a pitcher is the 3-6-1 double play, in which the pitcher must get over and cover first base to receive a throw from the shortstop. This play is similar to the cover first drill except that the throw is delivered much harder, on a more difficult angle, and many pitchers forget to cover in this situation. Lastly is the double play turned in a bases-loaded situation, in which the pitcher fields a come backer, throws home to the catcher, who then throws to first base. All of these double plays can be crucial in getting a team out of a potentially bad inning. Coaches should set up double play drills by hitting ground balls on the infield without runners on base initially. As the players develop quickness and consistently deliver accurate throws, coaches can put runners on base to give pitchers/infielders repetitions in these scenarios.

 Administrative Time-Out

One technique coaches can utilize to simulate game situations is to put runners on the bases while infielders execute different plays. For safety purposes, all runners must be wearing a helmet and treat the situation as if it is a game. The coach can have signals with the runners (separate and simpler than the team signals) to pressure the defense. With four players rotating in as runners and nine players on defense in the field, the remaining position players can work on position-specific fundamentals or hitting drills with an assistant coach before rotating in as a defensive player or base runner.

Pickoff Moves

Pickoff to First Base—Right-Handed Throwers

Pitchers pitch from the *stretch position* with a man on first base. This position enables them to throw over to first base with a *spin move* or deliver a pitch to the batter. The pickoff move requires quickness and accuracy, not power or strength. Right-handed pitchers with great pickoff moves have exceptionally quick hands and feet.

 Teaching Tip

Coaches often command their pitcher to "Focus on the batter" because he devotes too much attention to pickoff attempts. By implementing slide steps, step-offs, and simply holding the stretch position for varied lengths of time, pitchers can mitigate the opponent's running game. Baseball has no clock, so a rule against holding the stretch position for several seconds straight or until the batter calls time-out does not exist.

Three Steps to Success

1. Step off the pitching rubber with the right foot.
2. Jump turn toward first base while rotating the shoulders and hips.
3. Throw the ball like a dart from the right ear position to the first baseman.

For a right-handed thrower, various techniques can be implemented to hold runners at first base (Figure 1-32). Pitchers do not need to pick off base runners in order to be effective at controlling an opponent's running game. First, a pitcher can hold the stretch position for varied lengths of time to break the base runner's rhythm. The base runner is hoping to time the pitcher's move to get a *good jump* off the bag. The more varied the pitcher is in throwing to first base, holding the stretch position, and *stepping off* the pitching rubber, the more difficult it becomes for the base runner to get a good jump.

Figure 1-32. Right-handed pickoff move

A pitcher can also vary his delivery to the plate to further frustrate the base runner. On some pitches, he can lift his leg as in his normal delivery. On other pitches, he can *slide step* to take less time to deliver the ball. During a slide step, the pitcher does not lift his leg up to waist height, but rather uses *knee-to-knee mechanics* (with the glove-side knee quickly moving toward the throwing-side knee) and slides the landing foot close to the ground for a quicker release. The key is for the pitcher to find the proper balance between focusing on the batter and keeping the base runner in mind. Some pitchers, even at the major league level, will not bother to hold the runner close at first base because it is not a facet of the game that they effectively execute.

Conversely, some pitchers spend too much time focusing on the base runner. With his attention divided, a pitcher may walk the batter or throw too many hittable pitches. Many younger players in particular, once leading and stealing are introduced, become infatuated with attempting pickoff moves. This approach slows down the game and dulls the game for many of the players on the field. Furthermore, many of these pitchers' pickoff throws are wild, and the runner ends up advancing on overthrown balls anyway.

Administrative Time-Out

One item that coaches should always keep in their pocket is a stopwatch. In the case of holding runners, coaches can time their pitcher (and the opponent's pitcher) for how long it takes him to throw to the plate. The watch must be started when the pitcher breaks his hands or makes his first move to the plate and stopped when the catcher receives the ball. A pitcher that is 1.2 seconds or faster is extremely *quick to the plate*. 1.6 seconds or more is slow and will not be fast enough to give the catcher a realistic chance to throw out most prospective base stealers. Coaches should use the stopwatch discreetly in games.

In-Game Strategy: Cat and Mouse Game—Pitcher and Base Runner

Some avid baseball fans appreciate the game within a game between the pitcher and base runner at first base, while others find that it makes baseball slow and boring. From a strategic standpoint, it can determine whether a runner gets into scoring position and ultimately puts the offensive team ahead. Much of this battle involves breaking the opposition's rhythm. The pitcher may step off the rubber, throw over to first base numerous times with varied pauses, or throw a pitch out. The runner and batter may call time-out as the pitcher gets set, jump around to distract the pitcher, or devise other distracting tactics.

What is a balk?

Technically, a balk is when the pitcher deceives the base runner. However, it is a paradox as being deceptive is the goal of a pitcher's pickoff move. Nonetheless, specific pitcher movements will result in a balk call and advance runners one base each. The pitcher must come to a *discernable stop* in his *set position*. He also cannot start then stop and restart his motion, flinch his hands, legs, or make any movement that would imply that he is throwing to home plate. Some pitchers will develop a *balk move* in which they make slight movements with their feet to make the runner believe that they are throwing to first base or home plate, and then do the opposite. This move is, by rule, a balk, but a skilled pitcher can disguise these subtle movements.

Pickoff Drills—Right-Handed Throwers

Quick Feet Drill

This drill requires a gym floor or any flat ground area. Coaches can put down four pieces of tape. Two pieces should be put where the pitcher's feet are in the stretch position, and two pieces are placed where his feet will be after his jump turn move. Next, coaches can time their pitchers on how long it takes them to replace their feet in making a jump turn. An effective pickoff move should take less than 1.0 seconds. Pitchers can also be prompted to do 5 or 10 repetitions in a row working on quickly popping their feet.

Pickoff Drill

During indoor workouts, the pickoff drill is terrific to get base runners and pitchers in game shape. In this drill, pitchers rotate on an indoor mound or a plastic pitching rubber as base runners take their leads from a throw-down base. Every third pitch or so, pitchers should throw a ball to home plate to keep the runners guessing. Moreover, pitchers must work on a deceptive or quick move to the plate on these throws home. This drill can also be done outdoors either on the infield diamond or other flat ground area.

1, 2, 3 Drill

A crucial aspect of effectively holding runners is for the pitcher not to reveal his quickest move on every pickoff attempt. This drill requires pitchers to use their best move when coaches call out "1," their second best move on "2," and a mediocre move when "3" is called. Coaches may use a 3, 2, 1 sequence to reinforce the point to pitchers that they should not show opposing teams their most effective move early in the game, or on the first throw over. Pitchers can successfully fool or lull the opponent's base runners by initially posturing a weak and/or slow pickoff move.

Pickoff to First Base—Left-Handed Throwers

A left-handed throwing pitcher can feature two different pickoff moves. The *step-off, snap throw* is a move in which the pitcher steps off the pitching rubber with his left foot and throws a snap throw over to first base. This move is rarely effective unless the base runner is not paying attention, or is looking at the third base coach's signals. Not only does this move require a quick left foot, but enough arm strength to throw hard from shoulder height. Pitchers should not make this move a priority as it works infrequently and does not hold the runner when they deliver the ball to home plate.

The more readily used left-handed pickoff move is where the pitcher lifts his right leg and leaves the runner confused as to whether he is throwing to first base or to home plate. Left-handed throwers face the base runner from the stretch position, which is a completely different dynamic than that of the right-handed pickoff move. The effectiveness of a lefty pickoff move depends a great deal on body lean, deceptive hanging of the right leg, and looks at or away from the runner. An excellent left-handed move will not only pick off base runners, but also have runners *going back to the bag* on pitches home to the batter. Teaching pitchers this move can be time-consuming and difficult as some pitchers innately grasp it while others are awkward and too mechanical. *Unlike the right-handed pickoff move, which requires athleticism and quickness, the left-handed move incorporates guile and instinct.*

Pickoff Drills—Left-Handed Throwers

Cone Drill

For a lefty to develop an effective move, he must be comfortable holding his leg in the balance point position. For that reason, balance beam drills are good

Three Steps to Success

1. Lift the right leg to balance point and hang the leg without giving the runner indication of where the throw will go (Figure 1-33).
2. Provide alternating head looks between home plate and first base several times during the right-leg hang.
3. Make a sharp, strong throw to first base like a dart from the left shoulder-height or ear area.

Figure 1-33. Left-handed pickoff move

tools for the left-handed pickoff move. Aside from balance, pitchers must learn a *hard-to-read* body lean. Coaches can set up cones on the first baseline for pitchers to line up their right leg as they hang in the balance point position. The more comfortable pitchers are with hanging the right leg toward the middle of the 90-foot baseline, the more deceptive they will be.

Pickoff Drill

Similar to the right-handed pickoff drill, this drill includes base runners who are trying to read the pitcher. Coaches may want to have runners intermittently *run on the first move* of the pitcher. This drill will test the pitcher, first baseman, and shortstop in executing a quick throw to second base on a picked off base runner. Also, if the pitcher hangs his leg too long, then a speedy base runner may beat the throw to second base. Much like the right-handed pickoff drill, every few pitches left-handed pitchers must deliver to the plate and try to freeze the base runner.

How do left-handed pitchers typically balk in a game?

Left-handed pitchers can be called for a balk for several reasons. Much like a right-hander, they cannot move any part of their body once they have come to the set position. Also, left-handers may not throw over to first base if they break the imaginary line of the pitching rubber with their right leg, but must throw home instead. In addition, umpires will make a balk call if the pitcher breaks from his normal delivery to confuse the runner by committing his weight in one direction and throwing to the other.

 ### Teaching Tip

Many left-handed pitchers get in the habit of throwing opposite to where they are looking. Consequently, if the pitcher lifts his leg and looks at home plate, then he will throw over to first base and vice versa. This practice is known as the *90:10 rule*. 90 percent of all left-handed pitchers will do this, while only 10 percent will actually throw in the direction that they are looking. Coaches should review this rule with their pitchers and base runners to make sure they are aware of these pitcher tendencies. The great left-handed pitcher pickoff moves show a variety of looks at the balance point until the delivery.

Pickoff to Second Base

The pickoff move to second base is different than the pickoff at first base because no fielder is stationed at the bag awaiting the throw. Instead, the pickoff at second base is a coordinated, timed throw to the base with the second baseman or shortstop darting in for a quick throw. Typically, the pickoff to second is called for by the shortstop or catcher who sees that the runner is lackadaisical or taking a risky lead. The shortstop will flash his open glove to the pitcher to signal that he is going to break for the bag behind the vision of the runner. This pickoff is referred to as the *daylight play* because the pitcher will throw over when he sees "daylight" between the base runner at second base and the shortstop (Figure 1-34). Similar to holding runners at first base, the pitcher does not necessarily have to pick off the runner at second base. Rather, all pitchers should prevent runners from getting an aggressive lead and jump, which will enable them to score on a ball hit to the outfield.

Figure 1-34. Daylight play

The mechanics of a pickoff throw to second base require a reverse pivot in which the pitcher makes a 180-degree rotation toward his glove-side shoulder. For right-handed pitchers, the reverse pivot throw necessitates a shoulder turn toward first base, while lefties turn their body toward third base. Many pitchers do not complete a full 180-degree turn and must drop their elbow to establish an angle to throw to the second base bag. Inevitably, many of these throws sail into the outfield and enable the base runner to advance. Pitchers must place the throw on the third base side of the base, as that is where the tag and base runner will be approaching. Furthermore, pitchers should look in at home plate and not stare at the runner or shortstop in order to not tip off that a pickoff play may be on.

Three Steps to Success

1. Step off the pitching rubber while completing a reverse pivot jump turn.
2. Release a firm throw from throwing shoulder ear.
3. Make a low throw on the third base side of the second base bag for the middle infielder to apply the tag.

Figure 1-35. Reverse pivot pickoff throw to second base

Another form of pickoff at second base is the *inside move*. Unlike the reverse pivot jump turn move, the pitcher does not need to coordinate this pickoff with any teammates. Instead, the pitcher may sense that the runner is contemplating stealing third base. In this case, the pitcher lifts his leg and rotates from his balance point toward second base. If the runner is stealing on the pitch, the pitcher may spin and realize that the runner is already more than halfway to third base. As a result, pitchers who utilize this move must be ready to run at the runner to create a rundown situation, or throw quickly to the third baseman. The inside move is an easy move to learn and has a lower risk of overthrows than the reverse pivot pickoff. In order for the inside move to be effective, pitchers must sell the motion as a typical delivery to the plate in which their mechanics are identical to a normal pitch.

Aside from sensing that a runner may be stealing third base, defensive teams will also signal pitchers to use an inside move in potential bunt situations to see if the batter shows bunt as the pitcher lifts his leg. If he does square or pivot to bunt, defenses can prepare accordingly to defend the bunt on the next pitch. Another strategic time for an inside move arises when there is a 3-2 count with two outs and base runners are breaking on the pitch. Pitchers can occasionally pick off a runner who leaves for the next base before ensuring that the pitcher has delivered in this situation. Despite these tactical advantages for implementing the inside move, *pitchers must learn the reverse pivot jump turn as their primary move to second base because the inside move is ineffective at the higher levels and does not work unless the runner happens to be stealing on that particular pitch.* Additionally, once a pitcher has shown his inside move, it will be futile to use it for the rest of the game as base runners will be wary of it.

Administrative Time-Out

Coaches can devise indoor practice plans where pickoffs at second base are incorporated into the workout. Thirds drills with pickoffs at second base are effective to use once the team begins outdoor workouts. At some point before the season starts, coaches must build in these pickoffs within a team practice format. Outfielders, especially centerfielders, need to view all pickoffs so that they can understand how to back up these plays. Defensive situations and inter squad games are opportunities to practice player responsibilities during pickoff plays.

Conference Time

It is important for a coach to establish trust and rapport with the catcher/shortstop who relays pickoff plays to the pitcher and other infielders. Players enjoy this role of power, but, in the process, they can get overzealous. Coaches must communicate effectively with players about understanding the importance of proper situations (the score or inning of a game) when these pickoffs are appropriate. In addition, considerations must include the pitcher's propensities, how pickoffs may disrupt a pitcher's rhythm, and the momentum swings of a botched or overthrown pickoff attempt.

In-Game Strategy: Mound Visits

Coaches have a limited number of visits or "trips" to the mound. One strategy is to create a nonverbal cue with the catcher or infielder to call time-out and speak to the pitcher. This technique may help relax the pitcher or break the offensive team's momentum. Another technique is to change the sequence of pitches where the pitcher throws three consecutive off-speed pitches and gets back on track.

Why do some pitchers abandon the windup motion and throw strictly from the stretch position?

Many pitchers find that their mechanics are simplified and easier to control from the stretch position. In some cases, closers at the college and major league levels are seen only throwing from the stretch position because runners are on base when they enter the game. The stretch is an effective alternative for a pitcher who has wildness or body control issues, for example, a tall player who has not yet grown into his body yet. Pitchers and coaches should be aware that a degree of velocity loss may occur from the stretch position as well as a decrease in game day endurance.

The Mental Side of Pitching

Get Ahead; Stay Ahead

A question that all coaches can ask their pitchers during the pre-season is: what is the best pitch in baseball? While some may respond with their favorite pitch or one they wish they could throw, the correct answer is "strike one." By addressing this issue in a Q&A format, pitchers will learn that getting ahead of batters is the number-one priority. All they have to do is watch a complete game shutout or no-hitter to realize that well-pitched games share the same ingredient: pitchers getting ahead in the count. Conversely, pitchers who struggle to throw strikes and fall behind are more likely to walk opposing hitters, throw hittable pitches when behind in the count, or develop high pitch counts and be forced to leave the game early. Fielders also tend to play weaker defense and lose their concentration when pitchers are frequently falling behind in the count.

Work Quickly

Pitchers need to learn to find an effective rhythm. When examining the majority of Hall of Fame–level pitchers, it's evident that they work quickly. It does not mean that they rush their delivery or feel hurried, but rather they maintain an upbeat pace. More specifically, working quickly entails receiving the ball from the catcher and getting right to the rubber ready to start the delivery. Focus and concentration are key to this mindset. The eyes are in *tunnel vision* mode zeroed in on the catcher's glove, not wandering off to the dugout or stands. In the case of a rough inning or difficult stretch of the game, nothing is wrong with taking a walk to the back of the mound to gather composure. Yet, the overall approach should be to get the ball and be ready to go after the batter.

Major League Connection

Greg Maddux is a prime example of a successful pitcher who worked quickly. He pitched complete games that lasted less than two hours in length.

Keep the Ball Down

Aside from working quickly, pitchers should *work down in the strike zone*. Pitches, especially off-speed pitches, which are in the upper part of the strike zone, are regularly smashed for extra base hits. The rare exception is a pitcher with a dominant fastball that few hitters can get on top of. In certain counts and situations, a purposeful high fastball is a useful pitch. Nevertheless, a pitcher who keeps most of his pitches up will usually be knocked around by opposing hitters. In addition, most umpires will favor a pitcher who is consistent with his location and perhaps even call strikes on close pitches in that particular pitcher's tendency area.

Change Speeds and Eye Level

Once pitchers begin to throw strikes with consistency, disturbing the hitter's timing should become an area of focus. By changing speeds with four-seam fastballs, two-seam fastballs, change-ups, and other off-speed pitches as they develop, pitchers can effectively frustrate batters. Most all batters get into the box and *sit dead red*, look for a fastball to hit. Rarely will a hitter say, "I hate the fastball." More likely, a hitter will acknowledge that a pitcher's off-speed pitches or movement on the ball are his nemesis. In a given at bat, a strong complement to changing speeds is varying eye level on consecutive pitches. A low change-up or two-seam fastball contrasts well with a four-seam fastball up or out of the strike zone. By disrupting hitters' timing and comfort in the batter's box, pitchers will recognize that variety of repertoire brings success.

 ## Administrative Time-Out

At higher levels, most coaches believe in charting the tendencies of opposing hitters. Many hitters struggle with off-speed pitches. Some hitters do not take many pitches or are first-pitch swingers. Coaches should have several clipboards with *pitching charts* and *spray charts* that enable bench players to write down the pitch type, pitch count, and area of the field to which the batter hit the ball. In college and professional baseball, pitchers chart the opposing team the day before their next start so they can learn the lineup. At the lower levels, a team manager or bench player may have this duty.

Pitch Backward

In terms of breaking a hitter's rhythm, pitchers can develop strategies for pitch selection that surprise opponents. Certain counts are typically fastball counts, while other counts tend to be off-speed pitch situations. For example, most hitters are taught that a 2-0 count is a fastball count. In turn, if a pitcher can throw a change-up on a 2-0 count, he will induce outs by the element of surprise. Likewise in a 1-2 or 0-2 count, off-speed pitches are normally anticipated by the batter. A 1-2 fastball to a corner of the plate will freeze many hitters who may be looking for an off-speed pitch. The 3-2 count, especially with an *open base* (first base is not occupied, but a runner is on second or second and third), is a great time to throw an unexpected pitch. Obviously, pitchers must develop command and confidence with all of their pitches in order to pitch backward effectively.

Pitch to Strengths

In all sports, many athletes desire to play a position or perform a skill at which they are not proficient. For instance, a tiny second baseman desires to hit for power, a center on a basketball team wants to shoot long-range three-point field goals, or a football lineman craves running a fumble back for a touchdown. Clint Eastwood famously said as the film character Dirty Harry, "Man's got to know his limitations." Pitchers oftentimes do not throw their best pitch to hitters. In too many instances, fastball pitchers get beat by toying with off-speed pitches when they can dominate by primarily throwing fastballs. Pitchers must know their strengths and pitch accordingly. In a bases-empty scenario, nothing is wrong with throwing a second- or third-best pitch. With the game on the line and a man in scoring position, pitchers should rely on their strength, only get beaten by their best pitch.

Learn Hitter Tendencies

The first action that batters make before stepping into the batter's box is taking a couple of practice swings. Pitchers should watch for the level of these swings. Is the swing high or low? Good high-ball hitters will habitually take practice swings high in the zone, and vice versa for low-ball hitters. When the batter enters the box, does he stand close to or far from the plate? If he is far from the plate, he probably struggles with the inside pitch and likes pitches out over the plate. On the other hand, a batter who crowds or stands close to the plate prefers inside pitches. This hitter, as a rule, does not like pitches away from him and may be inefficient at covering the outer half of the strike zone as well.

Another clue about hitter tendencies involves how far up or back in the box they stand. This position may be difficult for a pitcher to see, so the catcher or a coach may need to communicate this information. Most hitters that struggle with off-speed pitches or *staying back on the ball* will move up in the batter's box, while batters who are concerned about catching up to a strong fastball will stand deep in the box as close to the catcher as possible. Many teams have a *first pitch fastball hitting* philosophy. In these cases, pitchers should expect batters to swing at the first hittable fastball thrown. Starting these teams or individual hitters that have this tendency with an off-speed pitch is a good tactic to counter this.

 ### In-Game Strategy: The Batter's Box

A hitter who stands up in the front of the batter's box may step out of the box upon making contact with the ball. Although oftentimes a difficult call for the home plate umpire, the batter should be called out. Coaches can alert the umpire to this situation if a specific batter is standing far up in the box. Not all fields, especially at the youth level, have batter's boxes lined for games. Some batters will wipe the box's chalk away with their feet as they get into the box as well. Coaches should expect this situation to arise when they have a pitcher on the mound with a below average fastball and a wide array of off-speed pitches.

Learn Base Runner and Team Tendencies

To generate offense some teams are very aggressive and use a great deal of bunting, hit and run plays, and stolen bases. These teams that play *small ball* must be recognized and pitched to accordingly. Coaches may decide to insert pitchers who are more crafty, deceptive, and better at holding runners on base against these highly aggressive teams. Pitchers should take note of which individuals on each team have excellent speed or the potential to steal bases. Typically, centerfielders and middle infielders that hit at the top or bottom of the batting order possess speed. Pitchers must utilize their best strategies for holding runners and varying their looks to the plate when these players are on base. Specifically, many base stealers display certain mannerisms or body twitches when they are about to steal a base. Body weight tends to shift to the right leg of would-be base stealers. Subtle arm or finger movements may also be apparent in base runners in these steal or hit-and-run situations.

 Teaching Tip

Coaches can assign several players on their team to steal opposing team signals. Many coaches teach techniques for detecting that a bunt, steal, or hit-and-run play may be on. Coaches may change the pace of delivering their signs, players may react differently upon getting a directive, and the team may tip that a certain play is on. At higher levels, teams have been known to videotape a coach giving signals and break it down in order to gain an advantage in future games against a particular opponent. Some view teaching the stealing of signs, in any form, as *bush league* or unethical baseball behavior.

Have a Game Plan

Pitchers want to get ahead of batters in the count. Many coaches and pitchers approach opposing batters whom they have never seen before by the book. This basic pitching philosophy is to throw "hard stuff" or fastballs inside and feature "soft" or off-speed pitches on the outside part of the plate. The reasoning is that hitters who lack bat speed will get *jammed* on inside fastballs, while batters who are quicker will struggle on outside, off-speed pitches as their bat will have already traveled through the hitting zone.

An underutilized strategy in an 0-2 count is to throw an inside, knee-high fastball that may catch the inside corner for a called strike three. At minimum, this pitch should move the hitter off the plate. In turn, on the following pitch, this approach will make the hitter vulnerable to an off-speed pitch on the outside part of the plate. The 0-2, inside fastball is also effective because many hitters who are behind in the count will be ready to dive out over the plate to hit anything close to a strike. This pitch will freeze hitters who are in a defensive mode, those sitting back and trying to spray the ball while not ready to turn on an inside fastball.

 In-Game Strategy: 0-2 Counts

Coaches have different philosophies on how to pitch a batter with an 0-2 count. Some coaches like to tempt the batter with an eye-high fastball as it looks easy to handle. Hitters may struggle to lay off the high fastball and will *go up the ladder* to chase successive elevated pitches. Other coaches prefer a breaking pitch on the outside part of the plate or in the dirt that the batter will feebly go fishing for. Perhaps most important is to learn a hitter's individual tendencies when he is in a defensive mindset. Pitching charts will many times be the best indicator of hitter weaknesses and how to approach an 0-2 count. It is important for the pitcher have a purpose with each pitch and not throw *waste pitches* mindlessly.

Develop a Positive Mound Demeanor

Like so many of life's endeavors, body language plays an important role for pitcher success. Specifically, if an umpire makes a call that disappoints the pitcher, he must not overreact. Likewise, when player errors cause the pitcher to give up runs or raise his pitch count, it is important for a pitcher to stay positive. No defensive player purposely makes an error, or wishes his pitcher to embarrass him. Conversely, pitchers should recognize and compliment a teammate on a sound defensive play that helps the team's cause.

Some pitchers achieve team support better than others, which is not a coincidence. Generally, these pitchers work quickly, throw strikes, and support their teammates in turn. It is not a fluke that highly successful pitchers are good team members, possess an upbeat mound demeanor, and demonstrate positive body language. These pitchers are skilled at eliminating distractions, such as belligerent fans, intimidating opponents, and off-the-field issues. Many pitchers simply do not possess the emotional make-up to survive being alone on the mound. Those pitchers who do survive have the ability to repeatedly focus on the task at hand and recognize that a pitcher's cognitive faculty is a key ingredient for success.

 ### Conference Time

Coaches should communicate with pitchers that their pitches need not be perfect. Rather, pitchers should focus on making good pitches: this distinction is an important point to stress. When a pitcher feels that he must make perfect pitches, he will walk batters. Ahead in the count, nothing is wrong with trying to hit a particular spot, but pitchers who get too cute or hung up in making the ideal pitch will repeatedly *issue free passes* (walks). Coaches can have their pitchers observe batting practice so that they can see that hitters make many routine outs on pitches thrown right down the middle.

Arm Maintenance

Daily Throwing Program

In an effort to build arm strength and avoid arm injuries, pitchers should have a daily throwing routine designed around their weekly, game appearances. Within a given week in-season, pitchers can expect to have one to two game appearances per week, two bullpen throwing sessions, three long toss days, and one or two days of spot drills. In addition, pitchers will be conditioning and working on other pitching drills that may or may not involve throwing a ball.

Sample Week for Pitcher A (Starter)

Monday: Game action—80 pitches as starter
Tuesday: Light tossing—35-foot spot drills
Wednesday: Long toss
Thursday: Bullpen session—25 pitches
Friday: Game action—25 pitches in relief
Saturday: Long toss—Spot drills
Sunday: Bullpen session—25 pitches

Sample Week for Pitcher B (Reliever)

Monday: Game action—30 pitches in relief
Tuesday: Long toss
Wednesday: Bullpen session—25 pitches
Thursday: Game action—40 pitches in relief
Friday: 35-foot spot drills
Saturday: Long toss
Sunday: Bullpen session—25 pitches

Note: One day is likely to be an off day (Saturday or Sunday in this schedule)

 ### Topic of Debate: Pitchers—Daily Throwing

Some coaches advocate four or five days rest in between pitching outings. This rest may include running, light tossing, or spot drills, but no strenuous throwing. However, other pitching coaches advocate a rigorous daily throwing schedule to boost arm strength and reduce injuries. Finding the proper balance of dealing with fatigue and building strength is a challenge. Historically, the Japanese have utilized an intense, daily throwing program to improve arm strength, durability, and overall mechanics. In addition, the highly successful Atlanta Braves' pitching staff of the 1990s implemented a daily throwing routine.

Three Steps to Success

1. Incorporate one to two bullpen sessions during each week.
2. Plan light tossing and/or spot drills on the day after a game appearance in which over 30 pitches were thrown.
3. Make long toss a priority for maintaining arm strength.

At the high school level and below, where there is less player specialization, pitchers ordinarily play other positions, which may limit the ability for coaches to develop regimented throwing programs. Nonetheless, on a daily basis, all pitchers can complete dry, mechanical drills along with their conditioning.

Should pitchers ice their arms after throwing?

As pitchers gain experience, they will develop a post-throwing routine that suits them. Some coaches believe that jogging will break down *lactic acid* in the arm, and that is all pitchers need. Other pitchers prefer icing for 20-minute periods several times after an extensive throwing experience. At the younger levels, many pitchers will be inserted in the game to play another position after coming off the mound. In these cases, pitchers will have to wait until the game is over to begin their icing and/or running program.

Conference Time

Players and coaches need to develop an open line of communication regarding arm fatigue and soreness. Coaches must be able to trust that their pitchers will inform them if they experience pain or general overuse so they can plan accordingly. Similarly, pitchers want to feel comfortable speaking up in these circumstances and know that their coach is cognizant of keeping their arm healthy. Given the high rate of *rotator cuff* injuries and incidences of *Tommy John elbow surgery*, this communication is usually lacking. Hopefully, as pitcher-coach communication improves, daily arm maintenance is emphasized, and sound conditioning routines are implemented, these throwing injuries will decline.

Therapeutic Bands—Surgical Tubing Drills

Dr. Frank Jobe of the Los Angeles Dodgers developed strengthening and preventative maintenance drills known as *Jobe exercises* (Figures 1-36 through 1-41). These drills are mainly used in rehabilitating thrower injuries and preventing future arm problems. Many strength coaches and physical therapists use surgical tubing or resistance bands to complete these rotator cuff exercises. These bands are colorful and commonly used during rehabilitation of any injured body part. The different colors reflect the varied resistance levels of the bands. Coaches can help their players maintain a healthy throwing arm and build arm strength by implementing these drills in to their daily practice routines.

Figure 1-36. Internal rotation

Figure 1-37. External rotation

Figure 1-38. Extension

Figure 1-39. Frontal raise   Figure 1-40. Lateral raise   Figure 1-41. Diagonal cross

 ### Administrative Time-Out

Coaches can require that all players carry a two- to five-pound dumbbell (depending on the age of the player) in their baseball bag. These dumbbells should be used to complete various Jobe exercises as part of the daily stretching routine before throwing drills begin. Another option is for coaches to get 20 empty tennis ball cans and fill each up with sand. These cans must be thoroughly taped up to prevent sand from coming out of the can. The sand-filled tennis ball can works as an effective tool for performing the Jobe drills without using surgical tubing, which is less conducive to fast, team-based warm-up activities.

Pitcher Conditioning

Running

A highly debated topic in baseball circles, especially within pitcher workouts, is the importance and type of running that players should perform. Historically, pitchers have run several miles throughout the week to build endurance and stamina to carry them into the late innings of a game. One reason that pitchers ran long distances is that coaches did not have enough time or staff to work with them. Accordingly, sending a pack of pitchers on a run together several times per week was administratively sensible. In addition, athletes who are more physically fit with less body fat are considered less susceptible to various bodily injuries.

Topic of Debate: Lactic Acid

In recent years, many pitchers are urged to run a distance workout on the day after they pitch to break down lactate or lactic acid. The goal is to limit arm soreness that might set in. Research is not concrete regarding how post-pitching running will affect lactate levels. Nonetheless, it is commonly expected that pitchers will run on the day of or day after their game performance. If the pitched game is over at a reasonable hour, pitchers can do their *distance day* of running on the actual game day. An intense, 30-minute bicycle workout or any strenuous cardiovascular workout where the heart rate is elevated can serve this purpose.

Aside from the distance running day, pitchers should be engaged in running drills to build their legs. In attempting to simulate the rigors of a game, pitcher workouts should be designed to emulate the duration and intensity of the pitching delivery. When developing this workout program, coaches must consider the different muscle fibers of the body. These muscle fibers are distinguished as *type I (slow-twitch) and type II (fast-twitch) fibers*. Type I fibers are linked to aerobic, endurance-based activities, such as distance running and long bicycle rides. Weight lifters and sprinters that require shorter, but more powerful uses for the body have more type II fibers.

The pitching motion, which lasts 10 seconds or less, is a type II muscle fiber activity. As a result, pitchers' weekly fitness routines must contain drills that emphasize type II fibers. Short, explosive running and plyometric drills are best suited to meet this goal. The following workouts can be implemented in variation to enhance pitcher muscle fibers and appropriate endurance training.

Running Poles

For conditioning purposes, pitchers may run from foul pole to foul pole along the outfield warning track, a workout known as *running poles*. These poles are approached differently by teams pending on the objective. Some pitchers will jog the poles, while other workouts require a more brisk, timed run. In an effort to exercise the type II, fast twitch muscle fibers, pitchers can sprint for 10 to 15 seconds from one pole to the centerfield area and jog to next the pole. Another variation of this drill is the *bow and arrow*. In this drill, pitchers will jog to the pole and down one of the foul lines toward the infield a certain distance before sprinting across on a straight line (the arrow) to the opposite pole. Based on age, coaches can use their discretion as to how far to have the players run the arrow. As players get older, the fields that they play on tend to expand in size, which makes for proper proportions to complete the poles and bow and arrow drills.

Hills

Athletes in a number of sports use hills as a conditioning workout. Running up an incline will intensively work pitchers' quadriceps, hamstring, and calf muscles. Baseball fields or training facilities that are not near hilly terrain can utilize a ramp in a safe area to get the benefits of the hill workout.

Administrative Time-Out

Coaches should devise conditioning workouts that are varied. In order to maintain that the fitness drills remain fresh and productive, coaches must be creative in drawing up daily activities. Otherwise, players will become mentally bored and their muscles will get too accustomed to the conditioning. Another reason for varying the workouts is to prevent injury. Overuse injuries will occur if the same muscles and tendons are drilled each day through repetitive exercises. The varied drills can be fun and team-based competitions should be implemented to make each exercise more interesting.

Explosive Running Drills

Sprints

Pitchers can perform a variety of conditioning workouts to enhance their fast twitch muscle fiber. Sprints that are run in the outfield from one foul line toward centerfield are effective. Second base is a useful measuring point as it is 90 feet (30 yards) from the first baseline. As the foul line widens moving toward the foul pole, the 90 feet does increase. During rainy days or out of season, the sprints can be completed on a track, gym floor, or turf field.

Stadiums

Coaches can also have pitchers run up and down the bleachers at a football field or indoor basketball arena. If bleachers are not logistically feasible, staircases may also be used. Professional and collegiate athletes have the benefit of using large stadiums for this conditioning workout. In terms of measuring the size of the step or whether to run up more than one step at a time, athletes must focus on a stride that will enable them to be explosive. If the stride is too short or long, the drill will be ineffective in fulfilling its purpose. Many players prefer to run up the steps or bleachers two or three steps at a time, but this can be dangerous, especially as they begin to tire.

Step-Ups

A more controlled workout can be done by having players use only the first step on the bleachers (Figure 1-42). On a whistle or verbal cue, players will step up and down from the stadium or bleacher step. The athletes must not let their feet stay on the ground or step for more than a split second. Coaches can time this drill for varied lengths of time in each set. For example, the first set might last 10 seconds, while the next set will not be stopped until the players work for 20 or 25 seconds. This variation keeps the players guessing how long the drill will last and adds an element of spontaneity to the workout.

 Conference Time

Many pitchers resist the notion that baseball players need to train or be in good physical shape. Coaches must communicate to all of their athletes, especially those with a poor physique, the relationship

Figure 1-42. Step-ups

between training and in-game performance. By providing examples of Hall of Fame–level pitchers, such as Nolan Ryan, Roger Clemens, and Tom Seaver, coaches can impress upon players that off-the-field workouts impact velocity, endurance, and injury prevention. Handing out or posting articles specifically dealing with peak performance levels related to pitcher fitness will validate this point.

Shuttle Runs

An agility-based drill that tests players' ability to sprint, stop quickly, bend over, and explode is shuttle runs. These exercises can be done on a gym floor, lined field, or tennis court area. Players should start in a base-stealing start with their right foot on the baseline. On a whistle or coach's command, they sprint 30 to 40 feet to another line or spot to stop, turn around, and sprint back to the baseline. Coaches can have the players pick up or drop a baseball at the turn, halfway point of the drill, or just have the players touch a line or cone.

Baseball Race

A challenging extension of shuttle runs is to place four or five baseballs on the lines of a football field or basketball court every 10 feet. Players will run out, pick up each ball one at a time, and place them on the line where they started from before running after the next ball. Coaches can time the players and require them to complete the activity within a certain period of time. Relay races can also be incorporated to make this drill a fun, teambuilding competition. As a reward, the winning team can be exempt from one or more of the planned races.

Pick-Ups

During the pre-season, many teams are forced to practice indoors. An excellent fitness and lateral movement drill for players to work on is pick-ups (Figure 1-43). This activity is done without a glove, and players must be partnered with another player or coach. One player will get down on a knee and roll a baseball on the gym floor so that it stays low and does not bounce up or hop. When rolling out the ball, the partner will alternate working the player to his right and left. This drill should push the pitcher to move laterally without crossing his feet over a 10-foot wide range. Players must stay low and not straighten up upon flipping the ball back to their partner. The speed that balls are rolled out will depend on the mobility of the players performing the drill. Sets of 20 to 30 repetitions should be completed before partners switch.

Figure 1-43. Pick-ups

Fartleks

The fartleks exercise is done on a track, but can be done around the edges of a fenced in baseball field or rectangular sports field. Players will jog the curves of the track and sprint the straight sections of the lap. On a field, players will find a section that they can sprint for 10 to 15 seconds and another section to jog for 20 to 30 seconds. Coaches can have different players rotating as the pacesetters for this workout. One game that can be played with fartleks is *catch the pack*. Pitchers will be set off in groups of four and have to catch the next pack or group of four doing their jogging phase of the drill. Prizes can be given out for the pack that performs the best throughout the workout.

Indian Run

Similar to the fartleks workout, an Indian run can be performed on a track or any sizable running area. Pitchers will jog in a single file formation and stay packed close together. On a coach's command, the player in the back of the line will sprint out to the front of the line. The more players involved in the drill, the longer the sprint will be. Optimally, this workout is conducted with 10 to 15 players. Players enjoy this team-oriented conditioning exercise.

Non-Traditional, Innovative Workouts

Given the fact that pitching requires balance, flexibility, and many different forms of bodily strength, some pitchers are using non-traditional forms of exercise to enhance their baseball physique: Karate, yoga, kickboxing, Pilates, dance, and other activities are among the innovative activities. These alternative workouts provide variation and, in some cases, a competitive component that attracts many athletes who seek an edge on the competition.

 Administrative Time-Out

Although players want to boost performance through off-the-field workouts, it is important for coaches to convey the importance of avoiding injury. For example, pitchers can tear their rotator cuff or develop shoulder problems if they are overzealous in the weight room. Players must be reminded that they are baseball players, not power lifters, boxers, or karate experts. While many players develop new athletic interests through alternative strength training, they should be guided carefully throughout this training process.

Sources/Further Reading

[1]Dickson, P. (1992). *Baseball's Greatest Quotations*. New York: Harper Perennial. P. 466.

[2]Berler, R. (2009) "Arms-Control Breakdown," *New York Times Magazine* (August 9, 2009).

[3]Dickson, P. (1992). *Baseball's Greatest Quotations*. New York: Harper Perennial. P. 41.

Marshall, M. (2003). *Coaching Pitchers* (Chapter 32: "Physiology of Exercise"). Retrieved from http://drmikemarshall.com/FreeCoachingBaseballPitchersBook.html

HITTING

Chapter 2

*The one unbreakable rule about hitting is this: if a
batter hits well with his own particular stance and
swing, think twice—or more—before suggesting a
change. There is no one correct way to bat, and so of
course there is no one correct stance to look for.*

—Stan Musial[1]

In baseball circles, the statement "If you woke him up in the middle of the night, he could get right out of bed and hit" describes the "natural" hitter. Hitting is a skill that some players instinctively possess regardless of their physique or athletic prowess. Babe Ruth, the most dominant hitter of all-time, was known to show up to the ballpark after a long night of beer drinking and gobble down several hot dogs before games. Certainly, photographs and video footage of his overweight, plump body give credibility to these stories.

There are many examples of batters who have excellent form yet fail to perform well, likewise, players with flawed hitting fundamentals have succeeded by relying on sheer athletic ability or their instinctive knack for batting. However, Michael Jordan learned that athletic ability does not necessarily translate into success as a hitter. The basketball legend batted a paltry .202 in 436 at bats at the AA minor league level.[2]

Major League Connection

Hall of Fame inductee Dave Winfield is a prime example of a player with unique athletic ability who prospered despite having a significant deficiency in his swing. Winfield's trademark *hitch*, characterized by dropping his hands as the pitch approached the plate, did not prevent him from outstanding offensive production. This hitch, prevalent in adult men's softball leagues, is not a sound technique for baseball.

In contrast, New York Mets' highly touted rookie Gregg Jeffries came to the Major Leagues with a textbook swing. Having rehearsed his splendid mechanics with workouts, directed by his father, Jeffries possessed all of the traits of a future hitting star. Despite his pure, fluid swing and solid baseball frame, he never dominated big league pitchers as baseball prognosticators anticipated.

Despite this evidence, *players can bolster their offensive performance at bat by implementing effective hitting techniques, proper mechanics, and a sound mental approach.* Therefore, while hitting may be largely determined by innate instincts, coaches can significantly impact their players' confidence level, swing efficiency, and effectiveness through various teaching points and drills.

Eye Dominance Testing

One of the first hitting activities that coaches can have their players perform is an eye dominance test, instrumental in making hitters aware of vision deficiencies that may hamper their ability to see the ball and quickly distinguish between fastballs and off-speed pitches. To administer this eye dominance test, coaches should have players overlay their hands and create a circle/oval shaped opening, or scope, with this configuration (Figure 2-1).

Next, players should select a visual target 15 to 20 feet away and capture it in their sight with both eyes through the opening made by their interlocking hands. Once players have the object locked in their sight, they should close

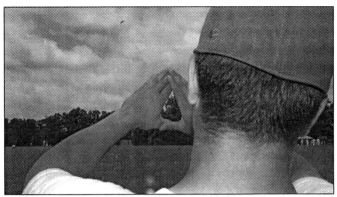

Figure 2-1. Using the hands as a scope

one eye to see if the object appears to move. If the object appears to move, it is likely that the closed eye is their dominant eye. To confirm this finding, the closed eye must be opened to test whether the object does not move upon closing the opposite eye.

Three Steps to Success

1. Overlay the hands to create a circular shaped opening.
2. Using the opening as a scope, focus on a target 15 to 20 feet away.
3. Close each eye to establish which eye is dominant by seeing whether the target moves or remains in a fixed spot.

With awareness of eyesight issues, players can take a far different approach to hitting. For instance, a player that is right-eye dominant can adjust his batting stance so that he has a full view of the pitcher with that eye. The eye closest to the pitcher (left eye for a right-handed batter) is the more critical of the two eyes in a batter's ability to track a pitch toward home plate. Furthermore, as he takes his stance in the batter's box, the position and angle of a hitter's head must be assessed along with eye dominance.

Administrative Time-Out

Players are required to get a physical examination in order to be eligible to play interscholastic sports. This physical entails an eyesight test, which coaches should carefully review. If necessary, coaches may recommend that a player see an eye doctor to obtain prescription glasses or contact lenses. Many players are known to have *holes in their swing* or blind spots where they struggle to hit pitches in certain areas of the strike zone. Eyesight problems can play a role in these instances and should be ruled out with a thorough eye examination.

Teaching Tip

Coaches can have players wear eye patches that cover their dominant eye while they take batting practice, enabling them to experience how important it is for them to be aware of their eye sight deficiencies and, in turn, make hitting adjustments accordingly. Ted Williams' remarkable success as a hitter is partly attributed to his reported 20/10 vision. By emphasizing to players the importance of vision, experimentation with different head tilts in their stance, and *seeing the ball* well, coaches can ensure this integral component of hitting.

Conference Time

Many adolescents are unwilling to wear glasses, worried about their friends or teammates poking fun at their glasses. Coaches can provide examples of professional athletes who need glasses or protective eyewear to make their players feel more comfortable. Prescription sports sunglasses have a more athletic look than traditional glasses. Most of all, when players witness the boost in performance that improved eyesight yields, their concerns about peer opinions will quickly disappear.

The Basics of the Swing

Grip and Bat Selection

When holding the bat, hitters can line up their *door knocking knuckles* for proper alignment of the grip (Figure 2-2). It is important that players not have an *overrotated top hand grip*. In this case, their top hand overrotates on the bat handle with the top of the wrist closer to the knuckles of the bottom hand (Figure 2-3). This grip provides less bat control and ultimately limits contact hitting proficiency. Players can slightly rotate their top hand in the opposite direction so that the tips of the fingers of the top hand are closer to the door knocking knuckles of the bottom hand. This grip will provide more bat control, but less power for hitters. The pepper drill (see Hitting Drills section later in this chapter) is an excellent activity for hitters to experiment with grips and develop a comfort level in holding the bat the proper way.

Figure 2-2. Proper grip on bat

Figure 2-3. Improper grip on bat

By selecting a bat that is too long or heavy for their size, many young players are at a disadvantage before even swinging at a pitch. Coaches can have players hold the bat out horizontally extended at shoulder height for 10 to 15 seconds to check whether it is too heavy. If the player struggles to hold the bat (at the knob) parallel with their shoulder for this period of time, then a smaller bat is more appropriate. Some of the game's greatest hitters, including

Ted Williams and Tony Gwynn, prefer small, light bats. Barry Bonds hit many of his 762 career home runs while *choking up* (moving his hands closer to the barrel) and thus shortening his bat length.

 Administrative Time-Out

Coaches can bring a wide variety of bats to practice so that players can find a suitable bat to use. Many teams in aluminum bat leagues have their players swing wood bats during batting practice, scrimmage games, and off-season workouts. This technique works as an effective training tool so that hitters learn to hit the ball off the sweet spot of the bat. Wooden bats have less room for error and require hitters to make contact with the ball off the barrel of the bat. Often, players will not use their game bat in practice so that it does not break or *go dead*.

Stance

Throughout Major League Baseball history, players have had success with a variety of batting stances. Some players are comfortable hitting from a low crouch, while others stand tall with their hands held above their head. Ultimately, hitters must find their own way after devoting hours and hours to practicing what works for them. Regardless of a player's particular style or batting posture, certain necessary elements are needed so that a hitter can effectively get his bat into the *hitting zone*.

A great deal of hitting starts with the feet. Many hitters that struggle to make consistent contact suffer from poor balance and stride length, both of which stem from the feet. As with so many athletic skills, the batting stance should have the feet at shoulder-width apart or slightly wider. Players can jump off the ground with their feet shoulder-width apart and land in a balanced, bent knee posture to find an effective athletic position. Some players widen their stance by moving their feet further apart to prevent an overly long stride. The key is to achieve a balanced base where hitters can explode their hips from the starting position.

 Is it advisable for players to spend a lot of time practicing switch-hitting?

Switch-hitting can be effective for players who struggle seeing the ball or handling off-speed pitches. Hitters must realize that since most pitchers are right-handed, if they choose to switch hit, then they will be batting left-handed 70 to 80 percent of the time. In addition, many coaches will not be able to give them equal swings in practice from both sides of the plate. Switch-hitting should only be utilized if the hitter is productive, not for a unique marketing gimmick or novelty.

Another crucial component to the stance involves the hands and the height at which the bat is held. *Players should keep their hands at least as high as the top of the strike zone.* If the hands start below the strike zone, then it will be difficult for a batter to catch up with chest-level fastballs. This positioning will result in pop ups, fly balls, and swinging through pitches. A guideline for coaches is to have players hold their hands somewhere between the height of the top of their head and their armpit (Figure 2-4). Ultimately, players must find their individual preference for the exact height of the hands without a mandate from coaches.

Figure 2-4. Balanced stance—
45-degree bat angle

Three Steps to Success

1. Stand in an athletic position with the feet slightly wider than shoulder-width apart.
2. Make sure the hands are above the strike zone and not lower than armpit level.
3. Use a bat angle that suits the goals of the hitter for power or contact emphasis.

 ### In-Game Strategy: Studying the Hitter

Many coaches and experienced catchers will carefully watch the stride and hands of an opposition's hitters and pitch them accordingly. A player who holds his hands low in the stance will be susceptible to high fastballs, while a player who strides *in the bucket* (off to the side or away from the pitcher) will struggle with the outside pitch. An awareness of changes in a hitter's stance, such as choking up or widening the feet, may give a coach the opportunity to move the defense in.

 ### Conference Time

Young players tend to emulate professional players or their TV idols by copying their stances. These "ESPN stances," as seen on *Baseball Tonight*, can hamper players from reaching their potential. Coaches should explain that Major Leaguers possess superior athletic ability and strength, which allows them to have mechanics that are nonconventional, but effective. In particular, the high leg kicks of players such as Ichiro Suzuki and Gary Sheffield should not be duplicated by players who do not have their remarkable hand/eye coordination and bat speed.

The angle at which players hold their bat varies from batter to batter. Some hitters will hold the bat vertically so that the knob is pointing directly at the ground and the top of the bat is facing the sky (Figure 2-5). Others will keep a *flat bat angle*, where the bat is on a horizontal plane (Figure 2-6). Players can also hold the bat at a 45-degree angle, which is somewhere in between upright and flat (Figure 2-7). Some players even hold the bat past upright with the top of the barrel tilting forward, which requires the hitter to generate great bat speed to get the bat into the hitting zone (Figure 2-8). A common problem, which slows the bat's arrival to the contact phase of the swing, is when hitters *wrap the bat* behind the head in their stance (Figure 2-9) or during the *load* process.

Figure 2-5. Vertical bat angle   Figure 2-6. Flat bat angle

Figure 2-7. 45-degree bat   Figure 2-8. Forward tilt   Figure 2-9. Wrapping the
angle   bat

A flat bat angle is the one in which the bat is closest and fastest to the hitting zone, while the vertical or forward tilt positions are further from the point of contact. Nonetheless, some hitters prefer the vertical angle as the bat feels lighter and provides an opportunity for more torque and bat whip than the flat angle. Hitters must find a bat angle that coincides with their goals at the plate. A player who wants to generate more power can utilize a vertical bat position, whereas players looking to maximize contact hitting should have a flatter bat angle in their stance.

What are the most common flaws in players' swings that need correction?

Many hitters at the youth level drop their hands, step in the bucket, *pull off the ball* with their body and head swaying out of the batter's box, possess an extreme uppercut, and prematurely remove their top hand from the bat. Causes of these mechanical issues are limited upper body strength, fear of being hit by the ball, and poorly thrown batting practice with slow, looping pitches.

Administrative Time-Out

Computer software programs are available that enable coaches to superimpose the stance and swing of their players with those of successful Major League hitters. Although it is important to caution players about copying the ineffective fundamentals of the pros, analyzing the positive aspects of successful players' swings is worthwhile. Coaches can also hang a bulletin board on the dugout fence or outside their office with the purpose of pinning up photographs and baseball card pictures of players in the proper hitting position for their team to study.

Stride

A player's stride is the trigger that moves his weight in the direction of the pitcher during the swing. It is imperative for coaches to emphasize that hitters must *get the front foot down early*. Otherwise, batters will be late in getting their swing through the ball. The stride should begin no later than when the pitcher releases the ball. Players can remember the four S words—*short, soft, straight*, and *soon*—to help with their stride. Specifically, the stride should be short in length, soft when landing on the ground, straight toward the pitcher, and completed soon enough for the swing to be performed effectively.

Three Steps to Success

1. Utilize a short stride of three to five inches.
2. Focus on a soft landing with the front foot that will not jolt the body.
3. Get the stride foot down early so the swing can be completed on time.

Major League Connection

Houston Astros' star Jeff Bagwell started with a wide stance and used a front foot stride that actually went backward. Bagwell surprisingly amassed 449 home runs in his career with these unique hitting mechanics.[2]

Teaching Tip

Players will commonly overstride or *step in the bucket* (named for the bucket of water put down by coaches to discourage hitters from stepping in the direction outside of the batter's box). Coaches can tie hitters' legs together with a short piece of string or tubing to limit stride length in practice. Hitters can monitor their stride on their own by sweeping the batter's box with their feet and looking at footprints after each pitch. Home plate can also be used as measurement to regulate stride length. Batters can simply make a mental note of where their stance starts in relation to the edges of the plate before and after they swing.

Rotational vs. Linear Hitting Styles

Hitting styles fall under two categories: rotational and linear. Rotational hitters, as the name implies, rotate their hips as the primary generator of power. This explosive turning motion provides the inertia for the bat to come through the hitting zone. Linear hitters' swings, in contrast, move in a forward direction with less emphasis on rotating the hips. Instead, the weight shifting movement from back to forward generates the momentum for the swing.

 ### Topic of Debate: Hitting Styles—Rotational or Linear?

When debating which style of hitting is best for a player, coaches can consider the particular body type and frame of a player. Furthermore, as his body moves forward 6 to 18 inches through the swing, a linear hitter's head drifts. This factor may limit the number of players who can still make consistent contact using this method. In both cases, hitters must let the legs and hips provide the power for the swing. Coaches should be careful not to expect team uniformity in hitter fundamentals. While some absolutes are ascribed to hitting, players can have the freedom to find their own way while incorporating aspects from linear and rotational techniques in their swing.

Major League Connection

Barry Bonds had a classic rotational swing. This approach enabled him to create immense power by rotating his hips through the swing, while limiting his *head drift*. As a result, Bonds' vision of the ball was extraordinary.

Alex Rodriguez utilizes a linear approach to hitting. His body moves forward greatly from start to finish throughout the swing. Despite moving toward first base when hitting, Ichiro Suzuki also manages to have remarkable success.

The Three Phases of the Swing

Phase One: Short Phase—To the Ball

Regardless of a hitter's approach, he must be *short to the ball*. The swing from the start to contact with the ball in the hitting zone is short and compact (Figure 2-10). Players should strive to be as quick as they can in *throwing the hands* and the head of the bat toward the ball. Many players load in the beginning of this phase by moving their hands back before coming forward to make contact with the ball. The load should be completed *slowly and early* to ensure that rhythm is not disrupted and the bat gets to the hitting zone on time.

Figure 2-10. Phase one of the swing

Phase Two: Contact Phase—Stiff Front Leg, Bent Back Leg

At the time of contact, hitters should have a *stiff front side* (stiff front leg). During this contact phase of the swing, the back leg should be bent (Figure 2-11). The lower the pitch, the more bent and perpendicular to the upper body the leg will be. At contact, the arms form a triangle in relation to the body or V-shaped configuration. The hands are in a *palm up/palm down position* with the top hand facing up and the bottom hand holding the bat with a downward posture. The back foot should rotate with the heel lifting up so that the hips can turn through the swing. Many coaches call this motion *squishing the bug* with the back foot. It is important that hitters do not allow this back foot to slide forward as it must be firmly planted to provide a strong base from which to hit.

Figure 2-11. Phase two of the swing

Phase Three: Extension—Through the Ball

During the final phase of the swing, hitters should come through the ball and get extension (Figure 2-12). Keeping the ball on the barrel of the bat for as long as possible is an effective mental image for hitters to work on. This technique will encourage an efficient follow-through after contact has been made. Hitters must not prematurely extend the arms during the swing; otherwise, casting or a sweeping action will occur.

Figure 2-12. Phase three of the swing

Teaching Tip

Coaches can implement a variety of innovative drills (see Hitting Drills section later in this chapter) to reinforce proper mechanics for the three phases of the swing. For rotational hitters, the hip drill is effective in helping players incorporate their hips in the swing. A medicine ball is useful for having players explode their hips (see Medicine Ball Drill in Chapter 1). Hitters can hit basketballs or volleyballs off a tee to work on coming through the ball. These balls are heavy and force the player to work on powerfully extending through the extension phase of the swing. Additionally, linear hitters will find this drill particularly useful as it requires a strong move forward.

Should players use a load or coiling mechanism in their swing?

The load is a movement back with the hands, hips, or legs that provides hitters with a device for timing and power, much like a hammer being taken back before it comes down to hit a nail. Loading up is effective so long as the hitter completes the load in time to get the bat through the hitting zone and does not lose balance in the process. Frequently, hitters will wrap the bat (Figure 2-9) during the load process, which may cause the bat to be late into the contact phase of the swing.

Hitting to the Opposite Field

Players at all levels do not always see or want to understand the importance of hitting the ball to the opposite field. For a right-handed batter, this means focusing on hitting the ball to the right side of the field. Various situations arise in games in which a ground ball to the right of second base effectively advances a runner from second to third or scores a runner from third base. Moreover, many off-speed pitchers try to induce batters to hit ground balls to the pull side as part of their strategy. In addition, players who gain a reputation for being *dead pull hitters* will have defenses and pitchers stymie their pull-side hitting tendencies by shifting the fielders over or throwing outside pitches.

In-Game Strategy: Situational Hitting

Hitting to the opposite field is advantageous when a base runner is on second base with no outs. The hitter's goal is to drive the runner home or at minimum advance him to third base with less than two outs. In another situation, a runner will be at third base with less than two outs. The infielders will, in many cases, concede the run as long as the ball is not hit to the third baseman. These runners will not be able to advance if the ball is pulled or hit to the left side of the field. These *situational hitting* scenarios require hitters to have the ability to hit to all parts of the field and can dramatically impact the outcome of games.

Several techniques can be implemented that help players hit the ball to the opposite field. Most importantly, hitters must wait for the ball to travel or *get deep* on them in the batter's box. By doing so, the pitch will be hit off the back leg and directed toward the opposite side of the field. It is significant to note that the barrel of the bat is not ahead of the body; rather, it lags and trails behind the hands and front leg. Secondly, hitters must not open up their hips, but rather they should stay *closed with the frontside* in trying to shoot the ball the other way. Lastly, pitch selection is an important factor. Inside pitches are difficult to hit to the opposite field unless the batter is adept at pulling his hands in close to his body and pushing the ball. This technique of getting *the hands inside the baseball* is difficult to master.

Three Steps to Success

1. Wait for the pitch to travel deep into the stance so as to hit it off the back leg.
2. Make sure the front hip stays closed.
3. Keep the hands inside the baseball to create bat lag to hit the ball the other way.

Major League Connection

Derek Jeter successfully gets his hands inside the baseball. He can shoot both outside and inside pitches to the opposite field with his *bat lag* and compact mechanics.

 ## Conference Time

A challenging aspect of coaching is teaching unselfish, team play. Many players are overly concerned with their batting average and other statistics. Coaches must address the importance of *productive outs* to help the team. Hitting a soft ground ball to the right side that advances a base runner from second to third base will help the team, yet lower a hitter's batting average. By fostering open discussions with the team, creating a leader board for sacrifice bunts/runners advanced, and having players congratulate teammates for quality at bats, coaches can effectively encourage an unselfish hitting approach and team spirit.

Hitting Drills

Soft Toss Drill

An excellent drill for hitters to isolate their mechanics is soft toss (Figure 2-13). This partner drill entails flipping a ball from three to five feet away in a kneeling position toward the hitter. It is important that the flipped ball be tossed diagonally, underhand toward the belt buckle of the batter. The goal of the hitter is to hit a line drive straight in front of him. The toss can also be directed at the front or back knee of the hitter to simulate inside/outside pitches. Yet, *flipping the ball toward the back knee can be dangerous as inexperienced batters may hit the ball in the direction of their partner.*

Figure 2-13. Soft toss (side)

A variation of this drill is *rear soft toss* in which the ball is tossed from behind the batter (Figure 2-14). This requires that the hitter wait until the ball travels into the hitting zone. By forcing the batter to keep his hands back before committing to swing, rear soft toss is effective at simulating off-speed pitches and working on opposite field hitting. While the pitch is coming from the opposite direction that it approaches in a game situation, the drill reinforces the concept of staying back and waiting on the ball.

Figure 2-14. Soft toss (rear)

Administrative Time-Out

Coaches should set up practices so that hitters can work on hitting the ball to the opposite field. Batting practices can incorporate fun situational hitting scenarios for prizes in which a runner is put on second base and the batter must move him over to third base. Soft toss and tee hitting drills should be performed with an emphasis on hitting the ball off the back leg. Rear soft toss is a more difficult drill, where the ball is tossed from behind the batter, so he must wait until the ball crosses the hitting zone to swing (Figure 2-14). This approach teaches hitters to let the ball travel before swinging. From an administrative standpoint, coaches must be aware of grass being torn up in areas where players perform soft toss. In addition, chain link fences will get damaged and have poles that pose a danger for soft toss hitting.

One-Hand Hitting Drills

Players can use a short, light bat to complete these activities. This *half bat* tool enables hitters to emphasize the proper use of the top and bottom hand when hitting. A batting tee or soft toss should be used to implement one-hand drills. These isolation drills can be performed standing up or on one knee. The top-hand drill is designed to help players find the proper swing path of the top hand/arm. In particular, this exercise focuses on ensuring that players do not drop their back shoulder when swinging. In addition, hitters can work on being short and quick to the ball with the top-hand drill.

Bottom-hand soft toss and tee hitting drills are especially effective in helping hitters work on hitting the ball to the opposite field. Players should focus on keeping their hand inside the baseball with the barrel of the bat lagging behind the knob. It is important for the barrel of the bat to stay level as many players will drop the barrel and hit underneath the ball.

Double Tee Drills

A batting tee is a valuable tool for players to refine their swing mechanics. Unlike batting practice and other drills, the ball is stationary and can be placed in specific spots of the stance. Also, players do not need a team or partner to utilize a batting tee as they can hit by themselves into a net or padded area and work independently on their swing. Double tee drills enable players to simultaneously put two balls into a hitting drill so as to focus on plate coverage and quick reactions to various pitch locations.

The *inside-outside tee drill* can be executed individually or with a partner (Figure 2-15). The double tee is set up so that one ball is on the inside portion of the plate, while the other ball is placed on a tee on the outside half of the strike zone. The hitter will take his stance over the tee, not too far behind it. As the hitter begins the short or load phase of the swing, his partner will command "outside" or "inside" to prompt him to hit one of the two balls. One of the keys to this drill, and all tee drills, is for the hitter to look straight ahead and visualize that a pitch is approaching from the pitcher's mound and react quickly to the pitch location.

Figure 2-15. Inside-outside tee drill

Players can also work on the *line drive tee drill*, which makes for fun competitions (Figure 2-16). In this drill, two balls are placed in a direct line separated by two to four feet. The hitter will try to hit a line drive off the rear tee with the first ball that will knock the second ball off the front tee. By focusing on line drive hitting, players will be motivated to develop the proper swing path.

Figure 2-16. Line drive tee drill

Conference Time

Young players sometimes view batting tees as juvenile because it reminds them of playing in tee ball leagues. Coaches must explain that the stationary ball allows for players to fine tune and refine their hitting skills outside of a team setting. Moreover, many professional players spend hours doing *tee work* in hitting tunnels on game day. Some players bring a portable tee to game locations and hit in the open field. Although this requires players to fetch the balls off the field, it enables hitters to visualize the scenery and background at that specific ballpark to prepare them for a live game.

Front Toss Drill

In simulating a pitched ball from the mound, coaches should utilize the front or short toss hitting drill (Figures 2-17 through 2-19). Coaches can stand, sit on a bucket, or kneel on the ground while flipping balls underhand from 10 to 15 feet away from the batter. The coach or partner flipping the ball must stand behind a screen to protect against line drives and ground balls hit back at him. This drill is specifically geared for working hitters on the inside and outside portions of the strike zone. Given the slow velocity and consistent accuracy of the flipped ball, hitters can effectively focus on their mechanics in this drill.

Fence Drill

Many players prematurely extend their arms or *sweep* (referred to as casting) early in the swing before making contact with the ball. One method for combating this problem is for players to swing in front of a fence. Before starting

Figure 2-17. Front toss (on a knee)

Figure 2-18. Front toss (on bucket)

Figure 2-19. Front toss (standing)

the drill, hitters must *measure up* by putting the knob of the bat against their chest while placing the end of the bat against a fence or padded wall (Figure 2-20). Once they have measured up (roughly 20 to 34 inches depending on the length of the bat), players swing with the goal of not hitting the fence/wall in front of them (Figure 2-21). This drill forces the hitter to keep his hands close to the body, develop *short to the ball* mechanics, and turn the hips properly. Hitters will be induced to utilize an inside-outside swing as opposed to coming around the ball rotationally. It is important for hitters to step straight when striding and avoid stepping in the bucket so as not to comprise the effectiveness of the drill.

Figure 2-20. Measuring up

Figure 2-21. Swinging—fence drill

Hip Drill

In an effort to incorporate hips into the swing, players can cross their arms or put a bat behind the back and exercise rotating the hips (Figures 2-22 and 2-23). The bat should be placed on the back just above waist height and held by the arms just below the biceps. The barrel of the bat should be on the side that the hitter bats from. Consequently, a right-handed hitter will place the barrel below the right bicep with the knob on the side of the left hip. The player will turn his hips using the bat as the steering wheel. The hip drill is excellent for players to warm up and for instilling a muscle memory of *popping the hips*.

A variation of this drill that can be performed by younger players involves swinging at a pitch (Figure 2-24). The hitter will put his bottom hand behind his back and grip the bat with both hands. The bat will be held in an awkward position on the right hip (for right-handed batters). A coach or partner will flip or soft toss a ball to the batter who will try to hit the ball from this unconventional standing position. Hitters will have to turn their hips in order to make contact with the ball. *Players should not be concerned with where the ball is hit, but rather on the turning of the hips.* By incorporating a ball in the drill, many lower-level players will find this version of the drill more exciting.

Figure 2-22. Without a bat

Figure 2-23. With a bat

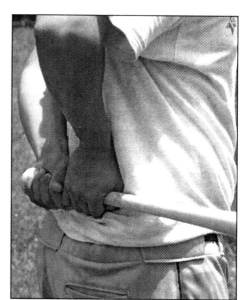

Figure 2-24. With a swing

Pepper Drill

One of the oldest, yet most beneficial hitting activities for players to practice is *pepper* (Figure 2-25). Pepper, as the name implies, involves the batter peppering pitches to other players situated in a semi-circle formation. Players will rotate in as the hitter in a group of two to six players, while the other participants practice their defensive skills and feed pitches to the batter. This drill tests hand-eye coordination, bat control, and plate coverage. It is important for players to throw accurate pitches to the batter so that he can hit the ball to each of the players in the semi-circle.

Players frequently derive games within the pepper drill to keep it fast paced and fun. For instance, if the batter hits a line drive that is caught by one of the

Figure 2-25. Pepper drill

fielders, then he moves to the field and the fielder comes to bat. If a player makes an error on a batted ball, he will have to move to the end of the semicircle and be last to hit. Pepper games should be set up in a safe manner and focus on the goals of the drill—clean defense, spray hitting, and proper mechanics.

Major League Connection

Major League baseball teams have banned players from playing pepper at stadiums to protect fans from injury and the grass from getting ripped up around the field.

 ## Administrative Time-Out

Pepper games are effective when played properly. Coaches must monitor these games and make sure players do not get too silly with the variations of the drill. Additionally, it is important for hitters to be wearing a helmet at all times during this activity even though the players are not throwing the ball full speed. Coaches can set up pepper drills at any location on the field with a fence behind the batter to block errant pitches. Pepper is especially effective when performed before a game so that players can get the feel of the bat hitting a ball.

 ## Teaching Tip

Players should gain confidence with contact hitting and overall plate coverage after playing pepper. Coaches who utilize the hit-and-run offensive strategy can observe their team's pepper games to view which players possess noteworthy bat control. It is important for coaches to stress that hitters take their normal grip on the bat and batting stance when playing pepper. Players commonly choke up too much or use poor mechanics in this drill. The pepper swing should be short and compact with just enough force to hit a firm ground ball to the fielders.

Situation Game Drill

For this drill, coaches will call out a count and situation to which the hitter must respond. For instance, a coach can call "Man on third, one out, 0-2 count." In this scenario, the batter will try to hit a sacrifice fly to score the runner from third base. Situation games can be created for indoor batting cages or at outdoor batting practice. Players or groups of hitters may be awarded points for each situation that they successfully execute.

Vision Drills

Players can perform a variety of activities that emphasize eyesight and vision when hitting. In particular, many of these drills are suited for indoor practice and can be implemented in the off-season. Furthermore, daily indoor practices in northern climates present a challenge for coaches in terms of keeping their team motivated for weeks at a time. As a result, coaches can devise daily hitting groups and stations in which one area of focus at each practice centers on vision.

Colored Ball Drill

Coaches can paint or mark batting practice baseballs with dots of various colors. As hitters swing at pitches, they can call out the color on the ball. These colored balls can be used for soft toss drills or traditional batting practice. The size of the colorful dots can be varied to make it challenging for the hitter. A variation of this drill requires that players respond differently to each colored ball. For example, a red dot may be a take (no swing), while a blue dotted ball should be hit to the opposite field.

Read the Fingers Drill

In this activity, players will have a partner who will stand 60 to 70 feet away and go through the pitching windup without a baseball in hand. As the player gets to the release position, he holds up a certain number of fingers for his partner to call out. This exercise helps the hitter get accustomed to reading the pitcher's release point and fingers/grip on the baseball.

 ## In-Game Strategy: Studying the Pitcher

Before stepping into the batter's box, hitters are constantly trying to gain some advantage. Many coaches will encourage their players to watch from the dugout for a pitcher's release point and the manner in which he may grip or tip off certain pitches. Hank Aaron was known to cover his face with his hat and look through the eyelids to isolate the pitcher's actions. Players are instructed to *read the seams* of an incoming pitch to detect whether a fastball, curveball, or some other off-speed pitch.

Timed Number Drill

In adding variety to indoor hitting workouts, coaches can devise a sheet with rows of numbers on it. These numbers may be handwritten or typed with different sizes and colors. Some of the numbers can be upside down or sideways. Players will be timed by a coach or a teammate to see how fast they can correctly read all of the numbers on the sheet. The player who completes this activity in the shortest amount of time can win a prize. This drill will also quickly show a coach which player(s) may have eyesight issues.

Seated Toothpick Drill

For this activity, players can sit on a chair or bucket with a toothpick in their hand. Their partner will hold a straw in front of them for the player to place the toothpick in. After each repetition with the toothpick, the partner will quickly move the straw to a different location in front of the player. This drill should be completed with both hands and test vision in front of the right and left eye.

75-Foot Hitting Drill

Batting practice sessions and team hitting drills throw balls to players at distances ranging from 5 to 60 feet. Hitters get accustomed to these drills and distances. By throwing pitches to players from 70 to 75 feet away, hitters will have to track the ball for a longer time. In addition, this drill will help players that struggle to wait on the ball. A pitching machine or coach with a strong, accurate arm can be utilized for this drill.

Alternative/Nonconventional Drills

Major League Connection

Sadaharu Oh, the all-time professional record-holder with 868 career home runs, used a samurai sword in his training. In swinging at a straw dummy, he writes, "I swung the sword as I would a bat. It felt right. The straw flew in all directions.... It is possible to fall into the habit of a harmless game when you repeatedly swing a baseball bat; that can never happen with a sword." Oh's remarkable career was aided by his innovative training with a Japanese warrior's balance, mindset, and sword. Certainly, practice techniques that are culturally derived vary from country to country, but Oh's success with unique training activities gives credence to nonconventional hitting drills.[3]

Water Resistance Training Drill

In order to work on bat speed and swing fluidity, players can complete a hitting workout in a pool. By swinging in water, hitters' bats are not able to whip through the hitting zone as they normally do. Rather, batters are forced to utilize their hips and legs in the swing. Gregg Jeffries utilized this training technique as a supplement to his daily hitting drills. This resistance swing training is welcomed by players as a change-of-pace practice technique, especially on hot summer days.

Axe Drill

A valuable demonstration for coaches to show players regarding the swing is the power at contact with arms bent versus fully extended. Ted Williams' book,

The Science of Hitting, has an excellent illustration of this important concept.[4] Coaches can have players put their hand out against a bat pushing out at contact with arms bent and arms extended to evaluate to difference in force with each (Figures 2-26 and 2-27). The axe drill reinforces this point by having players use an axe to chop down a tree at the base (Figure 2-28). Although cutting down a tree may not be feasible, coaches can hang a tire from a branch on a tree so that it hangs at the contact level of hitters' swings. In addition, durable mats can be used for players to swing into to feel the proper arm bend and V-shaped configuration on contact. *Zingbat*® is a product that strives to teach players these swing mechanics through the sound of a rubber piece sliding into a metal cylinder at the top of the bat.

Figure 2-26. Bent arm demonstration

Figure 2-27. Extended arm demonstration

Figure 2-28. Axe drill into mat

Should coaches teach hitters to get extension in their swings?

Hitters want to attain extension, but not during the contact phase of the swing. If extension of the arms occurs at contact, the batter will be sweeping the bat through the hitting zone. This approach makes the hitter susceptible to inside pitches and greatly diminishes the force and bat speed of the swing. Instead, hitters should strive for arm extension in the final phase of the swing as they finish.

Wiffle Ball® Drills

Light, plastic Wiffle balls or golf balls are excellent training devices. These balls do not fly straight and require hitters to focus intensely on the ball. Game bats can be used for these drills, but over time may destroy the plastic balls. Wiffle ball pitching machines are affordably priced and will guard player/coach arms against the damage of throwing these light balls.

Corn Kernel Soft Toss Drill

On game day when soft toss drills may not be allowed to be performed into the fence at an opponent's field, players can flip corn kernels or small pieces of pasta to each other. These drills are excellent at building player confidence as the baseball looks gigantic compared to a tiny piece of corn.

Weighted Broomstick Hitting Drills

Players can swing a bat with a small diameter to work on contact hitting. Most broomsticks are too light to simulate the weight of a baseball bat. Easton® makes a *Thunderstick*, which is the length and weight of a typical bat, yet the barrel's width is that of a broomstick. This durable hitting device can be used by the entire team for batting practice and other hitting drills.

Mental Approaches to Hitting

Ted Williams said, "The hardest thing to do in sport is hit a baseball."[5] Although many athletes and fans of other sports will debate this claim, hitters in baseball are considered proficient if they achieve their goal just three times out of 10. If a quarterback, jump shooter, or tennis player had a 30 percent rate of success, he would be considered terribly ineffective. Given this fact, hitters must understand from the outset that quite often baseball players experience failure.

 ### Conference Time

One of the most important aspects of coaching is building player confidence. Hitting, typically the activity that players enjoy the most, brings a great deal of player frustration and dejection. Coaches must be aware of which players are particularly sensitive. After practice, these athletes may need one-on-one counseling sessions or extra batting instruction. Dynamic techniques that coaches devise to foster positive thinking among their players will be utilized and remembered later in the professional and personal lives of these athletes.

Preparation Before the At Bat

Hitters can learn a great deal in their pre-at bat preparation, while in the dugout and on-deck circle. Several facts should be acquired during this process. All hitters must be aware of the arm angle or arm slot from which a pitcher throws. Is he throwing straight over the top, three quarters, or is the delivery sidearm? Next, players want to find out the variety of pitches in the pitcher's repertoire. Not only is it important to know which pitches are featured besides the fastball, but the type of movement that these pitches possess. Does the fastball run in or away from the batter? Can he throw his change-up for a strike? If so, how does it move, and how much slower is it than his fastball? Does the curveball break *12-to-6* (as on a clock), or does it slide across the plate?

In addition to pitch variety, hitters should study pitcher tempo. Many pitchers work quickly, while others take more time in between pitches. Also, batters must recognize the sequence that each pitcher features. Some pitchers will start batters with a first pitch fastball every pitch, while others may be less predictable. Pitchers may utilize a certain pitch when they have two strikes on a batter to put him away, including a specific pitch location. Perhaps, most importantly, can the pitcher throw strikes consistently, and with which pitch(es) can he do so?

Teaching Tip

Coaches must stress to players the importance of concentration while in the on-deck circle. Many players lose focus and socialize or do not use this time wisely. This time is an opportunity to work on relaxation breathing techniques, watch for positioning of defensive players, and the opposing pitcher's mechanics. Players should also consider their walk to the batter's box and routine before actually stepping in to hit. Some hitters take practice swings, sweep the dirt in the box, or adjust their batting gloves to get in the proper mindset before an at bat.

Three Steps to Success

1. Determine the pitcher's arm slot for releasing the ball.
2. Recognize pitch variation, movement on the ball, and strike percentage.
3. Watch for pitcher tendencies and tempo on the mound.

In-Game Strategy: Breaking the Pitcher's Rhythm

When a pitcher is dominating an offensive team, coaches will frequently use tactics to break his rhythm. Some hitters will take extra time getting into the batter's box, call time-out as the pitcher starts his windup, or walk over to the third base coach to chat. In addition to these mental notes, on-deck batters must remember to communicate whether to slide or not with incoming base runners to home plate.

Administrative Time-Out

Coaches should set up batting practice workouts with the purpose of simulating game situations. Each player can be issued a number, which will determine his rotating role during the practice, such as fielding, a hitting drill, on deck, shagging foul balls, or batting on the field. Hitters can use on-deck time to mirror their actions on game day. It is also important for hitters to work on specific goals during batting practice, such as moving runners over, bunting for a hit, or driving a runner home from third base. Coaches can devise point system games to maintain hitter accountability for *BP* (batting practice).

Developing an Approach to Hitting

In formulating an approach to an at bat, hitters must know what their goal is. For different players, this goal will dictate different mindsets. The lead-off batter must try to get on base any way possible and perhaps see as many pitches as he can, while a clean-up hitter is expected to drive in runs. These goals will also vary each at bat according to the game situation. A sacrifice bunt on the first pitch may be fitting in one inning, yet later in the game with a wild pitcher on the mound, taking several pitches may be more appropriate.

Aside from these specific scenarios, hitters must know their strengths and develop a strategy based on those strengths. For example, a hitter with tremendous power may be looking to swing at any fastball in his *hot zone* or wheel house. On the other hand, a light hitting second baseman could strive to work the pitcher deep in the count and move the runner(s) over with a ground ball. Sometimes, players' roles are communicated through their spot in the batting order, but hitters need to have a game plan based on the game situation and their individual abilities.

 ### Conference Time

Coaches should communicate with each player about his role on the team. This discussion inevitably will focus on offensive potential and contributions to the team. It is important to stress that each player's role is vital to team success. Whether it be working to get on base via bases on balls or driving in runners as a gap hitter, players should understand what is expected of them and how their at bats impact effective play. While hitters' roles can change based on physical development, players need a concrete view of how to approach an at bat.

 ### Topic of Debate: First-Pitch Swinging

Many coaches advocate their hitters be aggressive and freely swing the bat on the 0-0 pitch. These coaches claim that the pitcher is trying to get ahead in the count and will groove the first pitch to the batter. In their mind, this pitch may be the best pitch the batter sees throughout the entire at bat, and, therefore, he should be ready to *jump on the first pitch*. Some coaches prefer for their batters to take a pitch or even a strike before swinging at a pitch. They believe that while the 0-0 pitch may look hittable, it will move or tail just enough to prevent solid contact. In addition, teams that take a lot of pitches wear out opposing pitchers and draw more walks. Certainly at younger levels, pitchers possess less effective control and may struggle throwing three strikes before walking most hitters.

In a 1993 article, Thomas Boswell analyzed nearly 100 of the top hitters in baseball and found hitters bat about 70 points higher and have a higher slugging percentage by 130 points when swinging at the first pitch. Broadcaster Tim McCarver showed during the 2000 and 2001 World Series that Major League hitters bat over 100 points lower with two strikes on them in the count. Eric Bickel and Dean Stotz compiled a great deal of research on hitter performance in various counts. They conclude that "batters are just as likely to get a hit off a pitch thrown for a strike when they are ahead in the count as when they are behind!" Based on this data, it is more pivotal for batters to swing at strikes and hittable pitches rather than fixating on the count.[5]

Major League Connection

The dominant New York Yankees' world championship teams of the late 1990s were masterful in *going deep in the count* and seeing many pitches in each at bat. This philosophy helped the team draw walks and knock out many starting pitchers. Ted Williams was a strong proponent of hitters not swinging at a pitch unless they had already seen it. Williams advocated taking the first pitch as a player and later as manager of the Washington Senators. Not surprisingly, Williams' .482 mark for career on base percentage ranks first in Major League history.[4] Nonetheless, many professional hitters have attained tremendous success as *first-ball, fastball hitters*.

Guess Hitting

Most hitters are taught to look for a fastball and react to off-speed pitches, which makes sense at early ages, as the fastball is thrown on almost every pitch. Yet, as players develop and face pitchers with a variety of pitches in their arsenal, guess hitting can be a useful strategy. Specifically, with less than two strikes and a crafty pitcher on the mound, looking for a particular pitch type or location will be beneficial. Furthermore, hitters who have achieved success with hitting fastballs will provoke opposing pitchers to throw many off-speed pitches until these hitters prove otherwise.

When utilizing effective guess-hitting strategies, hitters must be disciplined enough to not swing if a pitch is delivered that they are not looking for. Therefore, if a hitter is guessing that a curveball is coming on the first pitch of an at bat, then he must not swing if a fastball is delivered. By expecting a particular pitch, hitters' timing and mindset will be different, which requires that they lay off a pitch that is not what they are *sitting on*.

Hitters either sit on a fastball or off-speed pitch when guess hitting. However, pitch location (inside or outside) is another aspect of this strategy. With a 0-0 count, hitters can look for a particular pitch in a specific location. As the count deepens and the hitter has two strikes on him, he must expand his focus to all pitches in any area of the strike zone. Hitters who are facing a team or pitcher for the first time should expect to see off-speed pitches if they are batting in the middle of the lineup. Guess hitting is particularly valuable for the hitter who struggled with a specific pitch in his first at bat of a game, which the opponent will continue to feature against him.

 ### In-Game Strategy: Scouting of Hitters

Scouting of opponents provides coaches with an evaluation of hitters and their success in handling different pitches. Coaches at the high school level and beyond call pitches and will refer to these scouting reports for pitch selection. Batters that hit in the third, fourth, and fifth spots in the lineup are generally given a steady diet of breaking balls and other off-speed pitches until they show proficiency hitting these pitches.

Three Steps to Success

1. Look for a specific pitch type in a particular location early in the count.
2. Be disciplined enough not to swing at a pitch unless sitting on that pitch.
3. If demonstrating success versus a pitch type, expect a different pitch to be thrown.

Conference Time

Meetings should be held with coaches and each of their players regarding hitting strategy. Many players are not comfortable guess hitting as they have had success looking for the fastball and reacting to other pitches throughout their entire baseball lives. With the exception of a few, highly talented hitters, guess hitting becomes crucial when facing top-level pitchers. Batters who sit *dead red* (expect the fastball) and try to react to off-speed pitches will have off-balance swings and hit the ball weakly to the pull side or not make contact at all.

Should batters guess with two strikes on them?

Most coaches will not be comfortable having hitters guess with two strikes on them. But, hitters can look for the curveball and merely foul off any incoming fastballs. Therefore, if fooled during guess hitting, batters can fight off pitches without trying to put them in play. In general, guess hitting takes time to master, and two-strike guess hitting may be reserved for experienced players.

Teaching Tip

Coaches can teach certain techniques to hitters that will make them more comfortable as guess hitters. Players should watch for the pitch sequence that the opposing pitcher uses against their team and different spots in the lineup. In addition, given that many young pitchers are predictable, hitters can zero in on the pitch that is likely to be in the strike zone. In batting practice, hitters can work on two-strike, defensive mode, guess-hitting strategies. Conversely, coaches can verbally ask what pitch or location a hitter is guessing in an 0-0 count, and then throw a pitch to that spot.

Slump Busters

Given that hitters have their own styles and body types, coaches should not attempt to create uniformity among their players' swing mechanics. Although certain fundamentals are necessary for a hitter to be successful, forcing players to follow a blueprint or specific recipe for batting is not wise. Rather, coaches can use batting instruction time for fixing glaring issues with player swings or work on the mental approach to hitting. When hitters are hot and experiencing great success, coaches should back off. Yet, during times of hitter frustration and struggle, coaches must take an active role. All players go through hitting slumps, where effective coaching becomes an important element in helping the batter get back on track.

When players are having a tough time at the plate, coaches can implement several techniques. Batting practice is an excellent time for coaches to conference with hitters before and after their round(s) of hitting. Video footage of players when they are swinging well and when they are slumping should be emphasized so that hitters can view mechanical differences of the two episodes. Coaches can also make changes in the batting order to take pressure off a struggling hitter or place him in a batting slot where more hittable pitches may be thrown. Most of all, discussions about proper pitch selection must occur to break the downward cycle of an out-of-rhythm hitter.

In-Game Strategy: Batting Order

Usually the second spot in the batting order will receive many fastballs because a speedy, base-stealing threat may be on base. In addition, the middle of the order is approaching, and no pitcher wants to issue a walk before these hitters come up. The seventh, eighth, and ninth slots of the lineup can take pressure off a pressing player as pitchers tend to relax and make more mistakes here. Also, coaches can signal for an in-game hit and run to force a batter to swing. Slumping hitters may be hesitant to swing or unable to *pull the trigger*. The hit and run can help a player forget about individual woes and get into the flow of the game by having to swing the bat.

Conference Time

During low periods, it is important for coaches to caution hitters about overthinking. The expression "Overanalysis leads to paralysis" applies here. Many struggling players will fixate on flaws with their stance or swing path and even adopt new, less effective mechanics. Coaches should utilize psychological methods to get their athletes into a better mental flow. Breathing and positive visualization techniques provide hitters with confidence during these periods. Players also should *get away from the game* when they leave the field and forget about their current struggles. Coaches can encourage players to go to a movie or change their off-the-field schedules to accomplish this goal.

Why do players go into a batting slump?

Like anything else, batting success has a cyclical nature. During a lengthy season, hitting highs and lows exist. The key is to limit the duration of the low periods with proper coaching intervention. Generally, slumps occur when players begin chasing pitches outside of the strike zone or get overly complacent and stop swinging at pitches that they normally drive. Sometimes, a well-hit ball or homerun can bring on a slump as the hitter may begin to try to do more than he is capable of at the plate. This mental state will manifest as a long swing, a collapsing of the backside, or other ineffective mechanics.

 Teaching Tip

When players have a prolonged cold spell at the plate, they usually experience alternating phases of being too aggressive or complacent. A fine line exists between a hitter demonstrating patience and anxiousness at bat. Coaches must discuss this balance with their hitters and get players to develop a rhythm during their plate appearances. Baseball does not have a fast-action game mentality, and the overall tempo is different than most other sports.

 Topic of Debate: Batting Practice—Live Pitching vs. Batting Machine

Pitching machines are useful in getting hitters many repetitions in the pre-season, especially during indoor workouts. However, once players begin facing live pitching in games, batting machines are less effective. Some coaches prefer the efficiency that machines provide to a practice. Although pitching machines enable coaches to show hitters lots of strikes in a short period of time, live pitching will better simulate the unpredictability of humans throwing pitches to players.

Sources/Further Reading

[1]Dickson, P. (1992). *Baseball's Greatest Quotations*. New York: Harper Perennial. P. 302.

[2]Baseball-Reference.com; Sports Reference LLC; 2000-2010. February 3, 2009.

[3]Oh, S. (1984). *A Zen Way of Baseball*. New York: Times Books.

[4]Williams, T. (1986). *The Science of Hitting*. New York: Simon & Shuster. Pp. 58, 83.

[5]Bickel, J.E. & Stotz, D. (2002). "Batting Average by Count and Pitch Type: Fact and Fallacy." *The Baseball Research Journal*. SABR publications.

BASERUNNING

Chapter 3

*Progress always involves risks. You can't steal second
base and keep your foot on first.*
—F.B. Wilcox[1]

Arguably, baserunning is the most exciting part of baseball. Whether it is an inside-the-park home run or stealing home, nothing excites fans more than drama on the base paths. Although natural running speed is a positive attribute, even a slower player can be an excellent base runner. In reality, effective baserunning can only be learned through game experience. Therefore, *more than any other aspect of baseball, baserunning as an instinctual skill is truly difficult to learn outside of live game action.*

Nonetheless, coaches should stress proper footwork, body positioning, and baserunning mechanics to help players develop into sound base runners. While in-game baserunning instincts may be tough to simulate in practice, numerous drills are effective at teaching the proper way to run the bases. Several skills—including the fundamentals of sliding, diving, taking leads, and rounding bases—must be covered by coaches in order to produce well-rounded players.

Major League Connection

Baseball legends Jackie Robinson and Pete Rose demonstrated how exciting baserunning can be. Robinson's ability to steal home and Rose's head-first slides brought a new, spirited dimension to the game. Moreover, their fearless, fierce style of running the bases helped energize their teams.

Baserunning Basics

Getting Out of the Box

When teaching players how to run out of the batter's box, coaches must stress the importance of utilizing the arms. Hitters should be explosive *out of the box* and achieve top running speed as quickly as possible. To do so, a hitter must immediately drop the bat, begin driving with the arms, and not watch the baseball. In youth leagues, coaches should be aware that many young players provoke warnings from umpires by throwing the bat aimlessly after making contact with the ball.

After running three steps down the baseline, players should peek over their left shoulder to check whether ball has made it through the infield (Figure 3-1). If the ball has not made it past the infielders, then the batter will run straight through the first base bag. On the other hand, if the batted ball is through the infielders, then hitters will *belly out* and *make a turn* at first base. Coaches should stress that players not slow down when peeking to see if the ball has made it past the infielders.

Figure 3-1. Peeking on sprint out of the batter's box

Teaching Tip

Coaches should instruct players to quickly look or peek at the infield to check whether the ball will be fielded and if a play will occur at first base. Three steps down the baseline is a basic guideline for teaching players when to peek, but other factors can determine proper timing as well. For instance, a hard hit smash versus a weakly hit ball will dictate how quickly the batter should check for the ball. In addition, younger players play on fields that are smaller in size, and, therefore, batted balls will take differing lengths of time to reach the fielders.

Running Through First Base

Upon quickly checking and realizing that a batted ball has not gotten through the infield, players should run through the first base bag. In doing so, it is important for the base runner to look straight ahead and not slow down before the base to watch the defensive play unfold. While maintaining speed through the base, a runner should hit the front edge of the base and simultaneously check for a possible overthrow by looking over his right shoulder.

After hitting the front part of the base, players should run through and break down 5 to 10 feet after the base. By breaking down, players will be able to react to an overthrow and quickly change direction to run toward second base. In the breakdown position, players are in a slightly seated, athletic position with the feet just wider than shoulder-width apart (Figure 3-2). The goal is to immediately slow down without losing balance or body control so that the runner can start toward second base on an overthrow as quickly as possible.

Figure 3-2. Breakdown position

Three Steps to Success

1. Peek to check whether or not a batted ball has made it past the infielders.
2. Run straight through first base while hitting the front corner of the base.
3. After quickly checking for an overthrow over the right shoulder, break down into an athletic position.

Administrative Time-Out

With a stopwatch, coaches should time their players *out of the box* during batting practice, scrimmages, and live games. An assistant coach or team manager can be responsible for logging player running times on a clipboard from home to first base. By keeping these times, coaches will help players strive to run faster and attain their personal best (*PBs*). Furthermore, if a player stares at the ball, does not run straight, or slows down at the base, coaches can use a concrete number to explain why proper technique for beating out an infield hit is crucial. 4.0 seconds is a benchmark time for college/pro players *down the line*.

 ### In-Game Strategy: Opponent Running Speed

An important element for coaches is to be aware of the running speed of the opposition. Coaches can time their opponents' players as they run down the line for an infield hit or ground ball out at first base. This reading will provide an indication of each player's ability to steal a base or lay down a bunt for a hit. Typically, players in the top and bottom of the batting order (first, second, eighth, and ninth in the lineup) possess *plus speed*, or the fastest running ability on the team.

Making a Turn at First Base

When a batter hits a ball that goes through the infield defense, he will *make a turn* and *round* first base. In order to do so, the hitter will belly out 20 to 25 feet before the base. At this point in the baseline, it is important for players to run toward the first base dugout area in a question mark shaped manner (Figure 3-3). This action will enable the player to maintain his full running speed while taking the proper angled turn toward second base. Otherwise, the base runner will have to slow down greatly or run toward right field before turning to approach the next base.

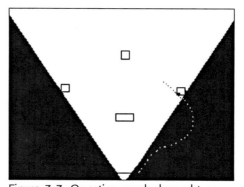

Figure 3-3. Question mark-shaped turn

Players should focus on hitting the corner of the base facing second base (left, inside corner) with either foot, so long as they do not have to break stride. While making this turn toward second base, players must focus their eyes on the ball and decide whether they can safely advance. During this phase, it is important for runners to watch for botched cutoffs and errant throws by the defense, as these errors may enable them to run to second base. Additionally, after rounding the base and taking their turn, players must continue to keep their eyes on the ball as they return back to first base.

Three Steps to Success

1. 20 to 25 feet before first base, belly out in a question mark–shaped angle.
2. Touch the inside corner of first base with either foot, so long as stride is not broken.
3. While keeping sight of the ball at all times, make a turn toward second base.

 ### How far off first base should players make their turn toward second base?

The size of the turn should be determined by the location of the ball and the arm strength of the player fielding the ball. The greater the chance for the runner to be thrown out at first base, the smaller the turn should be. Some basic guidelines for making a turn are: on a ball hit to left field, a 15- to 20-foot turn; a ball hit to centerfield, a 10- to 15-foot turn; and a ball hit to right field, a 5- to 10-foot turn.

 ### Conference Time

Coaches must stress the importance of not watching the ball as they run down the first baseline. Rather, as they come out of the box players should be encouraged to demonstrate their hustle and speed. Players can display that they know how to play the game the correct way and look like a ballplayer should when running to first base. In addition, attention to these finer aspects of the game and hustling out of the box are nuances that will impress potential college or professional scouts.

 ### In-Game Strategy: Making Turns at First Base

Ordinarily, teams at higher levels of baseball will have the catcher *trail* the batter as he takes his turn at first base. If the batter takes an overly aggressive turn on a single, the infielders may *throw behind* him for an out. In some instances, offensive teams will pinpoint which outfielders have the weakest arms during pre-game infield/outfield practice and instruct their speedy hitters to *think two* (try for a double) from the moment that they run out of the batter's box. However, base runners should avoid making the first out of an inning at second base.

 ### Administrative Time-Out

It is important at all times for coaches to ensure that an informed first base coach will be on the field. If no assistant coaches are available, then a player will have to fulfill these coaching duties. In either case, the first base coach must verbally alert base runners of how many outs there are, where the ball is, if the defense is throwing to the base, and to pick up the third base coach's signals. On a nonverbal basis, the first base coach should use his hands or arms to signal for a dive/slide into the base, making a turn, or to run straight through first base.

Taking a Lead at First Base

Upon getting to first base, runners have three responsibilities. Players must be aware of where the ball is, and know how many outs there are. Additionally, when getting the signs from third, runners should always have their heels on the base and with the coach visually confirm the number of outs. Most coaches will complete their set of signals with a clap to signify that the runner can take his lead. Although many players are excited and want to talk to the first base coach or motion to fans/teammates after they reach first base, it is important for them to focus on immediately getting this information.

 Teaching Tip

When taking a lead, players should establish a repeatable routine much like a free throw shooter. Every time they take their lead, base runners must develop a system that provides sequenced footwork and a uniform distance from the base. Players who merely jump out to their lead haphazardly will struggle to be consistent and be vulnerable to pickoffs and missed signals. Coaches can stress to all players, not just capable base stealers, that having a concrete routine for taking a lead will benefit them greatly.

The Primary Lead

The primary lead, as the name implies, is the initial lead that players take before the pitcher delivers the ball toward home plate. When taking their lead, players must keep their eyes on the pitcher at all times in case of a quick *throw over* to the base. Base runners should start with their heels on the base, facing second base, and take a step off with their left foot (Figures 3-4 and 3-5). Next, the right foot comes off the base as the player pivots and turns to face the batter with their feet in an athletic stance (Figure 3-6). Players will gain ground toward second base by bringing their left foot to the inside of the right foot and moving the right foot toward second base.

Figure 3-4. Heels on base Figure 3-5. Left foot stride Figure 3-6. Pivot to face home plate

Players should keep a leading stance at the height from which they will be running. With the knees slightly bent and the back upright, base runners should stay loose in their leading position. The arms should hang down with no tension, while the weight must be evenly distributed without leaning in any particular direction (Figure 3-7). As for determining the proper length of the lead, players must know that they can safely return to first base adeptly with a two-step move or dive back on a pickoff throw. On many fields, the oval-shaped grass cutout is a guideline for the approximate length of base runners' leads.

Figure 3-7. Apex of primary lead

Three Steps to Success

1. While stepping off first base with the left foot, keep the eyes fixed on the pitcher.
2. Pivot to face home plate as the right foot comes around and is placed so the feet are wider than shoulder-width apart.
3. Gain ground toward second base as the left foot comes to the inside of the right.

In-Game Strategy: Base Runners' Eyes

The eyes play an important role as base runners take their primary lead at first base. Those players who do not keep their eyes glued on the pitcher as they take their steps off the base can be picked off. Players who stare at the third base coach's signals while off the base also risk being *picked*. At higher levels, some players will quickly peek in to see the catcher's signals while in their lead. If an off-speed pitch is called, then the base runner may attempt to steal second base on that pitch, as it will take longer to travel to the catcher.

Teaching Tip

At the apex of the primary lead, players want to eliminate any tension in their body. Base runners will have to move quickly to their left to return to first base on a pickoff throw or explode to their right when going toward second base. In both cases, staying limber and fluid will aid in the process. Moreover, players should not stand too tall or crouch very low in their lead if they will be running at a different height than these positions. As with many fundamentals, players will frequently mimic the unique styles of professionals seen on television.

 ### What is the difference between a one-way lead and a two-way lead?

Sometimes, talented base stealers will utilize one-way and two-way leads. In a one-way lead, players will lean in one direction (either back to first base or toward second base) so as to get a better *jump*. For example, lead-off hitters who reach base may take a sizable primary lead to draw a pickoff throw, but will go back to the base on the *pitcher's first move*. This tactic enables runners to view and learn the pitcher's pickoff move early in the game. A two-way lead, which is more commonly used, enables the runner to readily move in either direction.

Major League Connection

Hall of Famer and base-stealing whiz Lou Brock was known to utilize a shorter, one-way lead when stealing second base. When not stealing, Brock could take a larger lead and lean back slightly toward first base. This strategy stymied pitchers.

The Secondary Lead

Once the pitcher has committed to throw a pitch to home plate, base runners at first base should take their secondary lead. In cases when the runner is stealing or running on a hit-and-run, the secondary lead will not be utilized. This *secondary* enables the runner to gain ground toward second base while keeping his eyes on the action at the plate. Players will shuffle in a lateral hopping motion two consecutive times to their right (Figures 3-8 through 3-12). Base runners should keep their shoulders square to home plate and use their arms to gain inertia during the process.

Figure 3-8. Step 1

Figure 3-9. Step 2

Figure 3-10. Step 3

Figure 3-11. Step 4

Figure 3-12. Step 5

The secondary is important for several reasons. First, it provides momentum toward second base that the runner will need to advance on a passed ball, wild pitch, or batted ball in play. Runners must get *good reads* on each of these scenarios to move quickly to second base. Getting the wrong read may result in an out at second base if the runner advances too slowly or even is forced out at first on a snagged line drive.

Three Steps to Success

1. When pitcher commits to throw home, shuffle laterally toward second base by gaining ground with a two-hop motion.
2. Keep the shoulders square to home plate and watch the play develop.
3. React by running to second base or returning back to first base according to the actions of the pitched ball and batter.

 ### Administrative Time-Out

Coaches can design practice drills that help players get proper reads during their secondary lead. Players must effectively learn how to judge balls in the dirt so they can advance on pitches that are difficult for the catcher to handle. *Dirt ball* reads can be worked on while catchers practice their blocking technique. Batting practice, inter-squad games, and baserunning drills are opportunities for players to work on this important skill. Not only will these activities aid players in reading balls in the dirt, but they will also help players react to ground balls, line drives, and other offensive developments. One way to teach this skill is to have runners at second base with no force play learn to hold on balls hit at them or to their right and to advance on balls hit to their left.

Teaching Tip

At the lower levels, many coaches will have their players advance on any pitched ball that hits the ground. Younger catchers generally lack the arm strength to throw the ball to second base consistently; in turn, nabbing base runners on dirt balls is highly unlikely. Also, it is during the secondary lead where coaches can teach players to *freeze on line drives* so as to avoid being doubled up. First base coaches must be vocal during the secondary lead in their effort to help base runners make the proper read on batted balls in play or wild pitches.

Getting Back to First Base

After taking a primary lead, players must be able to quickly return to first base on a pickoff attempt. Players can get back to the base in a standing position or dive back on their stomachs. In both cases, coaches should teach players the fundamentals to make this process faster, less taxing on the body, and safer.

When returning to first base standing, players can use the *California turn* technique. This method is a two-step movement in which the player crosses over toward first base with his right leg (Figure 3-13) and hops to the side of first base with the left foot. By returning to the base with the left leg, base runners do not give first basemen a large target to tag (Figure 3-14). Furthermore, the player can spin away from the tag as he lands on the base with his left foot (Figure 3-15).

Figure 3-13. Crossover step with right leg

Figure 3-14. Pop into base with left leg

Figure 3-15. Spin away with left foot on base

Many base runners get back to first base with improper footwork, which forces them to take a shorter primary lead than otherwise and leads to pickoffs. Common mistakes players make are approaching the base with the right leg (Figure 3-16) and taking small, choppy steps to the base. It is imperative for players to develop a uniform primary lead before working on the California turn.

Figure 3-16. Improper footwork

An alternative to returning to first base in the standing position is diving back to the base. Although this can be jarring on the body, it does allow for players to attain a longer lead. When diving back to the base, it is necessary for players to use proper footwork in order to avoid injury and get to the base quickly. *Players should dive back to the base much like an airplane landing, rather than like a helicopter descending.*

In order to dive effectively in to first base, base runners should pivot on their left foot and extend their right hand toward the base. During this 45-degree pivot, players must get low immediately on their approach to the base by placing their right hand in the dirt. Proper diving technique reflects gliding to the base in a low, fluid action. Players with poor diving form tend to flop on the ground and get low only as they finally reach the base (Figure 3-17).

Figure 3-17. Diving back to first base

 Teaching Tip

Coaches can effectively teach diving fundamentals to players by utilizing soft foam mats, wet outfield grass, or freshly raked infield dirt. The analogy of an airplane landing in a smooth, downward fashion helps players get a sense for getting low and quick on their dive back to first base. Diving and sliding drills can be completed in stages by having players start on their knees before having them stand up and complete the activity at full speed. By building up to a game-speed dive, players will avoid injury and gain more confidence.

 In-Game Strategy: Holding Runners On

Defensive teams will have the pitcher throw over to first base when a base-stealing threat is on base. These potential base stealers will strategically take a longer lead and need to dive back in to the base. Opposing coaches will look for body lean or mannerisms that may tip off a runner's intent to steal. Pickoffs and pitchouts will be signaled by coaches to contain these base runners.

Topic of Debate: Returning to the Base—Diving vs. Standing Position

Nimble, quick base stealers will benefit from diving back to the base on a pickoff attempt because it allows them to take a larger lead. Those base runners who have no intention of stealing bases should come back to the base standing up. Diving carries a greater risk of injury and can be physically exhausting. Also, players proficient at the California turn find that sizable leads can be attained without diving.

Stealing Second Base

Due to undeveloped catchers' arms and inexperienced pitchers, stealing second base at the youth level is not difficult; however, as players get older, it becomes more challenging. Base runners need to understand several important elements before attempting to steal second base. Moreover, stealing bases involves intuitive strategy and technical footwork that coaches should pass on to their players.

After taking a primary lead, players executing a *straight steal* of second base will watch the pitcher closely to determine when to take off. In the case of a right-handed pitcher in the stretch position, as soon as the pitcher's left leg is lifted, base runners can leave for second base. Many runners will focus their attention on the heels of the pitcher. If the left heel comes off the ground, then the pitcher must throw toward home plate and the runner can take off for second. However, if the right heel is raised then the pitcher can and most likely will throw a pickoff to first base.

Teaching Tip

Players have two methods for starting their move to second base as base stealers. Many runners utilize the *crossover* method by driving with their left leg and arm, while pivoting on the right foot toward second base. Others prefer to *open up*. When opening up, base runners will employ a *jab step* with the right foot, which entails turning the right foot and gaining three to five inches toward second base before even moving the left leg. In both cases, as they turn toward second base, players should explosively drive or punch with their left arm. Coaches can teach both techniques to observe which method works best for each individual.

When stealing second base off a left-handed pitcher, base runners must focus on the back shoulder and right leg of the pitcher. As the pitcher lifts his leg from the stretch position, base runners can view the body lean and the position the right leg has in comparison with the left. If the pitcher crosses the left leg or leans back with his weight as if he is delivering a pitch, then he cannot throw over to first base. Many left-handed pitchers will hang their right leg for an extended period or use varied looks with the head to throw off runners. The left-handed pickoff move elicits arguments over balk calls and is not a clear area of umpire judgment. These calls will vary, depending on the individual umpire and state/conference associations' interpretation of balk rules.

 ### In-Game Strategy: Base Runners' Timing and Rhythm

Pitchers will use a variety of tactics to throw off the timing of base runners. Many pitchers, in an effort to deter base stealers, will move their head intermittently, vary the timing to start their motion, and show different pickoff moves to runners. Base runners must not get stiff or lose their rhythm in their primary lead. Otherwise, the pitcher has won the battle and stifled the runner. In addition, many leagues mandate a two-man umpire crew at games, which affects the prevalence of balk calls and aggressiveness of pitchers' pickoffs. Sometimes, base stealers will mix in fake steal attempts to put pressure on the catcher and confuse the first baseman, who vocally alerts the catcher.

 ### Administrative Time-Out

Coaches can use a stopwatch to time each player running from a primary lead into second base with a slide. This time can be referenced to figure out whether the player has a reasonable chance of stealing second base. By adding the *pop time* (time it takes to throw to second base from home plate) of the opposing catcher to the pitcher's time to the plate from the stretch position, coaches can determine whether the base runner should attempt to steal second base. For example, if a catcher has a pop time of 2.15 seconds and the pitcher takes 1.5 seconds to deliver a pitch from the stretch position, then the base runner will likely beat the catcher's throw if he runs 3.65 seconds or faster to second base.

An alternative method for stealing second base is the *delayed steal*. This strategy is especially effective for base runners who do not possess noteworthy speed. As a result, the delayed steal works by using the element of surprise as middle infielders cannot react quickly enough to cover second base. *Base runners can execute the delayed steal by taking a large secondary lead and running to second base after completing the second lateral shuffle of the secondary lead.* Yet, if players take off too soon or do not complete a full secondary lead, the defense will be tipped off that the steal is on. At youth levels, players can also successfully complete a delayed steal by running for the next base just as the catcher throws the ball back to the pitcher.

 ### What can a coach look for that indicates whether a delayed steal will work?

When the middle infielders are not hustling in to back up the catcher's throw to the pitcher with men on base, a delayed steal is likely to work. In this case, the second baseman and shortstop will not get to the base on time to receive a throw and tag the base stealer. Also, when a catcher is lazily lobbing the ball back to the pitcher after each pitch, runners can safely advance to the next base if they take off as the catcher releases the ball. In addition, certain players that possess good baserunning instincts, or even those that may look slow of foot are good candidates.

Taking a Lead at Second Base

Unlike the lead from first base, the primary lead at second base involves striding out or walking off the base. Players can take six to eight strides off the base toward third base before pivoting 90 degrees to face the pitcher. The number of strides off the base will depend on the quickness of the runner and the ability of the defensive team to hold runners at second base. Furthermore, the specific game situation will dictate how aggressive or conservative the base runner should be in his primary lead.

Players must keep their eyes on the pitcher at all times while walking off the base. Some players dig a line in the dirt at the peak of their primary lead so as to create a marker for each time they get off the base. In addition, players should not look for the middle infielders in their primary lead, but rather keep their eyes fixed on the pitcher and listen to their third base coach for verbal directives. *Unlike the primary lead at first base, where a player's feet remain firmly on the ground in one spot, runners leading at second base should utilize a walking lead and always keep their feet moving.*

Three Steps to Success

1. Walk off second base six to eight strides, keeping the eyes on the pitcher at all times.
2. Make a line in the dirt as a guide for successive primary leads from the base.
3. Listen to the third base coach's directives for getting off or moving back to the base.

 Teaching Tip

With their eyes focused on the pitcher at all times, players should be taught to get their signals while on the base and then quickly walk out to their primary lead. Coaches must emphasize that the feet should not be stationary when leading off second base. Players can use a walking lead in which they slowly take small steps toward third base. Another technique involves *vaulting* with small lateral hops off or back to second base as directed by the third base coach. These vaults are smaller than the lateral moves of the secondary lead and, in this case, the base runner is gaining momentum toward third base in his primary lead.

 In-Game Strategy: Taking Leads at Second Base

Coaches may teach different strategies for determining the depth of the lead at second base. For instance, some coaches will teach a *straight line lead* while others have runners take a lead toward the hole at shortstop, closer to left field. This deeper lead or *angled lead* will give runners a better path when rounding third base and enable them to take a walking lead toward the pitcher for forward momentum. Some believe that the deeper lead gives pitchers an optical illusion that the lead is smaller than it actually is. In addition, this lead also makes it more difficult for the shortstop to sneak in for a pickoff throw behind the base runner.

Conference Time

Coaches must emphasize to players the importance of hustling back to the base after their secondary lead. Otherwise, when offensive signals are being delivered, the batter and/or other runners will have to wait unnecessarily. Also, catchers who possess a strong throwing arm may *throw behind the runner* and pick him off the base. Players may not be expected to quickly scamper back to the base at younger levels, but as they get older, the game speeds up and coaches' expectations for being alert greatly increase.

Administrative Time-Out

Coaches at higher levels may develop a system for players and coaches to deliver nonverbal communications regarding stealing catcher signals. First base coaches who can see catcher signs can stand with their arms crossed or on the hips to signal which particular pitch is coming. Base runners on second base can stand up tall or lean over to pass on similar information. Location for an inside/outside pitch can be relayed by subtly extending the right or left hand. Inexperienced players who verbally yell out pitches or hold up fingers to alert hitters may provoke the opposition to hide their signals or throw at the batter.

Stealing Third Base

In order to steal third base, players must have active feet before the pitcher commits to deliver the pitch. Given that the catcher's throw is only 90 feet to third base (as opposed to over 127 feet to second base), runners should obtain a sizable lead and an effective jump when stealing. As when stealing second base, runners are focused on the heels of the pitcher. If the heel touching the pitching rubber comes up, then the pitcher can step off or spin to throw a pickoff. Conversely, if the pitcher lifts his other foot (the glove-side foot) first, then he will deliver to the batter. On the other hand, it should be noted that with a runner on second base, it is legal for pitchers to perform an *inside move* in which they lift their left leg and spin to throw over to second base or run at the base runner.

In-Game Strategy: Stealing Third Base

Given that stealing third base requires much timing and instinct, many coaches will give specific players the *green light* to steal whenever they can get a good jump. Experienced runners on second base may also try to steal the catcher's signals with the intention of stealing on an off-speed pitch. Some coaches take off the green light when there are zero or two outs so that runners *do not make the first or third out at third base*. One exception to this cardinal rule is with two outs and a weak hitter at the plate. Coaches can strategize that the catcher may throw the ball into left field on the steal attempt and score the runner on the overthrow.

Teaching Tip

When holding runners at second base, coaches should teach players about the tendencies of pitchers. Many pitchers can be categorized as *one-lookers* or *two-lookers*, referring to the number of glances they typically show to runners on second base. If a pitcher does not stray from this habitual rhythm, runners can time his looks and steal third base accordingly. Players may also be instructed to watch for pitchers that implement an inside move to nab runners stealing third base. Most importantly, players can use batting practice or baserunning drills to learn walking leads and to keep active feet in their primary leads.

Conference Time

Coaches must conference with players so they understand that the green light is issued so that they can get a good, instinctive jump to steal a base. Coaches will only select players that they trust will understand the situation and know when to attempt a steal and when to be conservative. Runners at second base must be informed about in-game communication via the first and/or third base coaches. Commands such as "Off," "Back," or "Get another step" must be promptly responded to by all base runners.

Administrative Time-Out

It is important that all head coaches establish roles for the third and first base coaches, especially in regard to communicating with base runners on second base. Outside of the professional ranks, most head coaches coach third base and handle verbal commands to runners on second base. A number of teams utilize the first base coach to move down the line to a spot where he can easily view the middle infielders and communicate to the runner at second base if the defense is moving in to receive a pickoff throw at the base.

Taking a Lead at Third Base

When taking a lead off third base, players must be in foul ground at all times as a batted ball that hits them in fair territory will result in an out. Also, the initial lead should be short with small walking steps to gain forward momentum on a passed ball, wild pitch, sacrifice bunt, or infield grounder. *Most importantly, as the pitch crosses the strike zone, players leading off third base should be in a forward-moving position.* Because the timing of their secondary lead is flawed, too often runners on third base will start moving back to the base before the play develops. As a result, these base runners get poor jumps and do not score on plays in which they could easily cross the plate.

With the third base coach next to them in their primary lead, base runners should be alerted to how aggressive to act in each situation at third base. Nonetheless, base runners need to make good judgments of their own when reading plays developing on the infield. For instance, if the infield is playing back, the runner should be able to score on any batted ground ball unless it is hit back to the pitcher. Likewise, a wild pitch that kicks away from the catcher must be instinctively read by the base runner. Aside from knowing the number of outs, location of the ball, and signals, runners at third base should be aware of the positioning and strength of the outfielders' arms for scoring on a fly ball.

Three Steps to Success

1. To know whether to run on an infield ground ball, survey the depth of the infielders before the pitch is thrown.
2. As the pitch is delivered, take a short primary lead but an aggressive secondary lead with forward momentum.
3. Make a proper read on the developing play.

What are some common mistakes base runners make at third base?

Runners at third base must remember several basic guidelines, such as taking the primary lead in foul territory, returning to the base in fair territory (to block any pickoff throws back to the base by the catcher), tagging up on fly balls with less than two outs, checking the signals, reading the infielders' depth to judge whether scoring on a ground ball is possible, and having forward momentum as the pitch crosses home plate. In the excitement of a game, players often forget these baserunning basics and can botch a scoring opportunity for their team.

In-Game Strategy: Baserunning at Third Base

In youth leagues, many runners at third base will hop around or clap their hands aggressively in an attempt to distract the opposing pitcher. As players age and become more astute, they survey various elements on the field that may provide them with a scoring opportunity. Throughout the same at bat, defensive teams may vary the depth of each infielder to thwart the runner's chances for scoring on ground balls, and pitchers may use a rehearsed, timed pickoff throw to third base.

Stealing Home

The straight steal of home is an exciting and energizing offensive weapon. In order to execute this play, coaches must make sure the batter acknowledges with a clearly established confirmation signal that he will not be swinging on the pitch. Base runners from third base should try to get a long walking lead and an explosive jump as the pitcher starts his motion. The steal of home can provoke pitchers to balk or throw a wild pitch, which will also enable the runner to score.

Administrative Time-Out

For safety reasons, it is crucial that coaches have hitters use a signal to confirm that the steal of home is on and they will not be swinging at the pitch. Swiping the hand down the bat or adjusting the brim of the helmet are two examples of confirmation signals that can be utilized. Tactically, coaches should use a stopwatch to time the pitcher's windup motion to the plate. Pitchers who take 3.0 seconds or more to deliver a pitch, from the windup to the catcher, or who are intently deliberate in their motion, are prime candidates to be exploited.

Teaching Tip

Base runners who are stealing home or just trying to get a good jump off third base should watch for the pitcher's trigger that signifies he has started his windup and must pitch the ball. Some pitchers start with a movement of the hands, while others initiate the delivery by stepping back with their glove-side foot. Regardless of the mechanism, runners must learn what the trigger is and time the pitcher accordingly. Experienced pitchers will glance over at the base runner, vary the timing of their trigger, or step off the pitching rubber to freeze the runner at the base and prevent any forward momentum during the walking lead.

Major League Connection

Rod Carew, known for carefully studying pitchers' mannerisms from the dugout steps, stole home seven times in 1969, which ranks in modern history as the most steals of home in one season. Ty Cobb holds the career record with a remarkable 50 steals of home.[2]

Three Steps to Success

1. Learn the pitcher's trigger or device for starting his windup motion.
2. As the pitcher starts his motion to the plate, use a walking lead to gain forward momentum before taking off.
3. Run aggressively to home plate, and use a pop-up slide to the front edge of the plate.

In certain instances, base runners can execute a delayed steal of home plate, where players take advantage of a catcher that slowly lobs the ball back to the pitcher after each pitch is received. In addition, pitchers who are not focused as they receive the ball back from the catcher and turn their back on the field are susceptible to becoming a victim of this offensive strategy. In completing the delayed steal of home, the base runner will take an aggressive secondary lead and sprint for home as the catcher's arm goes back to release the ball to the pitcher.

In-Game Strategy: Stealing Home

Base runners contemplating the steal of home must make sure not to tip off the defense. Players who take too large a secondary lead may have to scramble back to third base, which can alert the defense that a steal is forthcoming. Although stealing home can be attempted with any number of outs, many teams reserve this play for when there are two outs and a struggling hitter at bat. With less than two outs, the risk of stealing may not be worth it as the run can score via sacrifice fly, base hit, or other offensive play.

How can defensive teams guard against the steal of home?

Pitchers should throw from the stretch position when coaches sense that the runner on third may try to steal home. Base runners will not have the time to get down the line and score off of a pitcher in the stretch position. Additionally, the third baseman can dart in for an occasional pickoff play. Pitchers should be aware of speedy base runners on third base and step off the rubber intermittently and *keep an eye on the runner* before each pitch.

Conference Time

Coaches must communicate to players the importance of learning signals and not displaying too much emotion upon receiving a particular sign. Specific players on a team may need one-on-one conferencing on this element of the game as they may struggle to identify signals or remain calm. Team leaders can hold after-practice conferences with players who have weaknesses in retaining signals. Highly strategic situations, such as the squeeze bunt or steal of home, require discreet emotional reactions on the part of players.

Specific Baserunning Situations

Tagging Up at Third Base

Runners on third base with less than two outs should tag up on all fly balls hit in fair or foul territory. When tagging up, players should place the toes or ball of their left foot on the corner of third base facing home plate (Figure 3-18). By using the left foot, players will be able to view the entire field and not be forced to turn their back on the developing play. A bent leg, athletic position is advantageous for exploding off the base when breaking toward home plate. In order to tag up and score in legal fashion, players must wait until the fielder catches or touches the ball before leaving the base.

An alternative method for tagging up is to start with the left foot behind third base on the left field foul line, while using the right foot as the contact with the base (Figure 3-19). This approach may enable players to push off the base more effectively by using the momentum of the left leg, starting before the ball is actually caught. The danger with tagging up in this manner is that an umpire may see the motion of the left leg before the ball is caught and assume that the base runner is leaving too early. Coaches can have their players clap their hands as the ball is caught and alert umpires of this technique in advance of a tag-up situation.

Figure 3-18. Tagging up at third base with left foot

Figure 3-19. Tagging up at third base with right foot

 ### In-Game Strategy: Tagging Up at Third Base

Quite frequently defensive teams will *appeal* at third base after a runner has tagged up and scored. Fans and players may claim that the runner *left early* from the base and should be out on the appeal play. Another tactic that sophisticated teams can utilize is to instruct the third baseman to obstruct the view of the runner who is tagging up. By quickly darting in to the line of vision of the base runner, the infielder may delay the runner's takeoff a split second, which can make a difference on a *bang, bang play* at the plate.

Specific Baserunning Situations

Hit-and-Run Play

As a base runner on first base who has been given the hit-and-run signal, several factors should be kept in mind. First, the base runner is not trying to steal second base, but rather is opening up a hole through which the batter can hit the ball. By running on the pitch, the base runner will prompt at least one of the middle infielders to vacate his defensive position to cover second base. Therefore, during a hit-and-run play, the runner must make sure not to get picked off first base. In addition, the runner must look in toward home plate on the second step of his move to second base.

This quick glance at the home plate area allows players to look for contact and decide how to respond. It is important for players not to stop or slow their pace in making this judgment. Glancing in at the batter is pivotal in determining whether to go back to the base on a pop-up or run to second base on a ground ball. One goal of the base runner is to advance to third base on a single to the outfield and score a ball hit to the gap or down the line. In the event that the batter swings through the pitch or misses the signal and does not swing, the runner will most likely be thrown out at second base from no fault of his own.

Three Steps to Success

1. To ensure that no pickoff occurs, take a conservative primary lead.
2. Glance in on the second or third stride to check for where the ball is hit.
3. Make a proper determination of which base to run to after the ball is put in play.

 In-Game Strategy: Hit-and-Run Play

Middle infielders communicate which player will cover second base on a steal attempt. Most teams use a nonverbal cue before each pitch to signify whether a player is covering the base or holding his fielding position. While using their glove to shield the signal, infielders commonly will show an open mouth or closed mouth to designate this coverage. During a hit-and-run play, the batter hopes to hit the ball to the area vacated by the infielder covering second base. Usually, the shortstop will cover the base when a left-handed batter is hitting, and the second baseman will cover with a right-handed hitter at the plate.

Squeeze Bunt Play

On a *safety squeeze bunt*, base runners at third base must read the play and advance accordingly. This bunt situation is a sacrifice in which the batter bunts with the intention of scoring the runner from third base as the defense fields the ball. Base runners must get an aggressive secondary lead off third base and make an instinctive, decisive action toward home plate or back to the base based on the effectiveness of the bunt.

When a *suicide squeeze bunt* is called, base runners should react in a manner similar to that of a straight steal of home. Unlike the safety squeeze, the runner is obligated to take off for home plate with the pitch, and must rely on the batter to get a bunt down regardless of pitch location. Base runners should take a walking primary lead and sprint to home plate as the pitcher is about to release the ball. It is important for runners not to leave too early, as the defense will be alerted that a play is on and can effectively defend the suicide squeeze attempt.

 Teaching Tip

Coaches should address a number of similarities between stealing home and running on a suicide squeeze bunt from third base. In both cases, runners must get an effective walking lead and a confirmation signal from the batter that he is not swinging without tipping off the defense. The major difference between the two plays is the timing of the departure from the primary lead. During a straight steal of home, the runner takes off as soon as the pitcher starts his motion, whereas players running in a suicide squeeze situation should leave for home plate only after the pitcher shows his backside in the delivery.

Trail Running

With men on base in front of them, base runners must pay close attention to what transpires at home plate and the decisions of the other base runners. As a *trail runner*, players may not be able to advance if the *lead runner(s)* choose to hold on a batted ball. For example, if a wild pitch is thrown with other men on base, the trail runner must make sure that the other runner(s) advance. Otherwise, he will run to a base that is already occupied and inevitably create a rundown situation that could stifle a big inning. Similar situations to be mindful of include balls in the dirt, tagging up on fly balls, ground balls with runners on second and third base, and *tweeners* (fly balls that fall between the outfield and infield).

Going Halfway vs. Tagging Up on Fly Balls

When there are less than two outs and a batter hits a fly ball to the outfield, an important aspect of the decision-making process for base runners occurs. Runners on third base will always tag up in this situation, while players at first base will ordinarily go *halfway*. The number of feet that the runner moves toward second base is not technically halfway (45 feet), but rather a distance that he feels he can safely return to the base without being thrown out by the outfielder catching the ball. In some cases, base runners will run past second base on a deep fly ball and have to hurry back to first base upon seeing that the ball has been caught. [*Note:* In this situation, on his return back to first base, the runner must retouch second base].

Infrequently, players can tag up from first base in situations where a deep, routine fly ball has been hit. For example, if the left or centerfielder is *camped under* a fly ball just in front of the outfield fence, it is likely that the runner will safely make it to second base on a tag up from first base. Universally, base runners at first base must tag up on any foul fly balls or pop-ups. If the fielder dives, falls down, or has a lengthy throw after making the catch, then the runner can successfully advance to second base. Players should not tag up on a fly ball if they cannot realistically advance from where it is likely to be caught.

 ### Administrative Time-Out

During the pre-game infield/outfield warm-up, coaches can have their team observe the defensive team's players. By taking mental notes of the arm strength, foot speed, and overall skill set of the opposition, base runners will have an easier time judging whether they can successfully advance to the next base on a tag up, *first to third*, or other developing situation. Given that two or three defensive players take infield/ outfield at each position, it is important for any observations to be connected to the specific starting players of the opposition.

The challenging aspect of the tag-up versus halfway decision occurs at second base. Players are often indecisive and thus unsure how to respond in this situation. A guideline that should help dictate their decision is the number of outs at the time that the fly ball is hit. With none out (one out after the ball is caught), players should be more aggressive in tagging up as getting to third base with less than two outs is a priority. Yet, with one out, going halfway may be more advantageous as the risk involved in getting to third base with two outs is not worth it. The exception to this guideline is on a deep or shallow fly ball, where the base runner can make a clear read as to the outcome of the developing play.

Sliding

An important fundamental for all baseball players to learn is the *figure-four* or *three-point slide*. When properly executed, this slide enables players to approach a base in a strategic fashion to avoid a tag and decrease momentum. Yet, if improperly completed, sliding can result in injury or an out on the bases. As the name implies, the figure-four slide entails players putting their legs in a configuration of the number four. Coaches should teach the slide in a progression of steps and on the proper surface.

Three Steps to Success

1. Squat down on the floor/grass with the fingers touching the ground (Figure 3-20).
2. Use the hands to pop into the figure-four slide configuration (Figure 3-21).
3. Raise the arms above the head with the hands in a clenched position (Figure 3-22).

Figure 3-20. Step 1   Figure 3-21. Step 2   Figure 3-22. Step 3

After players have completed several repetitions of the slide from a squatted position, they can progress to running before making a slide. Among the important factors to stress are sliding on the backside, not the knees or legs. Many young players will scrape their knees or legs when sliding when the buttocks should be the area of the body cushioning the landing. It is also crucial that players keep their arms raised and their hands clenched so as to avoid injury during the slide. (*Note:* When sliding during live action, players should not put a hand on the ground as done when learning the slide.) Lastly, players must properly time their slide so that they do not fall short of the base or slam into it too firmly.

COVERING ALL THE BASES

Players can hold batting gloves or dirt in their hands when running the bases. This will force them to keep their fingers clenched and protected when sliding and diving. Coaches can introduce sliding drills to players on wet outfield grass so that they learn the feeling of actually sliding. The muddy or discolored parts of players' uniforms are a good indicator of whether proper form is being used. If a player's pants by the kneecaps and shins are overly dirty then he is sliding on the wrong part of his body. Likewise, players with dirt on their backside are models of proper sliding form.

Topic of Debate: Sliding Into First Base and Home Plate

Players should watch the first baseman's feet to read whether he will come off the base to receive an errant throw. In this case, a slide into first base to avoid a tag is advantageous. However, sliding into a base does not actually speed up the running process. Yet, some players like to show hustle by diving into the base. In other scenarios, players will elect to dive head first on plays at home plate. While this maneuver may enable them to use their hands to slyly touch the plate, it may be more sensible to slide feet first toward a catcher who is wearing heavy protective gear.

Baserunning Drills

When learning how to run the bases effectively, live game experience has no substitute. Although, various baserunning drills are designed to build player instinct and baserunning competency. These drills simulate game situations and enable coaches to teach in-game baserunning fundamentals to players during practice time. Furthermore, *it is productive to design energized baserunning drills in which two or more players can run simultaneously so that players have limited time to idly stand around, waiting to run.*

Belly Out Drill

Coaches should have one group of players start at home plate while the other half starts at second base (eight or so players in each location). One runner will rotate in at each starting spot and run simultaneously to their destination. The runner at home plate will feign a swing and run out a double with an effective belly out and turn at first base. The runner at second base will take his primary lead and perform a secondary lead as the runner at home plate feigns a swing. After the secondary lead, the player will focus on bellying out and rounding third base properly before scoring. Coaches can do this drill until each player runs from both starting spots three times or for several minutes.

Beat It Drill

When teaching base runners how to properly beat out an infield hit, coaches can have players run one at a time from home plate through first base. By mandating that each runner peek to see the ball on the third step out of the box, hit the front corner of the base, check for the overthrow, and break down after coming through the base, coaches can teach players the necessary elements for running down the line. These *beat its* (beating out an infield hit) are also effective at helping players lower their times out of the box and can be timed by a coaching staff member.

Should players dive head first into a base or only slide feet first?

Although diving head first can lead to more injuries and bruises for younger players, diving head first is an acquired skill that, when executed properly, can help base runners avoid a tag and glide more precisely into a base. For example, the arms are exposed and can get scraped. Fingers can also be jammed or broken more easily on these slides. Furthermore, unless players land like an airplane (not a helicopter), head-first dives can knock the wind out of athletes. Players who slide feet first can utilize a pop-up slide, which enables them to quickly hop up and run to the next base faster than a head-first slide.

Three-Man Drill

Coaches can split their team in thirds (three groups of five or six players) and send a group to home plate, first base, or third base. In this drill, players will perform beating out an infield hit, running from first to third on a hit-and-run play, and tagging up from third base on an outfield fly ball. The runner from home plate will trigger the drill by feigning a swing, which will cue the runner on first base to take off for third base. When the runner from first base touches second base, the player on third base will leave from the base as if the ball has been caught in a tag-up situation. Coaches can add variations to the drill by having players perform other scenarios from these three locations, such as a running out a single to the outfield, dirt ball reads, and steals of home from third base.

Home Run Drill

This high energy, multi-skill drill starts with each player running to first base on a single to the outfield with an effective belly-out and turn at the base. Next, the runner will imagine that the defense is throwing behind him and dive back into first base. He will then quickly get to his feet and sprint to second base as if there has been an overthrow at first base. Upon approaching second base, the runner will execute a pop-up slide and head toward third base. At third base, the runner will perform a *hook slide* or *fade away slide* to avoid an imaginary tag. Lastly, the player will dash home and step on the plate in a standing position to complete the "home run."

Game Signals Drill

Coaches will line up four players at a time on the first baseline. The players will stand on the line as if they are on first base. The coach will flash signals, such as straight steal, delayed steal, hit-and-run, or no signal at all. After receiving their signals, all four players will take their primary lead. Next, a coach or pitcher standing on the mound will lift his leg as if he is pitching the ball toward home plate, and the runners will react accordingly. Occasionally, the pitcher can feign a pickoff throw to the base to keep the base runners alert.

Dirt Ball Reads Drill

This multi-player drill requires catchers and one or two infielders to simulate pitched balls in the dirt to which base runners must react. To start the drill, players will take a primary lead from first base (although the drill can be performed from any base). Next, a coach will pitch a ball in the dirt toward the catcher, who must block the ball and come up ready to throw out the advancing runner. Runners should only take off for the next base if the ball skips far enough away from the catcher. Coaches should mix in a pitched strike or pickoff move every five pitches to maintain the integrity of the drill.

Tag Up Drill

Coaches will hit fly balls to outfielders as base runners practice getting their secondary lead, tagging up, and advancing a base. Players can be put at any base for this drill and compete with the defense to see if they can run safely to the next base. Runners on first or second base should work on determining whether to tag up or go halfway on the fly ball. This drill can also place multiple runners on base simultaneously and help trail runners work on reacting to lead runner decisions.

In-Game Strategy: Trail Base Runners

Tagging up as a trail runner can play an important role in helping a team get a player in scoring position. With a runner on third base with less than two outs, many defensive teams will throw home on a fly ball hit to the outfield. This throw provides the other base runners with an opportunity to advance a base if they remember to tag up on the play. However, teams at the high school level and above may cut the throw headed to the plate and relay it to another base if they deem that there is no play at home. Trail runners must also know whether the *contact play* is on. In this scenario, the base runner on third base is running on the contact of any batted ground ball.

Pick Up the Third Base Coach Drill

To start this drill, runners are put on first and second base. Next, each runner will take a secondary lead and run toward the next base on an imaginary single or double hit to the outfield. As each runner approaches the base, he must *pick up* or look at the third base coach to see whether he is being held up or must advance further. Coaches must create signals for each runner using both arms. For example, the lead runner may be sent home even though the trail runner is being held at second base. Furthermore, it is important for runners approaching second base to learn how to pick up the third base coach while running full speed and touching the base.

Freeze on a Line Drive Drill

Base runners will take a secondary lead and react to line drives hit by a coach. Players must freeze on these line drives and only advance upon *seeing the ball through* the infield. The goal of this drill is for players to instinctively freeze on line drives and carry this learned response to game situations. Defensive players can work on doubling off base runners as they scramble back to the base.

Pickoff and Steal Drill

This indoor or outdoor drill requires a pitcher, first baseman, and several base runners. Each base runner will take a primary lead from first base and read the pitcher's actions from the stretch position. If the pitcher *goes to the plate*, then the runner will take off for second base. But, if the pitcher throws over to first base, then the base runner must return to the base with an effective California turn or dive. Pitchers must mix in pitches or feign a pitch to home plate every few repetitions to maintain runner uncertainty. This drill can be performed at all three bases, with or without coaches flashing signals.

Administrative Time-Out

Many of these baserunning drills can be set up indoors during pre-season workouts or days with inclement weather. Coaches must remember to have players wear helmets when a ball is used in the drill. For motivation, coaches can keep score of the players that execute properly and make effective baserunning decisions. Push-ups, extra running drills, or some other activity can be implemented for those players who make too many mental mistakes on the bases. In particular, the drills that incorporate decision-making, instinctive reads, or recognition of offensive signals can be used to tally player success rates.

Batting Practice Baserunning Drills

Like with so many other skills of the game, batting practice is an ideal time to simulate in-game scenarios and work on baserunning. After each hitter takes his round of swings, he should become a runner and react to successive hitters' at bats. For instance, from first base, the runner can work on the primary and secondary leads before reacting to a sacrifice bunt. Next, the runner and batter can execute a hit-and-run play. Most of all, the base runner should make proper reads on batted balls by the hitter, such as tagging up on fly balls, freezing on line drives, leaving at the right moment on squeeze bunts, and holding on ground balls when appropriate regardless of which base he is stationed.

Teaching Tip

Coaches should schedule a team visit from an experienced track runner/coach to model, discuss, and critique proper running form. Baseball is a sport in which players run, in many cases, 90 feet or less on a given play. Therefore, coaches must teach players to be quick, not fast, on the bases. The first two or three steps are pivotal in enabling an athlete achieve top speed as quickly as possible (Table 3-1). Players can run the bases or in the outfield while the guest critiques their form and models sound running technique. Plyometrics and *Reactions* are drills (see Chapter 8) that build explosive running speed, which can be performed in a team setting format.

Running Fundamentals Checklist	
What to Do	**What *Not* to Do**
• Lift the heel to the buttocks.	• Hold the breath.
• Relax the face.	• Move the arms from side to side.
• Lower the shoulders.	• Tighten the upper body.
• Use lollypop to pocket arm action.	• Slow down before the base.
• Lift the knees.	• Run in a jagged angle/manner.

Table 3-1. Running Fundamentals checklist

Mental Approaches to Baserunning

Coaches must communicate to their players on what the team's offensive philosophy is centered. Some teams run the bases in conservative fashion and expect extra base hits or home runs to power their offense. Major League manager Earl Weaver believed that "pitching, defense, and the three-run homer" was the best philosophy for winning baseball games. He was known for rejecting the strategies of sacrifice bunting, the stolen base, and the hit-and-run because "On offense, your most precious possessions are your 27 outs."[4]

Major League Connection

Baltimore Orioles' manager, Earl Weaver, was ejected from more games than anyone in American League history. In his career, he did amass 1,480 wins and a .583 winning percentage. In terms of in-game strategy, Weaver is famous for patiently waiting for the three-run home run to lead his team to victory.[3]

Despite Weaver's managerial view, many coaches take an aggressive approach with their team's baserunning abilities. His conservative stance is less plausible at the lower levels where catchers, pitchers, and defenses are not as skilled in defending offensive strategies. Accordingly, many teams will have base runners bunt, steal bases, and try to get an extra base whenever possible. Players on these teams will have more leeway to take risks on the bases.

Aside from understanding the team's offensive strategy, players must also be aware of the specific game situation. The score, number of outs, and skill level of an opponent will often dictate how aggressive a base runner should be. In a close ball game with a dominant pitcher on the mound for the other team, players should be more aggressive when trying to scrape a run for their team. Conversely, in a high scoring game with weak pitchers on the opponent's staff, players do not want to "take the bat out of their hitters' hands" and make an out on the bases. Specifically, base runners do not want to make the first out of an inning when a high percentage of batters are reaching base safely.

Another consideration for players when running the bases is an understanding of their individual role and abilities as a base runner. If a player lacks running speed and the potential to steal a base or advance to an extra base on a base hit, then he should not risk making an out. In particular, a player who is not planning on stealing a base should not take an overly aggressive lead that may result in a pickoff. Many examples can be found of players who lack running speed, but who can successfully read balls in the dirt or execute a delayed steal. Hence, all players must know their strengths and be mindful not to hurt the team with poor judgment or unrealistic expectations on the bases.

 ### Conference Time

Coaches should conference with their players regarding expectations on the bases. Several players on a team will inevitably desire the green light to steal bases freely, while others may feel content conservatively moving from base to base. This topic can be sensitive as slower, less athletic players may think that they have the ability to steal bases and run aggressively. Coaches can counter this perception by explaining additional strengths that they may possess and how they can make contributions to the team in other ways.

It is important for all base runners to learn the opposing team's defensive tendencies. For example, some teams implement trick pickoff plays or have a catcher frequently throw behind runners on the bases. Other defenses may have a fielder trail runners into each base or utilize an aggressive strategy to nab players on the base paths. Given this fact, runners should be aware of which specific teams may force them to be more conservative or alert on the bases. Similarly, some defensive teams do not focus on holding runners effectively. In these cases, players should be more aggressive and take advantage of baserunning opportunities.

 ### Administrative Time-Out

Scouting opposing teams becomes a priority at higher levels to help coaches communicate with their players about opponents' tendencies. In particular, learning the opposition's pickoff plays, style of holding runners on base, and defensive philosophy is beneficial. In the college and professional ranks, teams play each other in a three- or four-game weekend series, where they get familiar with each team's basic strategies and defensive tactics. Some coaches send an assistant coach to scout upcoming opponents, or are able to obtain scouting reports from other coaches.

Sources/Further Reading

[1]Dickson, P. (1992). *Baseball's Greatest Quotations*. New York: Harper Perennial. P. 469.

[2]Vass, G. (2004). "Stealing Home: A Lost Art in Major League Baseball." *Baseball Digest*.

[3]Baseball-Reference.com; Sports Reference LLC; 2000-2009.

[4]Weaver, E. (2002). "Weaver on Strategy: The Classic Work on the Art of Managing a Baseball Team." Brassey's. March 17, 2009.

BUNTING

Chapter 4

Learning to bunt takes a lot of time....
Managers get mad because someone didn't
sacrifice a man over, but very few managers
insist that their players learn to bunt.

—Maury Wills[1]

Along with the timing of pitching changes amongst armchair baseball fans, bunting is one of the top causes of in-game strategy debates and agitation. A sacrifice bunt attempted too early in a game, not executed properly, or not attempted in a close game may lead to questioning a coach's decisions. Some baseball managers, such as Earl Weaver, do not believe in sacrificing outs to move runners over. Yet, other coaches, especially those in Japan, will "sacrifice bunt" in the first few innings with the hope of snatching an early lead.

Since players executing a sacrifice bunt are giving themselves up at the plate to advance a runner, bunting is the ultimate selfless, team-minded play in baseball. In a society (and sport) that is largely focused on the individual, this aspect of the game highlights actions for "the good of the team." With player statistics translating into personal recognition and hefty contracts in the Major Leagues, bunting is not always endorsed by players. Nonetheless, many coaches are advocates of bunting in sacrifice situations, to score a runner from third base, or for a base hit. Therefore, players must learn proper fundamentals for a variety of bunting circumstances.

Typically, bunt situations exist with no outs and runners on first and/or second base. The goal of the bunter is to *drop a bunt down* that forces the defense to resort to ignoring the advancing runners and throw the batter out at first base. In this case, base runners can be moved into scoring position on second or third base with less than two outs. However, players can also bunt for a base hit with any number of outs or men on base. Some teams implement squeeze bunt plays to score a runner from third base with less than two outs. Also, bunting can be used as a tactic for surprising the defense or flustering a pitcher and inducing a fielding error.

The Sacrifice Bunt

Stance

In order to effectively execute a sacrifice bunt, players should be familiar with three different stances for this skill. These sacrifice bunting stances include squaring around, pivoting, and diagonal feet (Figures 4-1 through 4-3). In all cases, players should be in an athletic stance with their knees bent, holding the barrel of the bat at the top of the strike zone. Players must only bunt pitches that are in the strike zone and realize that drawing a walk will usually serve the purpose of a sacrifice bunt. In addition, it is important for hitters to keep their elbows in when bunting. The elbows should be flexible and enable the bunter to receive the ball on the bat much like catching a ball.

Teaching Tip

Coaches must emphasize to players the importance of bunting only at strikes. In particular, players who attempt to bunt high pitches will frequently pop out and possibly cause a double play. Bunters have a higher success rate on breaking balls or pitches down in the strike zone, as it is easier to get these pitches down on the ground. Many coaches mandate which stance that their players should use when bunting. Alternatively, coaches

Figure 4-1. Squaring around   Figure 4-2. Pivoting   Figure 4-3. Diagonal feet

can let players practice each of the three stances to find out with which they are most comfortable. Much like hitting, players should be limber and relaxed with no tension in their body when bunting.

Topic of Debate: Styles of Bunting

Traditionally, hitters were taught to square around when attempting to bunt. In response, opposing teams would pitch the batter high, inside fastballs, which made it difficult for bunters to get the ball on the ground or *pull the bat back* out of the strike zone. In recent decades, more teams favor pivoting or the diagonal feet bunting stance as turning away from an inside pitch and getting the bat out of the strike zone is easier with the feet in these positions. Despite this shift, some coaches still favor squaring around in the bunting stance.

Three Steps to Success

1. Get into an athletic stance with the knees in a flexed or bent position.
2. Utilize a method to turn and face the pitcher with the bat out in front of body.
3. Keep the top hand at shoulder height in upper portion of the strike zone.

Grip

As with the bunting stance, several grips can be adopted when holding the bat as a bunter. The bottom hand can be held at the knob or at the top of the tape on the handle of the bat (Figures 4-4 and 4-5). This hand is used as a rudder to steer the bat angle in the direction that the bunter wants the ball to go. The top hand should pinch the barrel of the bat with the thumb and pointer finger. Bunters should practice holding the bat without exposing the fingers of their top hand. Another method for holding the bat is to keep the hands together in the middle of the bat (Figure 4-6). Advocates of this method feel that bats that measure over 30 inches are more balanced and easier to control when held in this manner.

Figure 4-4. Bunting grip—bottom hand on knob

Figure 4-5. Bunting grip—bottom hand on top of tape

Figure 4-6. Bunting grip—hands together below barrel

In all cases, the barrel of the bat should be above the handle and tilting in an upward position. This position is more advantageous than a horizontal or level bat angle as the batter will be less prone to pop up. If he does pop up with the slightly tilted bat position, the ball is likely to travel into foul territory where fielders will not have an opportunity to catch it. Right-handed bunters can use their bottom hand to angle the bat so the top of the barrel is pointed in the direction of the second baseman when bunting the ball down the third baseline. For bunts on the first baseline, right-handed hitters can point the top of the bat toward the first base dugout. From the other side of the plate, left-handed bunters can use the third base dugout and shortstop as markers for pointing the tip of the bat to angle their bunts down either baseline.

What are the most common mistakes players make when bunting?

Many players will chase pitches out of the strike zone when bunting, which may lead them to pop up, laying down a bad bunt, or getting behind in the count. Players also forget to bend their knees to reach a low pitch and often drop the barrel of the bat to make contact. Other issues include running out of the batter's box before getting the bunt down, stabbing at the ball with the bat rather than *catching the ball with the bat*, and fearing the pitch hitting the hands.

Teaching Tip

When bunting, the analogy of catching the pitch with the bat helps players understand how soft their hands should be. Players want to deaden the ball when bunting, not hit it. The top hand is instrumental in determining the force of a bunt. It can hold the bat in a light manner so as to absorb the force of a pitch or it can exert itself to push a bunt past an infielder. Thus, the bottom hand can be viewed as the steering wheel, while the top hand acts as the engine. Players can practice their bunting stance and grip in front of a mirror to check for proper bat angle, stance, and grip on the bat.

Conference Time

Coaches should discuss the team's bunting philosophy with their players. Certain players on the roster may be better suited to bunt based on their spot in the batting order, running speed, and proficiency with the skill. In addition, hitters who are struggling or in a slump can bunt to get the feel of the ball hitting the bat. A bunt base hit is an effective way to get out of a hitting funk. Bunting forces batters to carefully focus on a pitcher's delivery, velocity, and movement, which can benefit them later in the game.

 In-Game Strategy: Bunting vs. Drawn-In Defenses

Defensive teams will practice strategies for protecting against a sacrifice bunt. Many teams will have the first and/or third basemen charge toward the batter to field the ball quickly and throw out the lead runner. Bunters should aim to direct their bunts toward the first and third baselines of the infield, not straight ahead toward the pitcher. Ideally, if a batter senses which corner infielder will be charging in or playing up, then he can angle his bunt toward the opposite line.

Bunting for a Hit

When bunting for a base hit, players should *show bunt* later than when in a sacrifice bunting situation. Rather than pivoting or squaring when the pitcher starts his motion as in a sacrifice bunting scenario, players should wait until the pitcher is about to release the pitch. Otherwise, infielders will charge in sooner and be able to field the ball in ample time to throw the bunter out at first base. Players can utilize two techniques for bunting for a base hit: the drag bunt and the push bunt.

Drag Bunt

The drag bunt is implemented by players who are trying to bunt the pitch down the pull-side foul line. For left-handed batters, a drag bunt down the first baseline is advantageous when the infielders are playing back or the pitcher falls off to the *third base side* (Figure 4-7). As their momentum moves toward first base, right-handed bunters will not technically drag the bat, but instead get the bat out in front of the body. Bunting down the third baseline when the third baseman is playing deep or the pitcher falls off the mound to the *first base side* provides an opportunity to reach base safely (Figure 4-8).

Figure 4-7. Left-handed drag bunt down the first baseline

Figure 4-8. Right-handed bunt down the third baseline

Three Steps to Success

1. Do not show bunt until the pitcher is releasing the ball.
2. Angle the bat so that the ball will be directed to the pull side of the infield as body momentum moves toward first base.
3. Bunt a strike on the inner portion of plate.

Major League Connection

In 1992, Brett Butler set a Major League Baseball record by successfully bunting for a hit 41 times in one season. Butler, a left-handed batter, was proficient at pushing bunts toward third base as well as dragging bunts toward the second baseman.[2]

 ### Administrative Time-Out

Coaches at higher levels of play who are involved in the grounds-keeping of their home field usually determine how the infield grass should be cut. The taller the grass, the slower the infield will play on ground balls. As a result, certain fields are more conducive to bunting than others. Coaches can also instruct an assistant coach or player to roll baseballs from home plate down the dirt baselines to see the slope of the infield when playing on a visitor's field. Some fields are pitched so that rolling balls tend to turn foul, while on other infields similarly bunted balls will stay fair.

 ### Teaching Tip

Footwork is an important part of executing a successful drag bunt. Left-handed batters can take their normal stride with the right foot and then pivot as the bunt is put down. Another option is pivoting the right foot to start the motion as the back foot comes off the ground to run toward first base. In both cases, the bat *drags* behind the body's movement down the baseline. As they make their move to run to first, right-handed batters must be careful not to step on home plate. Righties should not step back with their rear foot when pivoting, or else their body will get moving in the wrong direction.

Push Bunt

An alternative to bunting down the pull-side baseline is the push bunt, which is especially useful for speedy right-handed batters who draw third basemen in to play on the grass. A right-handed batter lays down a push bunt by bunting the pitch toward the second baseman (Figure 4-9). Much like a left-handed drag bunt, the goal is to get the bunt past the pitcher so that the second or first baseman has to run in and field the ball. Unlike a typical sacrifice bunt, where the batter wants to deaden the ball, the push bunt requires enough force to get the ball past the pitcher's mound.

Figure 4-9. Right-handed push bunt

Left-handed batters will place a push bunt toward the third baseman (Figure 4-10). This strategy is particularly effective when the third baseman is playing back or lacks mobility. Pitches in the middle to the outside of the strike zone are easier to push bunt toward the opposite side of the infield. Inside pitches can *jam* the bunter and induce a weakly hit bunt, or one that the pitcher can easily field.

Figure 4-10. Left-handed push bunt

Three Steps to Success

1. Do not show bunt until the pitcher is releasing the ball.
2. Bunt with force so that the ball will be past the pitcher on the opposite side of the infield.
3. Bunt a strike on middle/outer half of the zone.

Administrative Time-Out

Coaches must build time into their practices for working on bunt situations. Many games are won or lost on a bunt that is executed or defended in a pressure situation. Players must know what their responsibility is in each bunt scenario. Rainy day indoor practices are ideal opportunities to rehearse *bunt defense walk-through sessions*. Thirds drills are another productive method for practicing bunt defenses on each side of the field. To incorporate the offense, batters can practice getting down all types of bunts, to which the defense must react. Too often, finer aspects of baseball are not practiced, and teams fail to execute come game time.

 In-Game Strategy: Bunting Down the Third Baseline

Bunting for a hit down the third baseline with runners on first and second base is a sound strategy. Many third basemen *hold the base* in case of a steal of third and are slow to react on a bunt. Or, if the third baseman is too aggressive in charging during these situations, offensive teams can signal for a fake bunt with a steal of third base. This tactic is highly effective at the youth levels, as the shortstop will rarely rotate over to cover the base to receive the catcher's throw and tag out a runner stealing third.

 How do teams typically defend the bunt with runners on base?

Teams can set up a variety of plays to defend against bunt situations. Many defenses will have the pitcher quickly hop off the mound to cover all bunts on the third base side, while the first baseman is responsible for the first baseline. A more complex play is the bunt rotation, or *wheel play*, in which both the first and third basemen charge the batter to get the bunt quickly. At the same time, the second baseman rotates to cover first base as the shortstop sprints to third base. These bunt defense strategies are reviewed and diagrammed in detail in Chapter 8.

Squeeze Bunt

With a runner on third base or runners on second and third base with less than two outs, teams can *squeeze the runner(s) home*. The two types of squeeze bunts are: the *safety squeeze* and *suicide squeeze*. In both cases, the batter lays down a sacrifice bunt to score the runner, the major difference being the actions of the base runners.

In a safety squeeze bunt situation, the bunter tries to bunt the ball so that the runner can advance home as the defense fields the ball. This bunt is no different than a sacrifice bunt in that the runner reads whether he can advance based on the speed and location of the bunt. Additionally, the hitter squares or pivots early in the pitcher's motion so that he is not rushed in the bunting process. If the pitcher throws a high fastball or any sort of pitch to thwart the batter's bunt attempt, the bunter simply pulls the bat back and gets ahead in the count.

When a team attempts a suicide squeeze bunt, the runner breaks from third base as the pitcher lifts his leg before delivering the ball. The hitter must get the bat on the ball during the bunt attempt to protect the runner from being tagged out at home plate. Accordingly, the bunter must have effective bat control and the ability to bunt pitches in/out of the strike zone. Furthermore, the bunter should use a nonverbal cue to signal the runner that he is not swinging and will be bunting on the pitch. [*Note*: Some coaches have devised alternative names for this bunting strategy so as not to expose young players to the word "suicide."]

 Teaching Tip

Pepper is a terrific drill for hitters to work on for bat control and suicide squeeze bunting. Coaches can direct players to feed pitches to the bunter in the pepper drill that will challenge him to put the bat on the ball regardless of location. During this activity, players should show bunt later than a typical sacrifice just like in a suicide squeeze game situation. If hitters can make sure that the squeeze bunt is not grounded directly back to the pitcher or within the catcher's reach, then they are likely to score the runner from third base.

The Mental Side of Bunting

Even though bunting is generally used as a strategy to advance base runners and improve a team's chances of scoring, it can provide less visible benefits to players. Hitters who are experiencing a slump often find that bunting can help get them back on track. By forcing players to watch the bat hit the ball and positively impacting the team by advancing base runners, bunting can help a player get out of a mental rut. Moreover, a successful bunt for a base hit can provide a player with the sense that he is now out of his slump.

Bunting can also be an effective element of surprise that changes the momentum of a game. A squeeze bunt that scores the go-ahead run or a sacrifice bunt that is misplayed by the defense can energize the offense and put pressure on the opponent. Likewise, the first batter of an inning might bunt for a base hit, suddenly breaking the rhythm of a pitcher who has been cruising through the game. In particular, when a pitcher is dominating an offensive team or specific player in the lineup, bunting for a base hit is a clever method to get on base.

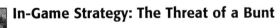 **In-Game Strategy: The Threat of a Bunt**

The threat of a bunt forces the infielders to play up on the grass. With a speedy hitter at bat, it is common for the first or third basemen to creep in to field a bunted pitch. This defensive positioning cuts down on the fielder's reaction time to a hard hit line drive or ground ball, giving the batter an edge. As a result, flashing a fake bunt during an at bat may draw in the defense and ultimately benefit a hitter.

When and where a player should bunt the ball depends on the opponent's defensive alignment. If a team's infielders are playing deep, then it may be an ideal time for a bunt. In addition, knowing the athleticism and arm strength of the infielders can help determine whether a bunt will be successful. In particular, a slower moving pitcher is a target for bunting. Conversely, nimble pitchers and third basemen are difficult to bunt against effectively.

Major League Connection

Greg Maddux won a record 18 Rawlings Gold Glove Awards in his career. Maddux was especially skilled at fielding bunts. Although not an ostensibly fast runner, he possessed great instincts in reading the angle of bunted balls from the pitcher's mound.[3]

Teaching Tip

Coaches and players should study their opponent during pre-game fielding practice and live game action to determine if bunting will be effective. Players should not wait until they step into the batter's box to decide whether to bunt or not. Instead, keeping tabs on the positioning and mobility of the infielders throughout the game will aid in this strategic process. In the event that a player knows he will be sacrifice bunting, he can practice pivoting or squaring ahead of time. Some players will work on these mechanics in the on-deck circle to help them mentally prepare for the in-game experience.

Conference Time

Upon receiving the bunt signal, many players will be disappointed, as they would prefer to swing the bat. Players may view the bunt signal as an indication that the coach does not have faith in their hitting ability. Coaches can speak with players who may be called on to bunt and stress the skill as a positive contribution to team success. Players need to take pride in executing a bunt for the benefit of the team. If a coach senses that a player is not giving full effort to get a bunt down, he may opt to remove him from the game.

Alternative Bunting Strategies

Slash Bunt

The slash bunt, also known as the *butcher boy* or *slug bunt*, is a solid strategy for making the defense more cautious of guarding against the bunt. Hitters will square or pivot to sacrifice bunt slightly sooner than normal. As the pitcher's hands break, the hitter pulls the bat back toward his rear shoulder and brings the hands together with a choked-up grip position on the bat ready to hit. Next, the batter attempts to hit a hard ground ball past the drawn in infielders. Although this play can also be executed as a "slash and run" with the runner in motion on the pitch, hitters must be disciplined in their pitch selection. This tactic is particularly effective when defenses run the wheel play and infielders charge the bunter in an overly aggressive fashion.

Three Steps to Success

1. Show bunt a bit sooner than a typical bunt so the batter has time to get the bat back.
2. Bring the hands together on the bat, and move the arms back toward the shoulder.
3. If the pitch can be handled, hit a hard ground ball past the drawn in infielders.

Four Phases of Executing a Slash Bunt (Figures 4-11 through 4-14)

Figure 4-11. Step 1

Figure 4-12. Step 2

Figure 4-13. Step 3

Figure 4-14. Step 4

Fake Bunt and Steal

This strategy is an effective tool for protecting a base stealer. Showing bunt places the bat in the vision of the catcher and temporarily makes him think that a bunt will be put on the ground. Likewise, the middle infielders may be caught off guard because of other bunt situation responsibilities and not cover second base as quickly. These factors can create defensive lapses of tenths or hundredths of a second that may enable the runner to steal second base safely.

In-Game Strategy: Swinging Through a Pitch to Protect the Base Runner

For helping a base runner steal a base, an alternative tactic to the fake bunt is for the batter to swing through a pitch purposely. This practice may not be advisable for younger players, as it teaches a negative skill. Nonetheless, a swinging strike stalls the catcher even more than a fake bunt. Although it puts the hitter behind in the count, most coaches will readily trade a strike for a runner moving into scoring position. Several college teams have executed the steal of home while having the batter swing through the pitch and above the sliding base runner.

Bunt-and-Run

Similar to the hit-and-run play, the bunt and run involves the base runner on first base running on the pitch. The hitter must make contact with the pitch and get the bunt on the ground. When using this strategy, the goal of the offense is to advance the base runners and, if possible, get a base hit. As the runner on first base takes off for second base, at least one of the middle infielders will vacate their position to cover second base, creating two advantages for the offense: the second baseman may not be able to rotate over to cover first base on a bunt fielded by the first baseman; and the shortstop will be unable to beat the base runner to third base on a bunt fielded by the third baseman. Consequently, this tactic is optimally utilized when the batter bunts successfully for a base hit toward the third baseman and the runner advances to third base.

Teaching Tip

The ultimate goal of the bunt-and-run is to move the base runner to third base. As a result, coaches should teach hitters to bunt toward the third baseman, giving the runner the best chance to advance. Since most hitters are more comfortable executing a push bunt rather than a drag bunt, coaches may reserve this play for left-handed batters. Base runners should pick up the third base coach when rounding second base. Bunts on the third baseline enable the base runner to see the play develop in front of them and determine if they can beat the shortstop to third base.

Bunting Drills

Hitters can improve their bunting skills and confidence by performing a variety of activities. *Many teams make the mistake of practicing bunting with the pitcher at close distances using slowly thrown pitches. It is important to simulate the bunting experience that players will encounter in a live game.* Bunting competitions, where players must read signals from the third base coach and execute various types of bunts while facing a pitcher off the mound, will translate into success on game day.

Bunt and Catch Drill

In order to reinforce the notion that hitters should catch the ball with the bat when bunting, coaches can strap or tie a fielder's glove to the barrel of a bat. This device teaches players that the bat is held firmly, yet not used to jab the ball when bunting. Players enjoy the challenge of trying to successfully catch the ball in the glove strapped to the bat.

Knock Down Drill

When practicing the squeeze bunt, coaches at the high school level and beyond should discuss defensive strategies that may be implemented. Many teams will throw a high inside fastball to prevent the batter from getting his bat on the ball in a squeeze bunt situation. To prepare for this scenario, as their hitters attempt squeeze bunts, coaches can throw tennis or sock balls *up and in* (high and inside). Hitters should offer at pitches that can be bunted on the ground and turn inside toward the umpire on pitches that will likely not be gloved by the catcher anyway. Players must hide the bat on this inside turn so that the pitch does not inadvertently hit the bat (Figures 4-15 and 4-16). This drill can be used within all hitting drills and situations.

Figure 4-15. Inside turn (front view)   Figure 4-16. Inside turn (rear view)

Hula Hoop® Bunting Drill

During batting practice or instructional bunting stations, coaches can place Hula hoops on the first and third baselines at which players aim. Hoops should also be placed in the location of effective push bunts, specifically past the mound toward the first and second basemen. Prizes or competition points may be awarded to those players who successfully land a bunt in the hoop.

Cones or helmets can be turned on the side and used as targets instead of hoops, especially when bunting indoors on a gym floor. Defensive players should make sure not to field the bunted balls until each bunt has finished rolling. A variation of this drill involves placing eggs at specific spots on the infield dirt or grass while hitters try to break them by landing bunts directly on top of the eggs.

Broomstick Bunt Drill

One training technique for bunting involves using a bat with a smaller barrel. Fungo bats, broomsticks, or any bat that has a thin barrel challenges players to be efficient with their bunting mechanics. With less room for error, these training devices require concentration, proper placement of the hands, and clear vision of the pitch. At higher pitch velocities, players can use metal stick bats that will not shatter on contact. As mentioned previously, Easton's Thunderstick is a thin metal rod bat that can be used for bunting or hitting drills.

Batting Practice Bunting Drill

In the course of team batting practice, players should execute at least two sacrifice bunts, a bunt for a hit, and each type of squeeze bunt. Lead-off hitters and speedy base runners can use several pitches to focus on push and drag bunts to both sides of the infield. In all cases, base runners (the previous hitters) should be on the bases for the bunters to advance. In particular, it is important for suicide squeeze bunts to be practiced with a runner, sprinting toward the batter, who flashes a nonverbal acknowledgement signal before the pitch is released.

Squeeze Bunt Drill

The team is split into three groups with players placed at second base, third base, and home plate. A coach will signal for a suicide squeeze, safety squeeze, or bunt for a base hit. While the batter bunts and then replaces the runner on second base, the runners must act accordingly. The key element of the drill involves the batter understanding which type of bunt play is signaled and reacting properly, which reinforces the point that hitters should only bunt pitches that are strikes unless a suicide squeeze bunt is called.

 Teaching Tip

The squeeze bunt drill enables coaches to teach trail base runners how to read the actions of the lead runner. In a safety squeeze or bunt-for-a-hit situation, the runner on third base may elect to hold the base. In this case, even if the bunt is good enough to allow him to advance, the base runner on second base must make sure not to run to third base. On a double suicide squeeze bunt, the trail runner may be able to advance to third base and at the same time realize that scoring is not a possibility.

Move 'Em Over Drill

Coaches will split the team in half with one group running at first base while the other group attempts sacrifice bunts to advance them. One bunter and base runner will be performing the drill at a time. The runner will take a primary lead, secondary lead, and advance to second base as the bunt is successfully put on the ground. Ideally, this high-energy drill will move quickly as each bunter quickly darts in to bunt one pitch and runs to the end of the base runner line. Coaches may continue the drill until every player correctly makes a sacrifice bunt to move the runner to second base. This drill can be completed with the base runners starting at second or third base as well.

Rapid Fire Bunt Drill

If available for this activity, coaches should utilize a pitching machine. Coaches will call out a situation, and players will execute the appropriate bunt. For example, a coach might call out "Man on first, none out," "Bases empty, third baseman playing back," or "Man on third, one out, suicide squeeze." In each scenario, the batter will bunt accordingly. A variation of this drill involves coaches flashing signals, which slows the pace and number of repetitions and which better simulates game activity. Indoor practice is an ideal time to rehearse drills of this sort.

Four-Corner Bunting Drill

By using each of the three bases and home plate, coaches can set up four bunting stations on the baseball diamond. Each station will utilize the base as an imaginary home plate with three to four players rotating in as a bunter. Besides bunting, player roles at each location will be fielding bunted balls, pitching, and catching. At each of the four stations, coaches will need a batting helmet, catcher's glove, and catcher's mask in order for players to practice different types of bunts. For instance, the group at home plate can work on sacrifice bunts, while first base focuses on suicide squeeze bunts. Second and third base can refine the push bunt and drag bunt, respectively. Ideally, a different coach will be at each location, instructing players on each type of bunt.

Sources/Further Reading

[1]Wills, M. & Celizic, M. (1991). *On the Run*. New York: Avalon Publishing Group.

[2]Curry, J. "Baseball: The Lost Art—Strategy of the Bunt; No More Easy Outs." *The New York Times*. August 17, 2003.

[3]Baseball-Reference.com; Sports Reference LLC; 2000-2009. April 22, 2009.

INFIELD DEFENSE

Chapter 5

*Pop flies, in a sense, are just a diversion for a second
baseman. Grounders are his stock trade.*
—Jackie Robinson[1]

Baseball is the only sport in which the defense has the ball. The pace of the game is controlled by the tempo of the defensive players, in particular the pitcher. Moreover, the nine defensive players on the field are defending against at most four, but often only one offensive player. Therefore, when viewing a game, spectators are focused on the demeanor, energy level, and overall competency of the defense. As a result, coaches must emphasize the important role defense plays in setting the tone for how the team is represented.

The old expression, "Pitching and defense win games," is evident at all levels of play. Even in the Major Leagues, the teams with the hottest pitching staffs and strong defenses usually win the World Series. Frequently, teams stacked with big-name offensive players are knocked out of the playoffs by scrappy defensive teams with effective pitching. Poor defense, chock full of errors and sloppy play, creates long innings and dejected players.

Teaching Tip

Coaches must emphasize to players the numerous ways that defense plays a role in team success. Long innings on defense enable the opposing pitcher to rest and gain strength to pitch longer into the game. Likewise, poor defense forces the pitcher to throw more pitches and makes coaches use their bullpen earlier than expected. Players must recognize that when they pick up a baseball to start their throwing that this sets the defensive tone for the entire day. On each game day, warm-up throwing and the pre-game infield/outfield routine is a revealing indicator of player concentration and team motivation.

Administrative Time-Out

During the warm-up throwing routine, many coaches will discipline players for making errors or throwing mistakes. Having the team run laps and do push-ups, crunches, or some other grueling activity can motivate an unfocused team to concentrate. Another option on game day is to use the infield/outfield pre-game fielding practice as a measure to determine the starting lineup. This approach may be administratively difficult as coaches must turn in their completed lineup cards soon after pre-game infield practice. Nonetheless, holding players accountable for their concentration on defense before games and practices is an important tool.

Fielding

Fielding Stance

One of the key components to achieving success as an infielder is to develop an effective ready position by getting into an athletic stance with the knees bent and feet wider than shoulder-width. The hands should be out in front of the body, not resting on the knees. Body weight should be on the balls of the feet, and the fielder must be prepared to move in any direction as quickly as possible (Figure 5-1). Infielders' eyes should be locked in on the catcher

Figure 5-1. Infielder stance

to read the signs and react to any batted balls from the hitting zone. To gain forward momentum toward the batter, some players utilize a slow, three-step walking movement as the pitch is being delivered.

Three Steps to Success

1. Get into an athletic stance with body weight on the balls of the feet.
2. Keep the hands out, and be ready to move quickly in any direction to field a ball.
3. Focus the eyes on the catcher and hitting zone to read the angle of the ball off the bat.

 In-Game Strategy: Pre-Pitch Positioning

Typically, middle infielders try to detect the catcher's signals for pitch type and location. This information will indicate where a hitter is likely to hit the ball and help them decide who is covering on a steal. Some teams have the middle infielders flash signals behind their back to outfielders so that they can get a better jump on fly balls with an indication of where the ball will be hit. Generally, assistant coaches are responsible for positioning defensive players based on hitter and pitcher tendencies from previous games or at bats.

Fielding Mechanics

As an infielder reads the ball off the bat, his goal is to take the most efficient angle to the spot where he will eventually field it. Ideally, he will have time to get in front of the ball with his body centered over it because if he cannot glove it cleanly, his upper body will knock the ball down in front of him. Proper fielding position entails the ball being fielded in the center of the body with the hands out (Figure 5-2). The fielder should be in a bent knee, athletic position with the head down and following the ball into the glove. Consequently, when approaching a ground ball, players should take a route that enables them to get behind it and *come through the ball* as they field and throw to a base. In cases where the runner has exceptional speed or the ball is hit far from reach, infielders may have to field the ball to their side to save time.

Figure 5-2. Ground ball fielding mechanics—vertical hands

Three Steps to Success

1. Find an angle, and approach the ball so that it is fielded in the center of the body.
2. Keep the hands out and glove on the ground so that the ball cannot pass.
3. Ensure that the head is down so that the button on the cap is visible to all, and the throwing hand comes down to cover the ball.

Teaching Tip

Coaches can use a number of memorable cues to help players understand proper fielding mechanics. The throwing hand should clamp down on a fielded ball just as a clamshell closes. An alternative to the clamshell analogy is an alligator chomping down on a piece of food. The button on the top of the hat should point in the direction of the catcher as the infielder looks down at the ball. This visual will help players stay down and not look up too soon to throw the runner out. A creative drill coaches can implement is to have infielders put the bill of their cap into their mouths. With the hat between their teeth, players will have difficulty seeing incoming ground balls over the hat. As a result, they will be forced to extend their hands effectively in order to see and field ground balls.

What are the most common mistakes infielders make that lead to errors?

Players must make a strong effort to *stay down on the ball* and not come up too soon. By bending at the knees (not the back), maintaining upright body posture, and keeping the glove on the ground, fielders can protect against ground balls getting past them. To guard against bad hops getting through to the outfield, infielders should also field the ball in the center of their bodies and not off to the side. When time permits, players should *get around the ball* and not field it off to the side to their backhand or forehand. Lastly, players must make sure to not *let the ball play them*; this occurs when their weight is back on the heels. In turn, they will not be able to choose a favorable hop to field the ball.

 ### Topic of Debate: Ground Ball Fielding Mechanics

Players may also field a ground ball with their hands coming together in a lateral motion. Rather than the throwing hand coming down on top of the glove hand as the ball enters the mitt, the two hands can be brought together from the side (Figure 5-3). This less common method accomplishes the same purpose of keeping the fielded ball in the glove and getting it out as fast as possible to make a throw. Proponents of this fielding motion feel that the horizontal glove action allows the infielder to field the ball while starting a shuffle step toward the target. However, critics of this method claim that without the bare hand clamping downward on the ball into the mitt, a greater risk of balls popping out of the glove can result.

Figure 5-3. Ground ball fielding mechanics—horizontal hands

Major League Connection

When imitating superstar Major League players, young players can learn poor fielding mechanics. Professional players may field the ball to their side on balls hit in the hole. In many cases, time will not permit them to field the ball in front of their body or throw from an ideal arm slot.

 ### Administrative Time-Out

An excellent training tool for infielders are paddles or table tennis racquets. By using these wooden, flat-panel boards as a glove, players quickly learn that they must utilize their throwing hand to field the ball. Coaches can make straps for the fingers, which can be attached to the back of the paddles. Several manufacturers make leather, flat-palmed gloves and bands that connect the wrists together for this same purpose. Early season drills can include ground ball repetitions with these paddles to reinforce the skill of bringing the throwing and glove hands together.

Conference Time

Youth-level players can have an experience that makes them *ball shy*. A pitched ball, line drive, or bad hop on a ground ball can unexpectedly hit a player and cause him to be afraid of the ball. Infielders who play back on their heels or retreat on ground balls may be playing scared. Coaches must be aware of this factor, and communicate with players accordingly. Ironically, players who are tentative in charging ground balls are more likely to experience a bad hop. Instead, they should be aggressive in fielding the ball and looking for the most advantageous hop.

Infield Throwing and Footwork

Upon fielding a ground ball, players must position themselves to make a strong, accurate throw. The arm angle that infielders use is different from that of outfielders or catchers. This difference creates a challenge for coaches, as players at most levels play multiple positions and must make adjustments to their throwing form. Unlike outfielders who throw completely over the top with *12-to-6 arm action* or catchers who throw from right behind the ear, infielders should utilize a three-quarter arm angle when possible (Figure 5-4). This arm slot enables players to get their arm back far enough to make a strong throw while also quickly releasing the ball.

Figure 5-4. Three-quarter arm slot

As for footwork when throwing the ball on the infield, players can implement a toe-heel shuffle step (Figure 5-5). This lateral movement provides infielders with momentum toward their target. Smaller than the outfield crow hop, the infield shuffle step allows for a fast release and simplified footwork. On certain plays, such as a slow roller or bunt, infielders may have to throw the ball on the run without systematic footwork and from a less desirable arm angle. Yet, in circumstances when time permits a fielder to get set and prepare a throw, infielders can use a shuffle step for a controlled move toward the target.

Figure 5-5. Infielder shuffle step

Three Steps to Success

1. Upon gloving the ball, bring the rear foot to the heel of the glove-side foot.
2. With eyes fixed on the target, the hands come together at chest level before the throwing arm goes back to a three-quarter arm slot.
3. After releasing the ball, body momentum moves toward the target.

 Teaching Tip

When teaching players the shuffle step, coaches can tell fielders to *replace their feet* as the toe of the rear foot approaches the heel of the glove-side foot. After fielding the ball, players should keep their eyes fixed on the base to which they are throwing. Furthermore, it is important for players to follow the throw with their body momentum after release. Many players make the mistake of pumping and bringing the ball back into the glove as they complete the toe-heel shuffle step.

Glove Side vs. Backhand Plays

Whenever possible, as mentioned, infielders should get their body squarely in front of ground balls. Yet, on balls that are hit softly, put in play by a speedy base runner, or hit to the extended reach of a fielder, players may have to field the ball off to their side. These ground balls are fielded to the glove side or forehand (left side for right-handed throwers) and backhand (right side for right-handed throwers). Learning proper footwork and glove action is essential to fielding these ground balls consistently.

When fielding ground balls to the glove side, it is important to bend the knees, open the glove completely, and maintain clear vision of the ball entering the glove. In some cases, fielders should utilize a crossover step with their throwing side foot to gain range (Figure 5-6). So, a right-handed thrower can cross over with his right foot to bend low to the ground and cover more ground on balls hit to his left. The angle of the batted ball and perceived time to get to it will determine whether a fielder instinctively crosses over with the throwing side foot or instead opens up/jab steps with the glove-side foot (Figure 5-7). On ground balls hit further from the fielder's reach, he can open up and take several quick steps to *get a favorable angle* on the ball.

Figure 5-6. Crossover step

Figure 5-7. Open up step

Three Steps to Success

1. Utilize a crossover step or open up to gain ground toward the ball.
2. Bend the knees so that the glove can get low to the ground.
3. Keep the glove open wide to maximize the surface area for the ball to be fielded.

Ground balls hit to an infielder's backhand are the most difficult to field for several reasons. Given that most fielded ground balls are thrown to first base, balls hit to the backhand side take the infielder away from his target. Even if he successfully gloves the ball, he may not have time to plant his feet and accurately throw to the base. Secondly, it is more difficult for an infielder to open the glove as wide when fielding to the backhand, causing a smaller chance of the ball cleanly entering the glove and a greater likelihood of the ball deflecting off the mitt. Lastly, players are usually less comfortable running to their backhand side and may lose vision of the ball temporarily as their arm crosses in front of their face to field the ball.

Despite these factors, players can use effective mechanics on balls hit to their backhand side. In these cases, the fielder can cross over with his glove-side foot or open up with his throwing side foot to gain ground to the ball. Depending on how far the fielder is from the ball will determine whether he crosses over or opens up. In both instances, he must bend the knees to get low to the ball and open the glove as wide as possible in the direction of the ball. At higher levels, coaches teach infielders to consider executing a backhand

V-cut with their weight moving toward the target at the completion of the cut before releasing the ball. On harder hit balls, they may only have time to plant with their rear (right) foot and throw.

Diving on the Infield

Similar to base runners diving back to a base after a pickoff attempt, infielders should dive low to the ground (as an airplane lands on a runway) with their glove arm extended. Whether diving to the glove side (Figure 5-8) or backhand (Figure 5-9) as the body hits the ground, the throwing arm should be positioned at chest level. This position will brace the player's landing, enabling the fielder to get the glove further extended toward the ball. After making a dive for the ball, players must quickly pop up to make a throw, cover a base, or receive a cutoff throw from the outfield.

Figure 5-8. Glove-side dive

Figure 5-9. Backhand dive

Major League Connection

Roger Dorn, played by Corben Bernsen in the 1989 film *Major League*, was ridiculed for not diving for balls within his reach. Portrayed as a pretty boy with a modeling career, Dorn was reluctant to risk injury. Later in the film, he is inspired by his teammates to dive for ground balls and helps the team defeat the Yankees and capture the pennant.[2]

 ### In-Game Strategy: Diving on the Infield

During a game, diving can play an important role in team success. With a runner on second base, infielders must make every effort to *keep the ball on the infield*. Diving or *laying out* in any manner to prevent the ball from rolling to the outfield prevents the base runner on second base from scoring. Teams that *get dirty* and dive for balls earn a positive reputation for "playing the game the right way." Diving is contagious and a spirited way for players to show how determined they can play. A diving play can inspire a team and quickly turn the momentum of a game.

Pop-Ups on the Infield

When fielding fly balls on the infield, various factors play an important role: body balance, judgment, wind, sun, communication, fences, and other considerations. Younger players tend to struggle with pop flies because they do not get a chance to practice these plays daily. Various drills and activities can be practiced individually or in a team framework that build player competency with pop ups on the infield.

When teaching pop fly defense on the infield, coaches should stress several mechanics to players. Fielders should use both hands when fielding fly balls and try to catch the ball at eye level. Players should be aware of wind direction so that they can make adjustments based on how far a fly ball may carry in the wind. Similarly, the sun can impair player vision of the ball. The glove hand and sunglasses should be used to shield the sun (Figure 5-10). Communication with teammates is crucial as infielder collisions can cause injury and errors. Players must also get familiar with field conditions, such as fences by the foul lines, dugouts, tarps, and other obstacles when running after fly balls.

Figure 5-10. Shielding the sun

 Teaching Tip

Younger players can be instructed in two methods for catching pop-ups. By stressing *thumbs up* and using two hands, players can gain confidence catching the ball at eye level (Figure 5-11). Some youth players that lack the confidence to catch the ball above their heads may also practice catching in the *pinkies down* position below their chest level (Figure 5-12). In both cases, the hands are touching so that the bare hand can collapse on balls that may pop out of the glove. Ideally, as they get more experienced, players will learn both strategies and get comfortable catching balls above their head.

 Administrative Time-Out

During practice, coaches should hit pop flies on the infield so that players can learn proper communication skills. "I got it," "Ball, ball, ball," and "Me, me, me" are commonly used expressions to call for a ball. It is important for teams to establish priority on fly balls when multiple players call for the ball. Routinely, the shortstop has priority on all infield pop-

Figure 5-11. Thumbs up

Figure 5-12. Pinkies down

ups, and the centerfielder directs outfield play. Outfielders should take charge when possible on shallow pop flies that are between the infield and outfield. Coaches must rehearse these communications through drill sessions to prevent injury and poor play. At youth levels, coaches that struggle to hit pop-ups can use a tennis racquet to maximize pop fly practice.

Conference Time

It is common for players to want to have priority on all fly balls. Coaches may have to meet with individual players to discuss team play. In circumstances where a talented player may feel that he is the only fielder able to catch high pops, team trust and unity can be broken. Sometimes, these skilled players are overly aggressive and range across the infield to make a catch. This behavior can cause a collision and make other players feel less valued. Coaches must intervene and use this situation as a teaching point regarding teamwork and sportsmanship.

In-Game Strategy: Pre-Game Pop-Up Preparation

During pre-game infield/outfield practice, coaches should hit pop-ups so that players can learn the wind, sun, and field conditions and work on communication at the same time. By hitting high flies near tarps and fences, coaches can help their team get adjusted to specific field issues. Certain league/state associations may put time limits on infield/outfield sessions, but coaches should do their best to prepare their team effectively with as many repetitions as possible.

How can coaches help a player who is fearful of catching high pop-ups?

Judging fly balls and possessing proficiency with catching high pop-ups is partially innate. But, at an early age, players can improve this necessary skill. Players at the youth level can lie on their backs and flip the ball up in the air or have a coach drop the ball down on them. Using tennis balls or soft baseballs to ensure safety, another method is for a player to toss the ball up in the air and spin around a couple of times before catching it.

Tag Plays

Infielders must develop proficiency at catching a throw and putting a tag down on a sliding base runner. Regularly, this fundamental is overlooked, but it plays a significant role during stolen base attempts, pickoff plays, and extra base hits. An effective tag can *sell the call* to the umpire that the runner is out, while a sloppy or tentative tag may induce an umpire to make a safe call on a close play. Therefore, it is important for coaches to teach their players proper form and technique when applying a tag.

As players anticipate receiving a throw, they should get in an athletic stance over the base with their knees bent and hands out (Figure 5-13). It is important to keep the eyes fixed on the ball, not focused on the approaching base runner. In addition, at higher levels, players should not give away to which side of the base the throw is coming, so as not to tip the runner and help him avoid the tag. Fielders should have *soft hands* when receiving a throw so that they can handle hops or errant throws. In placing a tag on the runner, players can implement a sweeping motion (Figure 5-14). This *swipe tag* enables fielders to quickly touch the runner and *show the ball* (within the glove) to the umpire (Figure 5-15).

Figure 5-13. Receiving the throw

Figure 5-14. Applying the tag

Figure 5-15. Showing the ball

Three Steps to Success

1. Straddle the base in an athletic stance with the knees bent and using soft hands.
2. Keep the eyes fixed on the ball without showing the runner where the tag will be.
3. Utilize a sweeping motion to apply the tag before lifting the glove upward to show the umpire the ball.

 Teaching Tip

As a runner is sliding into a base, many infielders, including catchers, struggle to catch cutoff throws that hop. These plays are difficult as fielders tend to be distracted by the approaching base runner. Coaches can work on this technique during practice by hitting one-hop line drives at fielders at their respective bases. Players can also throw one- or two-hoppers to each other before putting down a swipe tag. Players must be reminded to have soft hands in anticipating poor throws, apply a sweeping tag, and lift the glove to show the umpire that they have secured the ball.

 In-Game Strategy: Fake Tags

At most levels of play, umpires will penalize the defense for *fake tags*. This defensive tactic fools incoming base runners that there will be a close play at the base and may get them to slide. To prevent unnecessary injuries, fake tags have been banned by state and league associations. Some infielders will legally attempt to baffle runners by pretending that there will be a throw to their base by bending down in the receiving position even though no tag play is imminent.

Turning the Double Play

Infielders can rescue their team from a potentially game changing inning by turning a double play. A well-executed double play can not only save a pitcher from an extended inning, but also give the defense momentum before coming to bat. Coaches should review various throwing and footwork techniques with infielders to make them more adept at turning the double play.

When attempting to turn a double play, players must always make sure to get the first out. Sometimes, teams will get overly zealous and fumble the ball or force a throw, which may only fuel the offensive team. One method for ensuring the first out is for players to make strong *feeds* to the middle infielder receiving the ball at second base. These feeds can be delivered with the normal overhand throwing motion, underhand toss, or a backhand flip, also known as the *quarterback toss* (Figures 5-16 through 5-18).

Figure 5-16. Overhand feed

Figure 5-17. Underhand toss

Figure 5-18. Backhand flip

Aside from making a good feed to the middle infielder, players must be quick with their hands. The player feeding the ball must get it out of his glove quickly and utilize a short throwing arc in delivering the ball to his teammate. Similarly, the fielder receiving the first throw of the double play must be compact and quick in using his hands to catch and get rid of the ball (Figure 5-19). Players *making the turn* can implement a small, circular motion with their hands as they catch and throw to first base. Lastly, fielders should communicate which side of the base they will be throwing the feed to their teammate. By calling "inside" or "outside," infielders will be aware how to position their feet around the base (Figures 5-20 and 5-21).

Figure 5-19. The double play turn

Figure 5-20. Turn at second base (inside)

Figure 5-21. Turn at second base (outside)

In-Game Strategy: Double Play Balls

Given that double plays are such an important element of games, many runners will try *to take out* the middle infielder with an aggressive slide at second base. Most league associations below high school prohibit these slides. If an umpire deems that the runner intentionally interferes with a double play through sliding or another tactic, he will call an automatic double play. If a middle infielder perceives that a double play cannot be turned, he can fake to first base and *throw backdoor* by reverse pivoting and throwing to nab a runner at third base.

Administrative Time-Out

Players that play middle infield positions must use a small glove so that they can quickly get the ball out of the glove. Outfielders' gloves or oversized mitts will prevent a middle infielder from being as quick as possible at catching and releasing the ball. Coaches can use a stopwatch to time how quickly players can get the ball out of the glove after receiving a feed to start the double play. Indoor practice drills can utilize nets and *throw down bases* so that middle infielders can work on proper feeds and quick, compact throws to a target.

Teaching Tip

Communication is essential when turning double plays. Not only should infielders alert each other to which side of second base the first throw will be directed, but the first baseman should signal whether or not a second throw should be made. On plays where the trail runner will be safe at first base, the first baseman should put his arms up so that the middle infielders know not to throw unnecessarily. By communicating where the play is as soon as the ball comes off the bat, catchers are also a key component of starting the double play.

Run Downs

One aspect of infield defense that is scrutinized by spectators is the effectiveness of executing a run down. These situations arise when base runners intentionally or unintentionally get caught between two bases and try to avoid being tagged out by the defense. A well-orchestrated run down should take only one or two throws by the infielders. Base runners try to draw as many throws as possible hoping for an overthrow or dropped ball so that they can advance safely. Even Major League teams can struggle completing the task in five throws or fewer. Coaches can practice several teaching points with players to hone this challenging baseball skill.

Traditionally, teams initiate the first run-down throw by forcing the runner back toward the previous base. An infielder who recognizes a developing run down should pick and communicate a throwing lane to his teammate (Figure 5-22). "Inside" or "Outside" must be emphatically called so that the fielders have a clear path in which to throw when chasing down a runner. Secondly, players must promptly get the ball out of their glove and clearly show it to the fielder receiving the first throw (Figure 5-23). It is crucial that throwers do not run too fast during the run down or rush the throw as errors will occur. Lastly, the throw should be delivered straight from the ear much like a dart, not using a long-armed release.

Figure 5-22. Find a throwing lane   Figure 5-23. Clearly show ball

The fielder receiving the throw should be in an athletic position with his hands out ready to catch the ball. Additionally, he should call for the ball when he determines that it should be thrown to him. Finally, it is important for him to *close distance* or move forward as he receives the throw (Figure 5-24). Too often during a run down, receivers of throws catch the ball with the weight on their heels, which enables the runner to switch direction and prolong the run down. If players are trained to utilize this strategy, defensive teams will greatly enhance their chances of tagging out opposing base runners in run down situations (Figure 5-25).

Figure 5-24. Close distance   Figure 5-25. Apply the tag

Three Steps to Success

1. Establish a clear throwing lane and try to force the runner back toward the previous base.
2. Run in a controlled manner toward the runner, clearly show the ball, and utilize a dart-like throw.
3. When catching the ball, call "Ball" and close the distance by moving toward the runner.

Teaching Tip

When working on run downs, or *pickles*, coaches must stress communication. Players not only call for the ball, but also pick a lane for running the base runner down. Many coaches teach their teams to *run the offensive player back to the previous base* so that if the run down fails, they have not allowed a run to score or yielded an extra base to the offense. Nonetheless, using clear communication between players, a properly executed run down should focus on two or fewer throws. Sometimes, infielders will fake throws during the run down to trick the runner, possibly confusing the other fielders.

 Administrative Time-Out

Coaches must set aside practice time to rehearse this important team fundamental. To maximize space and time, several base paths can be used simultaneously to work on run downs. Catchers, third basemen, and pitchers can use the third base to home plate area, while pitchers, first basemen, and middle infielders practice between first and second base. Outfielders, wearing helmets at all times, can be used for running in the pickle. These drills and communications can be reviewed indoors and with multiple base runners on base as well.

 In-Game Strategy: Run Down Plays and Tactics

Offensive teams at the college level and lower will intentionally get into a run down as a tactic to help score a runner from third base. Defensive teams must practice a protocol for dealing with this situation. Clear communication technique and poised play are key elements of defending this effective offensive strategy. In cases where the offensive team inadvertently gets caught in a pickle, the runner's mission is to draw as many throws as possible so that all other base runners can advance and possibly create a botched throw by the defense.

Cutoff Plays

Frequently, infielders are required to execute relays or cutoffs on balls hit to the outfield. For effective defense on cutoff plays, infielders should practice sound communication, quick hands, proper footwork, and the ability to make adjustments based on the direction of a batted ball or throw from the outfield. When considering that every ball hit to the outfield involves setting up at least one *cutoff man*, these cutoff plays are a significant element of team defense.

Three Steps to Success

1. Run toward the outfielder with hands raised to provide an effective target.
2. Listen for directives to make positioning adjustments for alignment with the base.
3. Use feet to adjust to the flight of the ball and shuffle step for accurate relay throw.

Ordinarily, catchers are the vocal leaders on the infield and communicate to which base a throw from the outfield should be directed. Yet once the specific base has been established, infielders must communicate with each other to correctly line up for the throw. Infielders can command ("In," "Out," "Left," "Right," "Cut," "Hold," "Let it go"), stay silent, or call the number of a particular base ("One," "Two," "Three," or "Four"). The fielder manning a base should be the vocal communicator, as he can see the accuracy and strength of the outfield throw. However, the catcher, who can see the entire field, can overrule or change these directives if he sees another play develop worthy of the defense's attention.

As for positioning and stance on cutoff plays (Figure 5-26), infielders should run out on a straight line between the location of the ball and the receiving base with their hands extended above their head. While running out to his cutoff position, the infielder should be listening for directives to make sure he is properly aligned with the base. The feet are critical in adjusting to the angle of the incoming throw and implementing a shuffle step to help provide strength for the relay throw. Some players will utilize a *back* or *drop step* as they wait to receive an incoming cutoff throw to get their feet moving and create momentum toward the target. It is also important for players not to flip the ball from the glove to their throwing hand during *the transfer*, but rather make a short move with the bare hand into the glove.

Figure 5-26. Cutoff stance and throwing mechanics

Teaching Tip

Infielders who receive throws from the outfield as cutoff men must *adjust to the baseball*. For the fastest relay, the cutoff man needs to catch the ball on his glove side at shoulder height. Consequently, as the outfield throw is in flight, he should sprint to the spot where he estimates he will catch the ball at his glove-side shoulder. Throws received on the backhand side take too much time to make a quick transfer. Cutoff men should also *turn glove side* by rotating their body 45 degrees and starting their shuffle step before they actually catch the relay throw (Figure 5-27).

Conference Time

Cutoff plays require that all infielders learn how to be vocally assertive, especially catchers. Certain players on a team are more introverted than others and will be less comfortable in this role. Nonetheless, communication skills are essential for teams to nab base runners

Figure 5-27. Turning glove side

advancing on balls hit to the outfield. Coaches may choose to hold meetings with players to review the importance of affirmative infield commands. In addition, players may struggle to make in-game decisions on whether an outfielder's throw gets cut off or let go.

 ### In-Game Strategy: Double Cut Plays

On fly balls hit deep toward outfield gaps or down the lines, infielders may need to implement a *double cut*. This play utilizes an extra cutoff man to make throws from the deepest parts of the field more manageable. Without this additional cutoff man, an infielder may have to make a throw of almost 200 feet. Teams should practice which infielders are responsible for cutoffs and covering specific bases on balls hit to various locations along the outfield fence. Furthermore, with two or more base runners, infielders must make sound decisions for proper coverage.

 ### What are some common mistakes that players make on cutoff plays?

Many problems that occur when balls are hit to the outfield involve poor communication by the catcher or infielder covering a base. Players struggle to decide whether outfield throws should be cut off or let go. Habitually, effective outfield throws are cut because the catcher or basemen are in the cutoff mindset. These throws will travel much faster to a base if not cut off. In addition, because the infielders are not properly aligned with the base, many outfield throws are not accurate. Only a small percentage of youth baseball infielders understand how to move their feet and adjust to the baseball properly before cutting it off.

Administrative Time-Out

Coaches can rehearse cutoff plays by diagramming player positioning on a chalkboard or baseball field diagram. Each player must understand his responsibilities with multiple men on base and balls hit to each part of the field. Various drills can be used to reinforce these duties. By placing base runners on the bases and hitting balls to the gaps and down the foul lines, coaches can give their players practice with single and double cut play scenarios. Daily skill work with catch and throw transfer mechanics as well as cutoff drill speed competitions can help teams build proficiency of this important component of team defense.

Infield Drills

Box Drill

A commonly used drill to maximize infield ground ball repetitions is the box drill. Ideally, from several feet behind the baselines in foul territory, four coaches or pitchers will hit fungos to each infield position in a box configuration. The coach hitting from behind the first baseline closest to home plate should direct ground balls to the third baseman, while fungos hit behind the line closer to first base are intended for the shortstop. The two hitters on the third base side will provide ground balls in similar fashion to the first and second basemen. With four players assigned to receive incoming throws and flip balls to the fungo hitters, coaches can maximize repetitions.

Administrative Time-Out

Coaches must maintain safety during the box drill as several balls are in motion simultaneously. With balls being hit to infielders as other balls are thrown to the designated receivers, it is important to maintain clear, organized paths for each of the four infield positions. Another administrative issue regarding the box drill involves field maintenance. The grass area in foul territory next to the baseline will get worn out by fungo hitters. Coaches can put down protective mats for hitters to stand on during the drill. Similar mats can be used during batting practice so that batters and fungo hitters do not rip up grassy areas on the infield.

Groundball Mix Drill

Coaches should vary the type of ground balls hit to infielders. By interchanging slow rollers, high choppers, line drives, and backhand plays, coaches will keep their players versatile in handling various infield plays. These balls should be hit by a coach who can work individual players with specific weaknesses. A variation of this drill involves having base runners run from home plate and other bases to simulate live game action. As always, base runners must wear helmets in this drill to maintain safety.

Double Play Drill

With fielders at each infield position, coaches call out numbers, hit a ground ball, and players turn the double play. For example, if the coach calls out "5-4-3," he will hit the ball to the third baseman, who fields the ball, throws to second base, and starts the double play. Other double plays include: 6-4-3 (shortstop-second base-first base), 4-6-3 (second base-shortstop-first base), 3-6-3 (first base-shortstop-first base), and 3-6-1 (first base-shortstop-pitcher). Coaches should hit the balls rapidly so that the drill is high energy and players get as many repetitions as possible A motivating addition to the drill is for coaches to challenge players to turn 10 double plays without making an error.

Rapid Fire Drill

This fast-paced fungo drill has infielders take their positions and react to a number of ground balls in a short period of time. Coaches should hit five to seven consecutive ground balls to the same infielder with little time in between each fungo. The goal of the drill is to increase player reaction time to hard-hit balls. The drill is highly effective with two hitters rotating so that the infielder does not get a chance to rest. While coaches are trying to improve fielder reactions through high-speed activity, they must remember to practice in such a manner that does not risk player safety or create poor fundamentals through hurried repetitions.

Backdoor Drill

In order to teach infielders how to throw behind an overly aggressive base runner with runners on first and second base, coaches should set up a double play drill. When ground balls are hit firmly, infielders should attempt to turn a double play. Yet, when a ground ball is hit at moderate to slow speed toward any of the infield positions, the second baseman or shortstop *goes backdoor*. To do so, the middle infielder throws a full, long-armed fake toward first base as if trying to turn the double play. After throwing this fake, he reverse pivots and fires a throw to the third baseman, who applies a tag to the runner rounding the base. The third baseman can also verbally call "backdoor" if he sees a chance to nab the base runner, or a small chance of turning the double play on the slowly hit ground ball.

Count the Hops Drill

To foster concentration on the infield, coaches can have players count the number of hops a ball takes off the bat before reaching the glove. Infielders can call out the correct number as they field the ball before making a throw. This drill is particularly valuable during pre-season indoor practice in a gymnasium setting. Coaches can also have players partner up and bounce balls to each other to learn the skill before *reading balls off the bat*.

Diving Drill

When diving for ground balls in order to build player competency and confidence, coaches can set up practice drills for backhand and glove-side dives. These grounders can be hit or firmly rolled by coaches. It may take several repetitions for coaches to learn the range and wingspan of each player to determine where to place the ball. Coaches should err on the side of out of players' reach so that fielders extend to dive on each attempt. Players should focus on keeping each ball on the infield and popping up to make a strong throw.

Quick Hands Star Drill

Traditionally, teams practice the star drill during pre-game infield warm-up. The five infield positions throw the ball in a star configuration as quickly and accurately as possible. Typically, the catcher initiates the drill by throwing to the shortstop, who catches and throws to the first baseman. The first baseman receives the throw and fires to the third baseman, who delivers his throw to the second baseman. The second baseman completes the star by throwing to the catcher who continues the drill by throwing back to the shortstop. Coaches can use two or three balls in the drill at one time, which forces players to be ready to catch and throw the ball quickly. The goal of the drill is to rehearse transfer speed from glove to bare hand while maintaining the accuracy of the throw.

Short Fungo Drill

Coaches can help players work on getting their bodies in front of ground balls by having them start fielding in the kneeling position. By doing so, players will have to keep their shoulders square and core of body centered over the ball. Coaches can use soft safety balls for this drill. A variation of this drill includes having players start with their back to the infield and turning to field the ball after hearing contact. Some coaches favor the short fungo drill in which they hit balls to the infielders from a distance of 10 to 15 feet. This approach enables coaches to better control the direction of the ground ball and builds player reaction time.

Sources/Further Reading

[1]Kahn, Roger & Wismer, Harry. (1955). *The 1955 Mutual Baseball Almanac.* Garden City, NY: Doubleday.

[2]Ward, David. (1989). *Major League.* Paramount Pictures.

OUTFIELD DEFENSE

*No outfielder is a real workman unless he can
turn his back on the ball, run his legs off,
and take the catch over his shoulder.
Backpedaling outfielders get nowhere.*

                                                             –Joe DiMaggio[1]

Chapter 6

At the youth level, outfield defense usually consists of players staring at the ground, looking up at planes flying overhead, or "picking daisies" as thoughts wander. Compared to most sports that athletes play at a young age, baseball is a slow-paced game. Football, soccer, and basketball involve continuous action. These sports tend to be more appealing than standing in a grassy field, waiting for a ball to be intermittently hit in a player's direction. Therefore, coaches must work in techniques in practice and on game days to make outfield play more interesting for their players.

By stressing a proper ready position, having outfielders read signals from infielders relaying the pitch type, and communicating the correct number of outs and defensive positioning, coaches can keep outfielders involved. Moreover, outfielders will be more prepared to make a decisive play on a fly ball, line drive, ground ball, or back-up of an infield play with these teaching tools. Getting a good jump on a fly ball and throwing to the proper base are important outfield actions that are significantly impacted by mental judgments made before a pitch is thrown.

 Teaching Tip

In helping players (both infielders and outfielders) learn how to take a proper route to a fly ball, coaches can use soft, safety baseballs in pop fly drills. Short distance drills where coaches act as a quarterback and direct players to run to a spot are effective in training players to gain competence with *turning their back on the baseball*. To get a jump on balls hit directly over their heads, players must drop step to their backhand side 180 degrees and run straight back (Figure 6-1). Although this method may not be as natural as drop stepping to the glove side, it may help for recovering on fly balls that quickly change direction mid-flight.

Figure 6-1. Outfield drop step (backhand side)

Outfield Fundamentals

Outfield Stance

Similar to infielders, outfielders should be in an athletic position with the eyes fixed on the catcher as the pitch is being delivered: the knees are slightly bent, hands at waist height, shoulders squarely facing the home plate area, with body weight on the balls of the feet (Figure 6-2). Frequently, players are improperly instructed to put their hands on their knees, which puts them in a static position for too long. Instead, outfielders want to be loose and have the ability to quickly dash in any direction to range for a ball. When possible, outfielders should *be moving on the pitch*. When a catcher sets up in a certain location or the outfielder can see the flight of a pitch, outfielders should be moving in the direction in which the ball will likely be put into play.

Figure 6-2. Outfielder stance

Three Steps to Success

1. Get into an athletic stance with the shoulders square to home plate.
2. Place hands at waist level with the body loose, ready to react to a ball in any direction.
3. Rest weight on the balls of the feet while focusing eyes on the catcher to get a read on pitch location and bat angle at contact.

Fielding Mechanics

One of the keys to successful outfield play is *getting a good jump on the ball*. While much of this skill is learned over time and based largely on intuitive instincts, players can look for pitch location, hitter tendencies, pitcher tendencies, and wind patterns to help get a quick read on the ball off the bat. On balls hit to the glove side, to get an angle on the ball outfielders will open up or drop-step. The crossover step, as discussed during infield play, should be utilized for balls to the backhand side of the outfielder. In all cases, the goal of an outfielder is to *take a proper angle* or path and try to *get behind the ball*.

Fly Ball Defense

Most coaches start by explaining to their outfielders that *the first step should always be back when reading a fly ball*. The reasoning behind this philosophy is that it is easier and faster to run in than back on a misjudged fly ball. Furthermore, balls hit over the head result in extra base hits, which strike a harsher blow to the defense than a single landing in front of an outfielder. Ultimately, outfielders must strive to get correct reads on fly balls, as a step back on a ball hit in front of them can be costly as well.

Several other teaching points should be emphasized when practicing outfield fly ball defense. It is common for players to *drift* toward fly balls, which not only lowers the chances of ranging far for a catch, but also limits an outfielder's ability to get into a good throwing position. Instead, outfielders should practice *running to a spot*. This technique entails putting the head down and running to an area in the outfield where the fielder judges the ball will land. For many, this skill is challenging because it requires the player to be *blind to the ball*, which is uncomfortable. Until outfielders learn how to run to a spot, they will never maximize their range or effectiveness.

Major League Connection

Willie Mays is famous for his classic, over-the-head catches. Mays saved many games for his team by making these dramatic plays. More recently, Ken Griffey, Jr., Torii Hunter, and Jim Edmonds have earned a spot on highlight reels by making similar catches.

When running to a spot, players should tuck the glove arm close to the body as they pump their arms. Upon approaching the ball, with forward momentum, players should get behind the ball so that they can catch it at chin height (Figure 6-3). Too often, players will glove fly balls with their weight moving backward on the heels. This move commonly occurs when outfielders drift (Figure 6-4). As they make a throw to their target, drifting limits their ability to *come through the ball*. More significantly, if players *backpedal* toward fly balls, they risk not only catching in a poor throwing position, but also the ball tipping off the top of their glove.

Figure 6-3. Proper form (coming through the ball)

Figure 6-4. Improper form (drifting back)

 ## Administrative Time-Out

Batting practice is a terrific opportunity for players to practice running to a spot. Balls read off the bat in batting practice are the most realistic fly balls to game experience that outfielders can work on. Fungos hit by coaches are effective as well, but do not travel as true in flight as a batted ball. In addition, outfielders can move on the pitch during batting practice to get proper reads based on pitch location and catcher set-up. Given that daily batting practice is not always feasible or a productive use of limited practice time, coaches must set up other drills to help outfielders learn how to turn their back, run to a spot, and find the baseball.

Outfield Throwing Mechanics

Aside from getting behind the baseball and coming through the ball to generate power from the legs when throwing, outfielders should utilize a crow hop. Although many players struggle to learn the mechanics of a proper *crow hop*, it is worthwhile for coaches to take the time to teach this valuable skill. Players who possess a below-average throwing arm or who have to make lengthy throws should use the crow hop. However, players must crow hop only when they know which direction they are throwing and are coming forward as they field the ball.

When executing a crow hop (Figure 6-5), the outfielder's glove-side foot is ahead of his body. Body weight should rest almost entirely on the glove-side foot as the player explodes upward with the throwing side knee. During this process, weight transfers to the throwing side leg as the player releases the ball. In a step-by-step progression, coaches should teach players the mechanics of the crow hop. Otherwise, the timing and footwork will be off and actually inhibit an athlete's throwing ability.

Figure 6-5. Crow hop

The arm angle when throwing from the outfield should be *over the top* or *12-to-6*, as numbers on a clock. Players should get their arm as high above their heads as possible, using a four-seam grip before releasing the ball with a snap of the wrist (Figure 6-6). After releasing the ball, a player's momentum should pull him forward in the direction of the target. When possible, outfielders should set up several steps behind where the ball will land before they catch, crow hop, and release the ball. This set-up behind the ball enables players to use forward momentum as they come through the throw toward the target.

Figure 6-6. Outfielder release point

Three Steps to Success

1. Get behind the baseball and perform a crow hop before the throw.
2. Release the ball over the top (12-to-6) with a four-seam grip.
3. Enable momentum to pull the body forward toward the target.

Ground Ball Outfield Defense

When approaching a ground ball in the outfield, players must be aware of the specific game situation. With no base runners on base, outfielders must keep the ball in front of them. Balls in this situation can be fielded on a knee in *ground ball safety mode* to prevent the ball from getting past the outfielder and resulting in extra bases (Figure 6-7). With a runner on first base at the time of the pitch, outfielders should field the ball on the run so as to prevent the base runner form advancing to third base. This *intermediate ground ball approach* incorporates fielding with some caution, yet with an aggressive demeanor.

Figure 6-7. Safety mode

When outfielders must field a ground ball quickly to prevent a base runner from scoring the winning run, they are overly aggressive in manner. These *do-or-die* plays can determine the game's outcome based on how quickly and effectively the outfielder gets the ball to the catcher. Consequently, the outfielder must charge the ball at full speed, as caution or conservative play will take too much time. On these plays, field conditions, such as the quality of the grass, uneven ground, moistness of the field, combined with the velocity of the ball off the bat all play an important role.

 ### Topic of Debate: Outfield Ground Ball Mechanics

Usually, players are taught to field the ball off their glove-side foot in front of their body. This method enables an outfielder to explode into his crow hop faster because the glove-side foot is already in the forward position (Figure 6-8). Outfielders can alternatively field the ground ball with the glove-side foot back (Figure 6-9), which makes it easier to bend lower to field the ball. Though, when using this method, the ball is harder to track visually as it travels past the player's line of sight toward the rear foot. Both styles have advantages, and coaches can experiment with each to view, which helps their players perform best. In do-or-die scenarios, players must keep their glove low to the ground, especially on slowly hit balls that stay down. These high-intensity plays should be practiced regularly.

Figure 6-8. Glove-side foot forward

Figure 6-9. Glove-side foot back

Mental Aspects of Outfield Play

Player awareness of field conditions and game situation are integral elements to successful outfield defense. Outfielders must survey their position for the quality of the grass, firmness of the ground, rocks, and other debris in the area. In addition, the location and strength of the sun and wind should be accounted for. Players can jog along the outfield fence to check the footing in the warning track area as well as feel the fence or wall for stability.

Along with environmental and structural issues in the outfield, players must be aware of specific game situations. Before a pitch is delivered, players should think ahead and in a possible scenario know to which base they are throwing. The score and situation within a game may also be a factor in this decision-making process. For instance, if the tying run is at bat, then the outfielder will want to avoid making any throw permitting the batter to advance to second base. Likewise, when the tying run is on first or second base, outfield throws directed to home plate to cut down a runner tagging up from third may not be advisable. Rather, the focus should be on preventing the tying run from advancing further into scoring position.

Outfielders should be aware of the strengths and weaknesses of the offensive team. Knowing a player's running speed and power are valuable pieces of information. Certain players may be dead-pull hitters, while others tend to hit the ball to the opposite field. Fast runners in the batting order are more likely to be aggressive and consider an extra base. With two strikes, hitters may choke up on the bat and be less likely to hit for power. These factors and more must be considered by outfielders to increase their overall effectiveness.

 ### Conference Time

Communication between outfielders is essential. Similar to infield pop-ups, outfielders must know that the centerfielder has priority on all plays with a clear verbal system for calling for fly balls. Also, players should communicate with each other as outfielders run toward fences or other field obstacles. The number of outs, the score, and a hitter's abilities should all be discussed for each at bat. While coaches may position outfielders from the bench, teammates can also provide insight regarding outfield depth and positioning based on hitter/pitcher tendencies.

Major League Connection

In 1975, Boston Red Sox outfielder Fred Lynn became the first player to win the Most Valuable Player Award and Rookie of the Year Award in the same season. Lynn suffered injuries from outfield collisions, which prevented him regaining his production in later seasons.[2]

 In-Game Strategy: Positioning of Outfielders

Many teams will position outfielders based on the number of outs and runners on base. With two outs and runners in scoring position, teams may play more shallow in the outfield to prevent a bloop hit from scoring runners. Conversely, with bases empty, teams may move the outfielders back into a conservative position to guard against an extra base hit. When hitters fall behind in the count 0-2 or 1-2, it may be a good time to play more aggressively as hitters will shorten up. Outfielders playing in the opposite field should be shallower than pull side.

Outfield Drills

Quarterback Drill

Outfielders face a coach who pump fakes to the right, left, or straight over the head of the player before actually throwing a high pop to that area. The fielder will open up, cross over, or drop-step accordingly to take the optimal route to the ball. Outfielders should focus on proper footwork to attain the best angle to the ball in this drill. Ideally, the fielder's goal is to get behind the baseball, come through the ball, crow hop, and feign a throw back to the coach. This drill can be performed indoors and as a partner warm-up exercise.

Z Drill

As a follow-up to the quarterback drill, coaches will feign a throw in a given direction, and the outfielder will run to that spot. Instead of catching a ball in that area, players will pretend that they have misjudged the fly ball and quickly recover. The coach will throw the ball over the player's opposite shoulder so he can work on changing direction effectively. The key to this drill is for players to use correct footwork and turn blind to the ball as they recover to a misplayed fly ball. Coaches should ensure that outfielders simply turn their heads as they change direction rather than twisting their bodies to find the ball. To advance this drill, coaches can fake two throws and have players recover two times before catching the fly ball.

Shoestring vs. Overhead Catches Drill

Similar to the two previous drills, coaches will throw high pops in front of and behind players to foster quickness and competency on balls directly in front of and behind them. Coaches can flip the balls underhand or use soft, overhand tosses to work on players' range. Often, players struggle on fly balls that sink below the knee level because they are required to bend low to the ground while running full speed and during the process may lose sight of the ball. On fly balls overhead, players must gain confidence with the drop step, running with their backs completely turned to the baseball, and catching the ball with the palms facing up.

Feel for the Fence Drill

Players will face home plate and set up 10 feet in front of an outfield fence or wall. Coaches will pump fake in the direction of the fence as players run toward the hazard with their hand outstretched to feel for the fence. Most players use their bare hand to feel for the fence because they can remain square to the ball and field in this manner (Figure 6-10). When using the glove hand, players are forced to turn their bodies a minimum of 90 degrees to catch and throw the ball (Figure 6-11). Nonetheless, players must make sure not to get their bare hand cut or stuck on the fence. As a fun follow-up to this activity, coaches can have players attempt catches that rob hitters of home runs. Coaches can toss balls above the height of the fence as players leap to simulate these exciting plays.

Figure 6-10. Feeling for the fence—barehand   Figure 6-11. Feeling for the fence—glove-hand

Sun Ball Drill

At specific times of day on certain areas of the field, fly balls can be difficult to see in the sun. Coaches must teach players techniques other than wearing sunglasses for dealing with this situation. By turning their bodies 45 degrees and using the glove hand to shield the sun, fielders can better cope with fly balls descending from out of the sun. Initially, coaches should underhand flip low balls to their players so they gain a comfort level before hitting much higher fly balls. Coaches must make sure to have players run in all directions for fly balls while battling the sun to simulate game action. It is particularly useful to practice this drill on the game field at times of day when the sun begins to fall and is most difficult.

Superman Diving Drill

Unlike diving for infield ground balls, proper outfield form when diving involves extending with both arms. To practice this skill, a coach can set up lines of players to their right or left. A player approaches on a line in front of him, and the coach underhand flips the ball so that the outfielder can dive with full extension much like Superman flying through the air. Players should practice landing on their forearms as they extend, dive, and catch the ball (Figure 6-12). This drill can be performed in all directions, but coaches may have a tougher time making effective tosses at certain angles. When first introducing outfield diving drills, coaches can utilize wet outfield grass after a rainstorm to teach players how to glide after landing. Pole vault mats and other sponge-like cushions can be used for creating indoor diving drills.

Figure 6-12. Superman dive

Situational Ground Ball Drill

Coaches will hit outfield ground balls at different speeds and directions to outfielders. Before hitting each ball, the coach calls out a situation, which dictates how aggressively or conservatively the player will approach the ground ball. For example, if the coach calls out "Bases empty, none out," then the outfielder will field the ball in safety mode on a knee. However, if the situation is "Man on second, 2-2 score, bottom of the ninth inning," outfielders will aggressively charge the ball in a do-or-die scenario. The other situation for this drill is an intermediate ground ball in which the outfielder approaches a ball, looking to prevent the base runner from advancing to the next base.

Get the Angle Drill

With players in any of the three outfield positions, coaches hit ground balls to the gap or down the lines. Fielders must take an effective route to the ball and cut it off. Right and left fielders must try to circle around balls down the line and come through on an angle toward second base on their crow hop. All three outfield positions should work on taking a proper angle to the balls hit into the gaps. Additionally, players should communicate on ground balls that can be fielded by either outfielder. This drill can be performed with several fungo hitters or just one hitter with the fielders rotating to the three outfield positions.

 ### In-Game Strategy: Outfielder Priority on Fly Balls

Typically, the centerfielder calls for and fields any ball that he can get to. In cases where the centerfielder does not possess the strongest arm in the outfield, it may be advantageous to allow one of the corner outfielders to field a ground ball or fly ball with runners on base. Specifically, this concept applies on balls hit to the gap where an outfielder's momentum may carry him away from the base to which he is throwing. In turn, if two outfielders call for the ball, it makes sense for the fielder with a better throwing angle to the base have priority in fielding the ball.

Ball at Wall Drill

To practice fielding fly balls that carry over an outfielder's head and land on the warning track or against the fence, coaches should position players 20 to 30 feet in front of the wall. By throwing or hitting balls over players' heads against the fence, coaches can help familiarize players with quickly bending down, grabbing a ball with the four-seam grip, and throwing it to the cutoff man. Mechanically, players should turn their body perpendicular to the fence with the glove-side shoulder facing the target. The crow hop is vital on balls at the fence because outfielders must throw from a stationary position. A follow-up to this drill involves teaching players to work on fly balls that hit off the fence. On these plays, outfielders can start the crow hop and body momentum while playing the ball off the wall.

Communication Drill

Coaches should hit fly balls that fall between outfielders, which forces them to communicate on each play. These in-between fly balls, or *tweeners*, are common in-game situations and need to be reviewed and practiced. Players must work on vocal command cues, a priority system, angles to balls while avoiding collisions, and backing up teammates. This drill can be completed with two or three lines of outfielders. In either case, players should run to the back of a different line after each repetition to work on multiple defensive positions. Coaches can also include infielders in the drill to rehearse outfielders calling off infielders on shallow fly balls and develop an understanding of each individual player's range on the team.

Sources/Further Reading

[1]Dickson, P. (1992). *Baseball's Greatest Quotations*. New York: Harper Perennial. P. 112.

[2]Baseball-Reference.com; Sports Reference LLC; 2000-2009. May 1, 2009.

CATCHING

*A good catcher is the quarterback,
the carburetor, the lead dog, the pulse taker,
the traffic cop, and sometimes a lot of unprintable
things, but no team gets very far without one.*
—Miller Huggins[1]

Chapter 7

As the only player on the diamond that faces the entire field, the catcher has a unique role. Similar to a quarterback or point guard, the catcher is the on-field leader and spokesman. Given that he is the sole member of the defense able to see the positioning of players in relation to the ball and base runners, the catcher must verbally take command of all defensive action. Furthermore, the catcher is the coach's mode of communication to his team, be it pitch selection, defensive alignment, in-game bunt strategies, or whatever a coach deems appropriate. Therefore, a catcher must possess not only the physical tools to play this grueling position, but also have the intellect, communication skills, and vocal leadership to take charge of the team.

With such an important and diverse role on the team, catchers should be carefully selected by coaches. Catchers are involved with every pitch in the game and, in turn, are more likely to be injured than any other player. As a result, catchers wear heavy protective equipment, which adds to the taxing nature of the position. As the lead communicator with umpires and pitchers, the catcher is more influential than any other everyday player. When combining these factors with the responsibility of directing defensive throws and cutoffs to specific bases, receiving and delivering rapid coaching signals, and being the spirited, charismatic leader of the team, it is clear that the selection of catcher is one of the most important decisions for a coach.

Catching Fundamentals

Catching Stance

The catcher must be familiar with several stances. The first position is the signal stance (Figure 7-1). In this position, the catcher assumes a squat position with his back straight in an upright posture. The catcher should be relaxed and comfortable, while focusing on hiding his signals. To do so, the catcher gives the signal deep in the crotch area with the right hand flat inside the thigh. The glove hand rests on or below the left knee with the forearm on top of the thigh. The throwing arm stays tight to the body with the elbow in. Although the catcher should be looking straight ahead during the signal stance, in-game tactics can be used that may move his vision elsewhere.

Figure 7-1. Signal stance

Topic of Debate: Catcher vs. Coach vs. Pitcher Calling Pitches

Coaches who favor letting catchers *call the game* believe that players need to learn the art of pitch sequencing and studying hitters' strengths and weaknesses. Those coaches in favor of calling pitches feel that they are better suited to make these decisions and want to be in control of the game. The catcher has so many responsibilities to worry about and may not possess the experience or hitter tendency charts to make accurate pitch selections. Others view catcher signals as simply a method for not *getting crossed up* or confused by the pitcher and argue that the pitcher should have authority over pitch selection.

An essential stance that catchers must master is the ready or receiving stance (Figures 7-2 and 7-3). In this stance, the feet are slightly wider than shoulder-width apart with the weight on the balls of the feet. The catcher's body should be low and the arms semi-extended from the body while the target is given with a relaxed hand. Positioned squarely behind the plate with elbows situated outside the knees, the catcher should make no unnecessary movements while in the receiving stance. Catchers should assume a stance as close to the batter as possible and provide an effective target for the pitcher with his entire body behind the glove.

Figure 7-2. Receiving stance (bases empty)

Figure 7-3. Receiving stance (man on base)

Teaching Tip

While catchers should keep their bodies low in the receiving stance, they must not slouch. The rear should not be so low that catcher balance and mobility are compromised. Players should not jam the glove into the hand, but rather have a soft-handed approach. The throwing arm must be protected from foul balls by tucking it close to the body and behind the glove by putting it behind the back or grabbing the right ankle. Coaches who advocate protecting the throwing arm behind the glove claim catchers can block and throw the ball much faster from this starting position.

Routinely, catchers adopt a separate receiving stance for situations with men on base. In this stance, catchers are more prepared to throw out a base stealer and drop to block a ball in the dirt. By sitting up slightly higher, moving the weight to the toes of the right foot, and moving the right foot two or three inches back, the catcher will be better positioned to throw out advancing base runners. Some catchers prefer to have only one receiving stance and utilize this higher position for every game situation.

Receiving and Framing Pitches

Throughout the course of a game, a catcher can gain or lose several strike calls based on how effectively he receives pitches. Catchers must keep in mind several fundamentals when receiving, including keeping the glove hand away from the body and looking the ball into the glove without turning the head. They must also utilize soft hands by *giving with the pitch* and drawing the ball into the body, and angle the glove toward the plate without *pulling* it into the strike zone. By implementing the sway shift technique on close pitches, a catcher can get strike calls on borderline pitches by using his hips, arms, and legs without *stepping to the ball*. Home plate umpires will reward catchers with strike calls when close pitches are subtly framed. If a catcher has to move his glove or body significantly, then the pitch is likely to be called a ball.

Teaching Tip

Small movements with the glove hand and the lower body are important techniques for catchers to learn. On a close, low strike, the catcher can straighten his legs slightly to raise the pitch into the strike zone and catch the ball shallow (far away from the body). Conversely, the catcher can bend his knees a bit on a high ball near the top of the strike zone and catch the pitch deep (close to his head). Pitches below the waist should be gloved with the fingers pointing down. Whenever possible, catchers should strive to keep pitches in the strike zone by positioning the glove hand so that the palm of the glove stays in the zone even when the ball is not.

Aside from the sway shift, what techniques can catchers use when receiving?

When a pitch is too far inside or outside of the strike zone for a catcher to use the sway shift, the *step shift* can be implemented. In this scenario, the catcher steps to the ball while making sure not to cross the feet and keeping his body in front of the pitch at all times. The *shuffle shift* is a side skip step used when a catcher cannot reach the pitch with the step shift method. In all cases, the catcher must never cross his feet or his balance will be compromised and make throwing the ball extremely difficult.

In-Game Strategy: Arguing Balls and Strikes

Although umpires claim that arguing balls and strikes during games is not allowed, coaches and players use certain tactics to get borderline strike calls. Catchers can ask where a specific pitch missed so long as he does not turn around and *show up the umpire*. Coaches will irritate an umpire when questioning a strike call from the dugout, but can usually speak discreetly in between innings about an individual pitch. Catchers may use a nonverbal signal to alert coaches if a particular pitch was called improperly by the umpire. Umpires generally have personal strike zone tendencies that are influenced by their body height, which shoulder of the catcher that they crouch behind, and overall ball/strike philosophy.

Catcher Throwing Mechanics

While catchers at the professional level have tremendous "God-given" arm strength, coaches can emphasize a number of throwing fundamentals to their catchers. Catchers should catch and bring the ball to the right shoulder for a quick release. The wrist of the throwing hand should be relaxed as the hand grips the ball with a four-seam grip. With his eyes fixed on the target at all times, the catcher must make sure not to be flat-footed, but rather have his weight on the balls of his feet. His left shoulder should point toward the target with weight shifting from the right foot to the left as the throw is made. The catcher should step directly toward his target and make a fluid overhand throw, never dropping the elbow or throwing across his body.

Teaching Tip

Catchers must have a *shorter arc* when throwing to maintain a quick release (Figure 7-4). This throwing arc differs from that of other position players that have more time and can get their arm extended before throwing (Figure 7-5). Coaches must stress proper footwork with young catchers who do not have the arm strength to effectively catch and throw to any base. By introducing the *jab step, surfboard,* and other throwing techniques, coaches can give catchers a framework for delivering strong throws. At the Major League level, catchers possess enough arm strength to throw the ball to second base *from their knees* or standing with limited noticeable footwork.

In-Game Strategy: Throwing Out Base Stealers

When they expect the base runner(s) to steal, coaches and catchers may signal for a pitchout or fastball. Pitchouts are not always effective because pitchers struggle to make good throws, and catchers do not

Figure 7-4. Catcher throwing arc   Figure 7-5. Infielder throwing arc

regularly practice the footwork of this tactic. Given that offensive players may utilize the straight or delayed steal, catchers must have the mindset that every base runner is a potential stolen base threat. Throws to second base should be made above the bag on the first base side, while throws to third base should be on the second base side to nab a base stealer.

Major League Connection

Ivan Rodriguez won a remarkable 13 Gold Glove Awards and was selected to the Major League Baseball All-Star Team 14 times. Both of these accomplishments were aided largely by his incredible arm strength. Rodriguez possessed superior pop time and threw out a high percentage of *would-be base stealers*. Blessed with such a strong throwing arm, "Pudge" was able to thwart base-stealing attempts by throwing from his knees or using minimal footwork when throwing to second base.[2]

Catcher Throwing Footwork

Balance and sound footwork are key components to making consistent throws. Initially, these coaching points should be higher priorities than the speed of the release. Catchers should also practice throwing in full equipment, which helps to simulate game action. In terms of footwork, catchers can implement a number of techniques. Coaches can introduce catchers to the mechanics of each method and discuss which is the most feasible for them to adopt based on their size, arm strength, and foot speed. Moreover, the location of a pitch often dictates the catcher's footwork on his throws. Table 7-1 lists four catcher throwing techniques and the footwork for each.

Throwing Technique	Footwork	Advantages	Disadvantages
Sway	Catcher turns his right foot 90 degrees, shifts weight to his right foot, steps with the left foot, and throws to the target.	• Relatively quick method to get the ball to second base • No risk of stepping on the plate or losing balance	• Relies on above-average arm strength • Not a realistic method for most players at the high school level and below
Jab Step	Catcher quickly steps three to five inches with his right foot forward, moves left foot and shoulder on a line with target before releasing the ball in low position.	• Enables catcher to gain momentum by moving his feet • Quick jab step delays the throw only marginally.	• Catcher must square his left shoulder to target in small amount of time. • Difficult to execute when the batter swings at the pitch
Crow Hop	On a pitch to his left, the catcher makes a quick crow hop before squaring the shoulders and throwing to the target.	• Helps the catcher move his feet on the pitch off the plate • Provides leg motion to help propel the throw to the target	• Balance and compact footwork hard to master • Takes more time than other methods, and the runner may easily beat the throw
Surfboard or Jump Shift	Catcher uses a *jump pivot* to turn his feet and body from parallel to perpendicular with second base. This short hop incorporates a rotation of the hips and shoulders.	• The fastest technique for throwing the ball • Simple footwork and mechanics create fewer issues with balance.	• Requires an exceptionally strong throwing arm • Catchers must be able to stay low, or the hop will waste too much time.

Table 7-1. Catcher throwing techniques

Administrative Time-Out

During the pre-season, coaches should devise position-specific practices when catchers can work on footwork drills. Coaches can draw an upside-down "T" on the gym floor with tape, or in the dirt behind home plate to give catchers a starting point to place their feet. The T has one line to which the feet to start parallel and one line for the feet to finish perpendicular to second base. For each of the four throwing techniques practiced, coaches should make sure catchers' feet start and finish on this T configuration. The T should not touch home plate in either direction, as the catcher may slip if he throws while stepping on the plate. Throws should be practiced from both sides of the plate with left- and right-handed batters.

What are some common mistakes that catchers make when throwing?

Many catchers *come out of the chute* too quickly by rushing through the throwing process, leading to high throws. Frequently, younger catchers *flail* by dropping their throwing elbow, resulting in the ball sailing toward right centerfield on plays at second base. In many cases, catchers struggle to stay low and take too much time by standing straight up before releasing the throw. Balance is a major issue, as catchers must throw from a solid base. Not stepping on home plate or getting off balance should be points for coaches to emphasize. Players should also remember that a slower throw on target is better than a quick, wild throw.

Blocking Balls in the Dirt

A catcher's ability to block pitches in the dirt (Figure 7-6) is essential, especially on baseball fields where the backstop is not directly behind home plate. If the catcher does not possess strong blocking skills, base runners will easily advance into scoring position and pitchers will not be comfortable throwing low *out pitches*. A good mindset for catchers to adopt is to always anticipate a dirt ball. Ideally, when a catcher blocks a ball in the dirt, the ball will bounce directly in front of home plate so that he can quickly throw it to any base. In order to do so, the catcher's body should be square to the pitcher with his body weight shifted forward.

Figure 7-6. Blocking mechanics

Upon realizing that a pitch is in the dirt and must be blocked, the catcher should drop to his knees with his head down and eyes on the ball. The catcher's hands roll in a downward scooping motion so that the hands finish in between the legs. The elbows tuck inward toward the core of the body. During this process, the shoulders must be rounded so that the pitch will hit off the chest in front of the plate. Blocked pitches should be attacked by the catcher as he looks for a developing play.

Three Steps to Success

1. Drop to both knees with the head down, and stay square to the pitcher's mound.
2. Roll the hands downward while keeping the elbows close and inside the body.
3. Round the shoulders with the goal of knocking the pitch down in front of the plate to quickly make a play on the bases.

 ### Teaching Tip

Many young catchers get lazy and use their hands when blocking balls in the dirt. Instead, the upper body should be the area of focus for blocking dirt balls. The catcher should never backhand or stab at the ball, but rather quickly slide over in front of the ball with his knees together. Catchers must realize that they do not have to cleanly glove every pitch in the dirt so long as they can knock the ball down and keep it close. The catcher should drop to his right knee for balls to his right and drop on his left knee for balls to his left. While dropping, the shoulders turn to get around the ball to keep it square with the pitcher. Curveballs in the dirt tend to break away from the catcher and bounce toward the opposite shoulder.

 ### Administrative Time-Out

Catching equipment is heavy, expensive, and takes up considerable space. Consequently, many teams encourage catchers to purchase their own equipment and bring it daily to practice and games. By the time a player enters high school, he should determine if he is serious about catching and try to purchase his own gear. Coaches may want to acquire at least one extra set of catcher's gear in case a catcher is absent, his equipment breaks, or another player is inserted behind the plate on a given day. With hockey goalie–style masks, knee-saver leg pads, chest protectors, shin guards, gloves, and other items, large durable bags should be used to keep all of this equipment transportable.

Fielding Bunts

On bunted pitches, the catcher communicates where the play is and which defensive player has priority to field the ball. Given that he is the only fielder who can see the base runners advancing and knows the range and arm strength of the fielders, it is fitting that he is in command. As soon as the bunt is down, the catcher should bounce out from behind home plate. On plays that are his responsibility, the ball is fielded and pushed into the glove with the bare hand. Catcher throws made on bunt plays are typically overhand. However, in situations where the throw has to be made extremely quickly, the catcher may need to throw from a sidearm angle.

In-Game Strategy: Catcher Decision-Making

If a catcher senses that he will not be able to make a play on a bunted ball, he can let the ball roll foul and pick it up as soon as it crosses the foul line. Not only do catchers communicate which fielders should make the play on a bunt, but also to what base the play is directed. In addition, when a catcher fields a bunt or drops a third strike, he calls "inside" or "outside" to alert the first baseman from which side of the baseline the throw will be coming. This call helps diminish the chance of a thrown ball hitting the base runner as he moves down the line.

 Teaching Tip

Balls that have stopped moving should be pushed into the ground with all five fingers and picked up with a four-seam grip (Figure 7-7). Rolling bunted balls are picked up by catchers in a *dust pan* or bent over, two-hand sweeping motion (Figure 7-8). Bunts on the first baseline should be approached from the left side with the catcher throwing to the inside of the base. When balls are rolling on the third base line, the catcher can circle the ball and keep it in front of him before scooping it and making the throw. Alternatively, the catcher can play the ball with his back to the target, drop-step with the glove-side foot, and throw to the base (see the last photo in Figure 7-7).

Figure 7-7. Fielding a stationary bunt

Figure 7-8. Fielding a rolling bunt

Catcher Pop-Ups

As a pop-up flies upward, customarily, a catcher removes his mask quickly and holds it in his right hand. Once the ball is located, the mask is tossed in the opposite direction of where the ball is expected to land. However, with the widespread usage of hockey goalie masks, when catching pop-ups some catchers may choose to keep their mask on. The glove should be raised to help the catcher shield his eyes from the sun. Given that the catcher's glove is so small, he must use two hands at all times when catching pop-ups.

Foul pop-ups hit behind home plate will drift toward the infield. As a result, catchers should turn around and face away from the infield and let the ball carry back toward them. This *infield drift* should be accounted for on all pop-ups as well as wind, sun, dugouts, fences, and light poles. In addition, catchers can get jumps on foul pop-ups by having the awareness that outside pitches to a right-handed batter are usually fouled off to the right of home plate and inside pitches are popped up to the left. For left-handed batters, the opposite trend ordinarily holds true (Figure 7-9).

Figure 7-9. Catcher pop-ups

Conference Time

Coaches must meet with catchers to discuss communication and the decision-making process on pop-ups. Catchers should be aware of which fielders are the most sure-handed under fly balls so they know how to direct priority on these plays. Many teams discourage the pitcher from calling for pop-ups, even though he is commonly the best athlete on the field. Given that the catcher possesses the smallest, least flexible glove and wears the most bulky equipment on the infield, other players should try to get to as many pop-ups around home plate as possible. As for communication, teammates should stand up to protect and alert the catcher to how much room he has around dugout steps and other potentially dangerous infield structures.

Catcher Tag Plays

When preparing for a tag play, catchers should position their left leg so that the shin guard is parallel to the third baseline. Both legs should be flexed slightly with the left heel in front of home plate and toes pointing up the third baseline. On incoming throws from centerfield and left field, the catcher can set up in a more upright position with his arms relaxed at the sides to decoy the base runner. When receiving throws from right field, the catcher should give the runner the inside of the plate.

As the catcher prepares to apply the tag, he should watch the feet of the sliding base runner, and should only drop down when the runner goes down into his slide. It is important for the catcher not to lunge at the runner. The catcher's left shin guard is dropped and greets the approaching runner. As for the ball, the catcher must hold it in the throwing hand, tightly covered by the glove to prevent it from coming loose.

 ### Teaching Tip

Before attempting to make a tag, catchers should always wait for the base runner to commit to sliding, standing, or moving inside/ outside. On plays where the catcher receives the ball in advance, he should move up the line and apply the tag on the runner's left shoulder. One-hand tags can be effective, but may result in the ball popping out of the catcher's mitt or delay a throw to another base. Catchers must also consider the field conditions as a wet or damp field may force incoming throws to skip or affect the length of a runner's slide toward home plate.

 ### In-Game Strategy: Blocking the Plate

For years, when catchers were instructed to block the plate as incoming base runners approached, offensive players would attempt to *bowl over* the catcher. With the hope of dislodging the ball from the catcher's glove or opening the base line for future runners, players got psyched up for this high-contact part of the game. This practice has been banned at most levels below the professional ranks to avoid serious injuries and bench clearing brawls. For this tactic, players are penalized with automatic outs, ejections, and suspensions by most state and league associations.

Major League Connection

In the 1970 MLB All-Star Game, Pete Rose knocked over Cleveland Indians' catcher Ray Fosse. After this infamous collision at home plate, Fosse suffered a shoulder injury and never hit as well as he had previously. After this incident, Rose earned the reputation for highly aggressive, tenacious play.

Specific Catching Situations

Backing Up First and Third Base

On ground balls or base hits when no runners are on base, the catcher should back up first base. Catchers should take a proper angle to the ball on these plays so that they are in the position to catch an overthrow or ball that skips past first base. It is important for catchers not to run too close to the foul line; otherwise, he will not be *angled out* effectively for the overthrow.

On base hits to the outfield, the catcher should *trail the hitter* out of the batter's box and be alert for a backdoor throw behind the runner rounding first base. Additionally, on throws from left field to second base on a single, the trailing catcher provides a back-up on errant throws. With a base runner on first base, the catcher must cover third base on bunt plays fielded by the third baseman. In particular, offensive teams may attempt a bunt-and-run play with the goal of moving the runner to third base.

Base Runners on First and Third Base

The catcher and infielders must coordinate strategies for defending *first and third situations*. When the runner on first base attempts to steal second base, the catcher has several options. These include throwing the ball straight through to second base, directly back to the pitcher, immediately to third base, or to a middle infielder at the edge of the infield grass. Most of these tactics, as well as faking a throw to second base or having a middle infielder fake cutting off a catcher throw to second base, are designed to contain the runner at third base. It is essential for catchers not to lob the ball back to the pitcher since some teams implement delayed steal plays.

 ### Teaching Tip

Coaches should discuss with their catchers the specific scenarios in which offensive teams behave aggressively in first and third situations. With two outs, offenses tend to be more apt to send the runner from first base, especially with a less-skilled hitter at the plate. A close game with a dominant pitcher is also more likely to elicit risky baserunning tactics from the offense. Most of all, the arm strength of the pitcher, catcher, and infielders matched against the speed of the base runners will determine how aggressively the offense behaves.

 ### In-Game Strategy: Relaying Defensive Signals

During first and third situations, defensive teams have several methods for relaying signals. Most teams rely on the catcher to call time-out, step in front of home plate, and deliver a set of hand signals to specify where he will throw the ball on a steal attempt. At the youth level, with fewer screaming fans, teams may utilize a verbal signal system usually through a set of three to five numbers. In some cases, teams will have the shortstop or third baseman display the signals to the defense. Regularly, coaches survey the situation and relay the signals to the catcher.

Double Plays: Home to First Base

When the bases are loaded with less than two outs, the defense has the opportunity to turn a home-to-first double play. If the infield is playing in on the edge of the grass, the throw to the catcher can come from a variety of angles. Yet, with the *middle back*, catchers may receive throws from the pitcher, third baseman, or first baseman.

As the throw approaches from an infielder, the catcher drags his right foot across the plate, catches the ball with two hands, and throws to first base on the inside of the baseline. On quicker plays, such as *come-backers* to the pitcher or hard-hit balls to third and first base, the catcher can place his left foot on the corner of the plate, while providing a target on the first base side of the plate. As he makes the catch, the catcher pivots on the right foot and throws to first base.

 ### Teaching Tip

It is important for all position players to learn how to stretch with the proper foot on force out plays. Players should stretch with their glove-side foot, keeping the throwing arm foot touching the base or plate. Too often, middle infielders will race over to a base to receive a throw on a force play and stretch with the wrong foot. This move undermines the purpose of the stretch and makes the fielder less mobile to handle throws to different sides of a base. Coaches can have catchers and infielders receive throws in practice for both tag and stretch plays.

Throwing Behind Runners

When base runners take an overly aggressive secondary lead or are not focused on the bases, catchers can throw behind the runner. This throw requires a significant level of arm strength and may not be effective for players at the youth level. A *snap throw* from the kneeling position to first and third base can successfully pick off a base runner. A throw to second base, which is more than 35 feet longer than to the corner bases, may require the catcher to raise up to make the throw.

 ### Conference Time

Coaches may need to communicate with their catcher the appropriate situations to throw behind base runners. Many catchers like to show off their arms by frequently firing throws to each of the bases whenever a runner is on base. This practice can result in two problems. By throwing behind runners habitually, catchers will alert the offense that they must readily hustle back to the base after taking their secondary lead. In addition, the more throws that are made increases the likelihood of an overthrow into the outfield, enabling the runners to advance.

In-Game Strategy: Catcher Pickoff Plays

Teams at higher levels will institute orchestrated pickoff plays called by the catcher. Nonverbal signals such as picking up a handful of dirt or touching the top of the mask can signal that a pickoff play is on for the next pitch. In particular, some teams pick off to first base with a left-handed batter in the box, as this will block the base runner's view of the catcher's arm. The catcher will signal for an inside pitch, pivot to his right, and deliver a quick, snap throw to first base. Pickoffs to second base are effective when a catcher can throw from his knees to second base as if merely tossing the ball back to the pitcher. Middle infielders who back up catcher throws to the pitcher by *pinching in* behind the mound will not tip off the base runner if they routinely back up after every pitch.

Double Steals

With runners on first and second base, catchers must be able to react to a double steal. Although the throw to third base is shorter than the throw to second base for the catcher, he must consider several factors before deciding to which base to throw. For instance, the catcher must consider the running speed of both runners before making his decision. Also, catchers must be aware of the length of each runner's lead. If the runner at second base has a sizable walking lead and gets a good jump, then the catcher should only throw to second base. The runner on first base typically gets a late jump to second base because he must wait for the base runner on second to break for third before taking off. Furthermore, many trail runners do not run as hard when stealing, as they do not expect a throw directed toward second base.

Dropped Third Strike

With a dominant pitcher on the mound it is common to see a strike out on a ball that gets past the catcher. In these cases, the catcher must quickly grab the ball with four seams and throw to first base. The first baseman should communicate and give a target for the catcher to throw "inside" or "outside" the base line (Figures 7-10 and 7-11). This communication is important so that the catcher has a lane for throwing to first base that is not blocked by the base runner. Many of these plays are directed outside the baseline, except when the wild pitch or passed ball travels toward the third base side of home plate. Coaches should review with players the specific scenarios when a batter can and cannot advance to first base on a dropped third strike as it will eliminate unnecessary throws to first base that may cause overthrows and allow runners to advance.

Passed Balls/Wild Pitches

When a pitch gets by a catcher with men on base, he must hustle after the ball. On the play, aggressive base runners may attempt to advance two bases if the catcher is lackadaisical in retrieving the ball. In cases where the pitch goes *back to the screen* or backstop area, the catcher may have a long throw to third base. At youth levels, fields tend to be fenced in snugly behind home

Figure 7-10. "Inside" throw to first base   Figure 7-11. "Outside" throw to first base

plate to avoid catchers having to run back after every ball that gets by. Yet, at the collegiate and professional levels, catchers may have to run over 20 feet to secure a wild pitch. In all scenarios, catchers should sprint after the baseball, listen to their teammates' communications, and always anticipate the runner(s) to be advancing.

Intentional Walk

Many leagues do not require pitchers to throw four balls for an intentional walk, but rather simply award the batter first base. However, some associations require pitchers to actually throw four balls, as in the Major Leagues, which can cause problems for the defense. It is important that the pitcher and infielders do not forget about the base runners, as stolen base attempts may occur. Also, some pitchers struggle to throw accurate pitches to the catcher because these intentional balls are rarely practiced. To prevent wild pitches, catchers should stand upright in the catcher's box and extend their glove hand or throwing hand several feet outside of the batter's reach. Catchers should provide a large target and remind pitchers to check the base runners. Catchers can be called for a catcher's balk if they leave the catcher's box too soon to receive the pitch.

 In-Game Strategy: Dropped Third Strike

Game fields should be lined so that the runner has a lane in which to run halfway to first. Otherwise, runners may intentionally run toward the first baseman to obstruct his view of the throw. Catchers must also be aware when ball four gets away, as some teams may send the batter to second base, especially if a runner is on third. With the bases loaded, catchers can step on home plate to record the third out on a dropped third strike.

Mental Aspects of Catching

While catching is a physically taxing position, it also requires various mental capabilities as well. Not only is the catcher the verbal leader of the defense, but throughout the game he must also communicate strategy with his coach(es). More significantly, the catcher is the battery mate of the pitcher and must do everything possible to help him have an optimum performance. Whether it is calming down a pitcher with control problems, building his confidence, or recognizing a flaw in his mechanics, the catcher is instrumental in helping the pitcher succeed.

Catchers must always be aware of the game situation. Aside from knowing how many outs there are and communicating this information to his teammates, the catcher must know the score to help him determine how aggressive or conservative to be in directing defensive plays. Catchers should also be sensitive to specific points in a game when the offense may be poised to utilize a certain tactic. For instance, catchers may sense when a sacrifice or squeeze bunt play is possible and, in turn, call for a high fastball. The score, body language of the players, tendencies of the offense, or signals delivered by the third base coach can all play a role in helping a catcher make this instinctive read.

In addition to communicating effectively with his teammates and coaches, the catcher should develop proper rapport with umpires. Catchers must learn appropriate means for inquiring why a particular pitch was not called a strike or *where the pitch missed*. It is taboo for the catcher to turn around and ask an umpire about a specific call. Rather, he should face forward in his catching stance as if ready to receive a pitch and discuss the pitch so that no onlooker senses that he is questioning the umpire. Ideally, the catcher and umpire develop a mutual respect and working relationship, which may help the defense get the benefit of the doubt on close calls.

It is important for catchers to maintain emotional stability. Too often, catchers will have a difficult at bat and lose focus when returning back to the field. Coaches must emphasize to catchers that bad experiences when hitting should be left in the dugout while putting on their equipment. In particular, if the catcher deems that the umpire made a poor call during his at bat then he may carry his anger back to the field and hurt his team's chances of getting calls on borderline pitches. Moreover, if frustration over an at bat distracts him from effectively running the team or being aware of developing situations, the catcher will inevitably hurt the ball club.

Ideally, catchers can find a balance between being a spirited, vocal leader and a selfless, poised warrior solely concerned with team success. Traditionally, Major League catchers hit in the bottom half of the batting order, just ahead of the pitcher, and were expected to focus on their defensive roles, not offensive production.

Major League Connection

Cincinnati Reds' Hall of Fame catcher Johnny Bench played during the 1970s, when he was one of only a few potent offensive players at the catching position. Catchers commonly hit below .250, but were expected to possess a strong throwing arm and sound defensive skills.

Experienced catchers must learn to master many finer points of catching. Astute catchers will sense if a runner on second base or a base coach is stealing his pitch signs and relaying them to the batter. Similarly, catchers must be aware of batters peeking to learn pitch type or location. Not only should catchers be sensitive to these situations, but also possess plans to rectify them. Catchers may devise decoy signals for the pitcher or use a secondary pitch system with their pitchers and infielders. During night games, catchers may need to put nail polish or tape on their fingers to help pitchers see their signals. Several other intuitive actions that catchers may demonstrate include conferencing with the pitcher when he gets *crossed up* on pitch signals, walking to the mound when the umpire is hit with a foul ball, nonverbally signaling that a throw to second base is *coming down* before the inning starts, and calling time out to discuss poor play or to review bunt defenses.

Catching Drills

Barehanded Framing Drill

To help catchers learn to utilize soft hands when receiving, barehanded framing drills can be performed. Tennis balls and plastic golf balls are useful tools that can be thrown to a squatting catcher who must implement proper framing technique (Figure 7-12). Sway shifting and effective positioning of the glove hand should also be emphasized during these drills.

Figure 7-12. Barehanded framing drill

No-Hands Blocking Drill

Frequently, catchers inappropriately use their hands when blocking pitches in the dirt. When catchers get lazy with blocking fundamentals, they tend to reach for the ball and rely entirely on their hands. By practicing blocking drills with the hands behind the back, catchers can focus on proper placement of the upper- and lower-body parts (Figure 7-13). Coaches can also have catchers wear boxing gloves during these drills to protect their hands. This protection enables them to position the hands and arms in the correct manner in relation to the legs.

Figure 7-13. No-hands blocking drill

Situational Team Defense Drill

Perhaps the most important skill for young catchers to practice, as plays develop on the field, is their verbal directives to the defense. Coaches can help catchers refine this skill by setting up various defensive game situations and have catchers make the proper verbal command. With runners placed on the bases and alternating different numbers of outs, coaches can hit balls to the defense and have them make the play. Catchers will work on making the proper decision as to which base the play should be directed and who should have priority on the play. These decisions are difficult for youth-level catchers to determine, as many plays develop quickly and can have various outcomes. For example, by putting a runner at each base and hitting a ball to the outfield gap, coaches will test a catcher's ability to line up cutoff men and direct the throw to the proper base. This practice activity helps all players refine their anticipation skills, especially the catcher.

Administrative Time-Out

When setting up situational defensive practices, coaches must consider how to minimize player down time. With a 16- to 20-man roster, coaches can assign four players to rotate in as base runners. Soft toss, pepper, and tee hitting drills are productive activities to have four or five other players perform. During this time, pitchers can rotate in to throw 15 to 20 pitches off the game mound as the coach hits balls to fielders. Pitchers can utilize this opportunity to get comfortable with the mound and throw their full repertoire of pitches. In between pitches and executed plays in the field, an assistant coach or pitcher can hit fungos to fielders not involved with the play.

Timed Fielded Bunt Drill

Coaches can place balls in front of home plate in a V-shaped configuration and have catchers come from behind home plate to field and throw to a base. The balls should be spaced 12 to 24 inches from each other, and catchers should hurry behind home plate and squat down after throwing each one. The key with these drills is for the catcher to use proper footwork and determine whether to dust pan or use the bare hand to field each ball. Balls furthest from home plate should be approached first so that the catcher's feet do not get tangled on any stray balls. Coaches can also roll out bunts instead of placing stationary balls on the ground to simulate fielding a moving ball. To make this drill competitive, coaches can use a stopwatch to time each catcher.

Skip Tag Drill

Catchers are stationed at home plate ready to receive throws from the outfield. Base runners are positioned at third base to tag up on a fly ball or at second base to score on a single to the outfield. Outfielders should throw the ball on a bounce to home plate to test the catcher's ability to glove a short hop and place a tag on incoming runners. To spare outfielder arms, coaches can also hit one-hop fungos from 40 feet away toward the catcher as runners try to score.

Tile Drill

Numerous floor tiles are placed in the home plate area. As a coach hits pop flies to the catcher, without stepping on any tiles, the catcher must attempt to catch the ball. By directing the catcher to take his eyes off the ball to avoid the tiles, the tile drill helps catchers develop confidence in relocating the ball after having lost sight of it.

Combination Block Drill

While standing on the pitcher's mound, a coach fires balls in the dirt to be blocked with proper form. Coaches should move their throws in the dirt to the middle of the plate, left of the plate, and to the right of the plate. It is important for coaches to mix in a strike every few pitches to ensure that the catcher does not drop to his knees on a framed strike. In order to increase the speed of the pitch and force the catcher to quicken his reaction time, the coach can move closer to home plate. A variation of this drill involves setting up a hockey or lacrosse goal behind the catcher. The coach will try to throw balls in the dirt that get past the catcher for a goal.

Pop Time Drill

College and professional scouts will gauge a catcher's arm strength by checking his pop time when he throws down to second base in between innings. Coaches can have catchers try different footwork techniques with each of the four throwing styles explained earlier to see which method enables them to throw quickest to second base. A benchmark time of 2.00 seconds is what high school and college catchers strive to attain consistently. Ideally, coaches should also track the pop times of their catchers during game situations with a batter swinging on pitches. Catchers will periodically sit up or lean forward in an unrealistic manner to score a low pop time during this drill if no hitter is in the box.

Given that catchers frequently receive bullpen sessions from pitchers or perform different activities than position players, how can coaches adjust for this difference?

Coaches should be sensitive to the grueling nature of the catching position and the sacrifices catchers make to play the position. By providing catchers with several extra swings during batting practice or requiring fewer post-practice duties, coaches can lighten the load for catchers. Even so, catchers should not be babied or negatively take advantage of the down time in between catching pitcher bullpen sessions. Practicing *roll-outs* (rolling out bunts to properly field) or rehearsing throwing footwork are drills that can be performed individually.

Summersault Pop-Up Drill

In teaching catchers to be adept at catching pop-ups, coaches can have players complete a forward roll at home plate before running to the ball and making a catch. This drill disorients catchers for a moment before having to find the ball, adjust their body accordingly, and make the play. A variation of this drill involves a coach bumping or pushing the catcher as if he knocked into the hitter or umpire as he went after the pop-up. This fun exercise helps simulate realistic game action for catchers seeking to feel more comfortable with pop-ups. As a follow-up, coaches can hit (or throw for younger players) multiple pop-ups for the catcher to field in three-second intervals after the forward roll.

Timed Catcher Gear Change Drill

Although catchers will not be timed when putting on their gear during a game situation, it is beneficial for catchers to be able to put their equipment on quickly. Umpires and starting pitchers do not like waiting for the catcher to emerge from the dugout in between innings. Accordingly, during practice days coaches get more done when their catchers get their gear on quickly. Therefore, this timed competition does not simulate an on-the-field fundamental, but helps players become more efficient with their time. Catchers can start the drill as a hitter at home plate that makes the third out in a hypothetical inning. By sprinting down the first baseline, running into the dugout to put their equipment on, and hustling behind home plate, catchers simulate a game scenario. Coaches can time their catchers in this fun, competitive activity.

Sources/Further Reading

[1]Dickson, P. (1992). *Baseball's Greatest Quotations*. New York: Harper Perennial. P. 193.

[2]Baseball-Reference.com; Sports Reference LLC; 2000-2009. Jun 16, 2009.

TEAM PLAY

Chapter 8

*Finding good players is easy. Getting them
to play as a team is another story.*
—Casey Stengel[1]

Before developing practice plans and organizing various team events, coaches must formulate the team's philosophy. Coaches may even choose to post a mission statement that states the importance of team membership, commitment, safety, playing time, fundamentals, winning/losing, or whatever is deemed important. This statement can vary greatly depending on the age of players and the style of the coach (see Introduction for various coaching styles). For instance, one coach may have a team meeting to discuss what the philosophy should be, while another may dictate the goals. Regardless of the specifics within the philosophy, this chapter provides coaches with a foundation on which to base their program.

Many universities, high schools, and other institutions have a mission statement that allows participants to be aware of certain goals and central tenets that represent the organization. Before making a commitment to a baseball team, parents and players should know whether the team is focused on winning, learning fundamentals, or just having fun. This philosophy will also frame how a coach sets up daily practices. A coach who has pressure to win will gear in-season practice time toward strategy, game situation repetitions, and immediate performance rather than basic fundamentals and fun-filled activities. Furthermore, if winning is the top priority (as is at the college and high school varsity level), then the intensity level of practices, equity of playing, and commitment level will vary from that of a recreational team.

Administrative Time-Out

A major challenge for coaches is to provide equal swings, pitches, defensive repetitions, and attention to all team members. Within a particular practice the goal may be for every player to get 12 to 15 swings during batting practice. However, it may not be feasible. Frequently, the first 10 hitters get more time in the cage or batter's box than the last six receive. Some coaches will design batting practice in the same hitting order as their game day lineup. Others prefer to vary practice so that players are unaware of the batter order or starting lineups. Regardless, coaches should be aware of time constraints during practice and how this affects equality of repetitions and, in turn, players' attitudes.

Conference Time

It is imperative for coaches to discuss player roles with each team member. These conversations can take place as early as directly after tryouts to throughout the season. Typically, players have different views of their ability level and deserved playing time than that of the coaching staff; therefore, coaches should not only review game roles with players, but also practice roles. The last player selected for the team may not understand why he receives fewer swings compared to other players during batting practice. If this is the case, coaches must communicate this aspect so that the player feels like a valued team member and maintains a positive attitude to help foster strong team chemistry.

How can the coach motivate players to buy into the team concept?

Attempting to foster team unity and help players accept the notion that "There is no 'I' in team" is a significant obstacle for coaches. Given that player statistics, website exposure, post-season awards, newspaper stories, and college scholarship opportunities are largely based on individual achievement, coaches must work hard to build team commitment. In-season dinners/trips, teambuilding activities, and one-on-one conferencing can positively influence this process.

Practice Planning

When devising a practice, coaches must consider the following factors: time, space, and coaching priorities. Many school teams are restricted to practicing immediately after school, depending on field availability. College teams have a greater range of facilities and practice times. Recreation programs routinely rely on weekends and intermittent weekday afternoons for practices. In all cases, coaches must determine their goals given the allotted time that they have with their players. A three-hour practice, for example, provides more opportunities for individual skill work and game strategy than a 90-minute workout.

At the outset of their season, teams in colder climates will be forced to hold practice indoors, which may translate to sharing a gym with other teams and dealing with the issue of limited space. During this time, coaches must assess player ability for team selection as well as teach fundamentals. As a result, practice planning becomes more critical to deal with the pressures of setting up effective drills in a non-baseball field atmosphere. Even when practicing outdoors, many teams share field space with different sports teams or age groups of baseball teams. Communication with the other coaches vying for space is an essential component to ensuring safety and a productive use of practice time.

 Administrative Time-Out

Safety should always be a priority when setting up baseball practice. With hard baseballs and bats, coaches must stress to players the importance of being cognizant of those around them. Indoor practice magnifies these issues as balls can ricochet off walls and strike athletes in the head. Within crowded practice spaces, swinging bats and throwing balls at close distances leave little room for error. Organization and diligent practice planning are keys to overcoming these hazards. In addition, clear communication with players regarding these issues is essential.

Three Steps to Success

1. Be aware of how much time exists for players to practice.
2. Know what field or facility will be used for the practice and how much space is available.
3. Prioritize which skills, strategies, and activities should be performed.

Major League Connection

In professional baseball, especially at the Major League level, coaches have limited practice time. Although specialized coaches in areas such as hitting or pitching work with players one-on-one, managers do not hold full field team practices within the regular season. Pre-game defensive and batting practice comprise in-season practice.

Coaches may find it useful to draw a diagram of the space where practice will be held (Figure 8-1). On this diagram, letters, numbers, and/or names can be inserted to designate players, coaches, and activities performed. Within cramped quarters, rotating station drills are beneficial for rehearsing basic fundamentals, maximizing small areas of space, and keeping players motivated with a variety of drills. Every 8 to 12 minutes, a team of 16 to 20 players can rotate to each skill station and practice numerous skills.

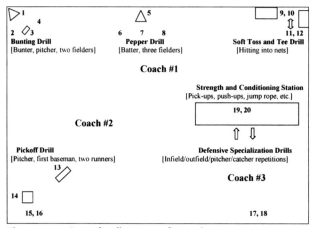

Figure 8-1. Sample diagram of practice space

Ultimately, coaches must decide on their priorities for each day of practice. Doing so requires finding a balance between instruction with basic fundamentals, player repetitions on various skills, and team rehearsal of synchronized plays. On a given day, a coach may want each infielder to get 100 to 150 ground balls and turn 50 double plays. These repetition-based practices are high energy and can include prizes or punishments for levels of success. Prior to starting the drills, coaches may review certain fundamentals; for example, proper glove action when fielding ground balls or footwork when turning a double play. A final component is the team coordination of these skills through verbal communication, rehearsed plays of deception, or reacting to base runner movements. *A coach's challenge throughout practice is to find the proper balance of teaching fundamentals, providing repetitions, and working on team coordination of in-game strategy.*

Effective tools for organizing practices that are productive and comprehensive are typed practice plans. Coaches may choose to print these out daily with colorful or highlighted fonts. Although typing practice plans is time consuming, it offers several benefits. Assistant coaches can be given a copy of the day's practice before it begins or emailed in advance so that they can be prepared to carry out their responsibilities successfully. Additionally, these plans provide coaches with an archive of practices that can be utilized in the future. Lastly, some coaches post the team's activities on a bulletin board at practice or during the school day so players will know what is expected of them.

Topic of Debate: Posting a Practice Plan

Some coaches do not believe in showing their players the day's practice plan ahead of time. While it may demonstrate to players how organized the coach is and enable them to prepare for the activities, it robs the practice of imagination. The element of surprise can provide a benefit when working with athletes, and a displayed practice plan may eliminate some the excitement associated with this. In the heat of a hectic season, some coaches may not want to allocate the time required to type daily practice plans. But rather, these coaches prefer to jot down the activities and teaching points for the day on a piece of paper to keep it simple.

Practice plans should detail numerous activities, including player equipment responsibilities, a warm-up/throwing routine, timing of drills, administrative reminders regarding transportation or team events, and conditioning workouts. Providing a daily mini-lecture topic, tip of the day, or quote is an effective vehicle for reaching players' cognitive side. By keeping this topic brief, coaches can address issues of baseball fundamentals, ethics and morality, individual motivation, or whatever the team requires. Posting this outline on a bulletin board at the field alongside relevant articles can help players understand the importance of the mental side of baseball. Moreover, by reporting to a bulletin board as they arrive to practice, players will be trained to focus as soon as they step on the field. This bulletin area also provides a spot to post team standings, statistics, goals, scouting reports of opponents, photographs of players with proper baseball mechanics, or merely a humorous baseball quote.

Regardless of the content, throughout the practice coaches should remember to diversify and keep the players moving to different drills and activities to maintain a high energy level. Baseball has lost many young athletes to faster paced, action sports where practices do not drag and down time is limited. Before beginning the practice planning process, coaches must consider the needs and interests of their players. The two sample plans provided in Tables 8-1 and 8-2 offer a framework for designing comprehensive, detailed practices.

Aside from designing daily practices, coaches should establish a warm-up routine for the team to access on all game and practice days. This routine must be brief and thorough to provide the players' bodies with an adequate warm-up. Normally, teams arrive to games only minutes before competition. Given this scenario, players need an effective, quick means to prepare for rigorous play. Unlike soccer, basketball, and hockey, where players' bodies are in motion, baseball requires athletes to react quickly from a static position. Minutes may lapse before a player is required to move extensively on the field. This stop-and-go nature of baseball makes players more susceptible to injuring muscles and tendons.

	Practice Plan #1	
	Next Game vs. Washingtonville High School (Saturday)	

Team/Practice Notes

Washingtonville game	Extended lead strategy and execution
Skills/drills to work on	Mini-lecture topic: Two-strike hitting

Pre-Practice Jobs (3:20 to 3:30 p.m.)

Screens: Fama (back-up) and La Padula	Balls: Koehler
Med kit: Laccetti	Cooler: Fama
Helmets: J. Matos	Water bottles: Meier
Bats: Bruzzese	Hitting mats: A. Matos
Bases: La Padula, DeRaffele, Cardone	

Activities Time	Skills	Description
3:30 p.m.	Warm-up, arms, cans	Jog to centerfield; complete dynamic warm-up routine; Jobe exercises, throwing arm stretches, long tossing (push-ups for overthrows)
3:50 p.m.	Plyometrics	
4:00 p.m.	Defensive situations	Oswald, Bruzzese, Cardone, Lopez throw off mound
4:45 p.m.	Mini-lecture: 1-2 count, zero outs hitting game	Runner on second base (last batted out) Hitters receive: 1 point for moving runner to third base; 2 points for RBI hit; 1 point for base on balls. 3 outs per team. 8 fielders; one feeder for coach throwing batting practice. Hitters run four poles for taking a called third strike; two poles for a swinging third strike; plus team poles for losing team(s).
5:50 p.m.	Clean-up, poles, and post-practice notes	

Post-Practice Jobs (6:00 to 6:15 p.m.)

Balls: Koehler	Med kit: Laccetti
Drag bases: Siegel and Meier	Helmets: J. Matos
Rake plate: Iacopetta	Bats: Bruzzese
Rake mound: Koehler and Coach Gurney	Bases: La Padula, DeRaffele,
Rake first baselines: La Padula and A. Matos	Cardone
Rake third baselines: Bruzzese and Cardone	

Post-Practice Notes

Discuss Washingtonville High School scouting report and bus departure time (10:30 a.m.)
Individual meetings: Bruzzese, Meier, Iacopetta

Go Hard or Go Home!

Table 8-1. Sample practice plan #1

Practice Plan #2
Next Game vs. FDR-Hyde Park High School (Saturday)

Team/Practice Notes
Playoff game and opponent (pitcher; defense)
Mini-lecture topic: Baserunning at second base

Pre-Practice Jobs (11:50 a.m. to 12:00 p.m.)	
Screens: Balliet and Erlick	Balls: Koehler
Med kit: Laccetti	Cooler: Fama
Helmets: J. Matos	Water bottles: Meier
Bats: Bruzzese	Hitting mats: A. Matos
Bases: La Padula, DeRaffele, Cardone	

Activities Time	Skills	Description
12:00 p.m	Warm-up, arms, cans	Jog to centerfield and complete dynamic warm-up routine; Jobe exercises, throwing arm stretches, long tossing (push-ups for overthrows)
12:20 p.m.	Mini-lecture baserunning	Players run out infield single; outfield single Four lines at first base and pick up signal/react to pitcher; Base running at second base; signals at third base and score
12:50 p.m.	Box drill and outfield fungos	Infielders take ground balls at second base and shortstop. Outfielders work on do-or-dies; over-the-shoulder catches.
1:15 p.m.	Thirds drills	Blind picks to first base; cover first drill; fake rotation throw first base; Pickoffs at second base; fielded bunts and throw to third base on catcher's call; lefty pick at third base
1:30 p.m.	Situations; soft toss; bunting	Situations with runners and pitchers throwing off mound; Players sub in to bunt/hit off pitchers Pitchers off-mound = Koehler; Lopez; Laccetti; Bruzzese; Players rotate to bunt drill/soft toss in bullpen
2:30 p.m.	Clean-up and post-practice notes	Review mental visualization techniques; discuss importance of sleep and eating properly prior to Saturday game day

Post-Practice Jobs (2:35 to 2:45 p.m.)	
Balls: Koehler	Med kit: Laccetti
Drag bases: Siegel and Meier	Helmets: J. Matos
Rake Plate: Iacopetta and Balliet	Bats: Bruzzese
Rake mound: Koehler and Coach Gurney	Bases: La Padula, DeRaffele, Cardone
Rake first baselines: La Padula and A. Matos	Screens: Fama and Erlick
Rake third base lines: Bruzzese and Cardone	

Post-Practice Notes
Positive mental visualization techniques
Sleep and nutrition leading up to Saturday's game

Table 8-2. Sample practice plan #2

Administrative Time-Out

Common baseball injuries include pulled hamstrings and quadriceps, calves, and groin muscles. Baseball requires quick reactions from a stationary position, such as dashing out of the batter's box, sprinting to a ball in the outfield, or rapidly reacting to a ball on the infield. These sudden movements can cause muscle tears and strains, especially in cold temperatures or if players have not warmed up properly.

 Topic of Debate: Warm-Up and Stretching Routine

Traditionally, before playing baseball players have jogged and stretched the major muscles for 15 to 20 minutes. In recent years, many teams perform some form of warm-up with few, if any, stretching of muscles. Rather, the warm-up routine is dependent upon getting the muscles and body loose. Proponents of this method do not believe intense stretching should take place until the end of the workout when muscles are ready to be stretched in a fixed position for several seconds at a time. Nonetheless, some teams jog and go through a sequence of static stretches in a traditional fashion before performing on the field.

Warm-Up Routine

Coaches can implement many variations of warm-up drills for their team to utilize. The key is for players to establish a daily routine in which all of the major bodily muscle groups get an adequate warm-up. While plyometric training is an important aspect of team performance, coaches should not combine these explosive exercises with the team's warm-up routine. In addition to light jogging, bunny hopping, or backpedaling in between these warm-up activities, the activities shown in Figures 8-2 through 8-13 can provide teams with a 10-minute systematic, structured method for preparing to begin a practice and/ or game play.

Figure 8-2. High knees

Figure 8-3. Backwards run (high knees)

Figure 8-4. Walking quad stretch

Figure 8-5. Carry over (carioca)

Figure 8-6. Walking leg cradles

Figure 8-7. Tin soldiers (walking)

Figure 8-8. Walking lunges

Figure 8-9. Lunges with a twist

Figure 8-10. Flat back lunges

Figure 8-11. Walking knee hugs

Figure 8-12. Hip arcs

Figure 8-13. Arm extension lunges

Teaching Tip

Coaches must stress that although the warm-up exercises should be completed in a timely manner, players should not speed through each repetition. These drills are set up so that players can perform each activity for 50 to 75 feet in separate lines. Players should always be in a *base stealing starting stance* and run to their right as on the base paths when the exercise permits. Even though athletes lined up in rows commonly will race to the end line, this should not be encouraged during a warm-up routine (Table 8-3).

Warm-Up Exercise	Muscles Recruited	Points/Mechanics of Emphasis
High knees	Hamstrings, quadriceps	Pump the arms, knees above the waist
Backwards run	Hamstrings, quads, calves	Upright posture, raise the knees
Walking quad stretch	Quadriceps	Look straight ahead, stay balanced
Carioca	Hip flexors, IT bands	Explode up with the knees on crossover
Leg cradles (walking)	Groin, hip flexors	Maintain straight legs, stay upright
Tin soldiers	Hamstrings, gluteus maximus	Hamstring extension
Walking lunges	Quadriceps, calves	Stay balanced and upright, bend low
Lunges with a twist	Gluteus maximus; SI joints (back)	Bend, perform a full turn with the arms
Flat back lunges	Quadriceps, lower/upper back	Maintain a flat back, shoulder to knee
Walking knee hugs	Quadriceps, hamstrings	Stay upright, bring the knee to the chest
Arm extension lunges	Lats, rotator cuffs	Maintain balance, bend low
Hip arcs	Hip flexors, groin	Maintain balance, stress flexibility

Table 8-3. Warm-up exercises

Plyometric Exercises

Plyometrics are a form of explosive, power training that can be used several times per week to enhance player performance. These drills work on the rapid firing of muscles. In turn, players must perform the exercises with a quick, responsive mindset. Many teams will incorporate plyometric drills into their warm-up routine, but these exercises can be completed later in a practice session as well.

Among the various lower body plyometric activities are high knees, kick backs, power skips/bounds, backwards high knees run, frog leaps, high strides, hopping over low hurdles, and box jumps. These drills can be researched for variation and proper form. The key is to keep them short and explosive in nature.

In the photographs shown in Figures 8-14 through 8-16, players are performing several plyometric exercises that can be conducted on a baseball field without other forms of equipment. Otherwise, agility ladders, mini-hurdles, elevated boxes, and cones are some of the training tools that can be used to build explosiveness. Within the context of a two- to three-hour, in-season practice, coaches may choose to direct players to complete their plyometric conditioning in several minutes time without setting up drills requiring equipment. Pre-season and off-season workout sessions are more appropriate times for extensive, more sophisticated plyometric training activities.

Figure 8-14. High strides

Figure 8-15. Power bounds

Figure 8-16. Rapid fire feet

Teaching Tip

Players should perform plyometrics and all running drills from a base-stealing start so that they get comfortable pivoting and running to their right as on the bases. Players need to focus on completing high-quality, explosive repetitions. During a plyometric exercise, athletes should never come to a *static position*, or stop, on the ground. The firing of the muscles will only be sharpened if players are immediately responsive upon touching the ground. Also, coaches should not implement plyometric drills on the same body part more than three times a week, as the activities will lose effectiveness, cause fatigue, and create a greater risk of injuries.

Reactions

 Excellent speed training exercises that incorporate on-the-field baseball actions with explosive quickness are reactions. Reactions are short sprints where players must respond to motion. This motion can be the movement of the player lined up in front of them in the drill or a coach who lifts his leg to simulate a pitcher delivering a pitch to home plate. To set up the drill, coaches should have players split into four or five lines in a base-stealing start from a primary lead position. The first player in the line sprints 30 to 60 feet, while the other lines must wait to run until he shows movement. Each player should not run until the player directly in front of him makes a move (Figure 8-17). By reacting to movement, players simulate the live game action of stealing a base.

Figure 8-17. Reaction sprints

 In-Game Strategy: Pre-Game Baserunning Preparation

Before games begin, many teams perform reactions for several minutes. Upon seeing the opposing pitcher warm up in the bullpen, coaches can have their players line up and react to the lifting of their leg in the stretch position. This activity usually takes place along the left or right field line on the side of the field where the team's dugout is located. Given the likelihood of a relief pitcher entering the game, coaches may pretend to deliver a pitch as a left-handed and right-handed pitcher with the goal of getting players' legs limber and ready to steal a base.

Administrative Time-Out

To simulate steals, delayed steals, and hit-and-run plays, players should properly respond to verbal directives when reacting to pitcher leg lifts from the stretch position. Coaches can designate an assistant coach or pitcher to direct these pre-game reactions. Prior to the game, head coaches are often busy with lineup cards, ground rules, and other administrative duties. Coaches can observe the reactions from the dugout or home plate area to watch for players working hard, which may prompt coaches to make a quick lineup change based on what they observe.

Establishing a Daily Throwing Routine

It is imperative for coaches to design and implement a system for organizing daily throwing. It is not advantageous to send players down the outfield line in pairs to play catch. But rather, players should have a progressive program that stretches their arm and strengthens it through the daily throwing process. As discussed previously, throwing is routinely the first baseball-related activity performed on the field. Therefore, coaches must see the importance of providing a structure and focus to players as they set the tone for a day of baseball performance.

Within Chapter 1, coaches are encouraged to have pitchers start their throwing on a knee. This approach isolates the motion and enables players to develop proper muscle memory for all of the moving parts involved with executing an effective throw. On practice days, especially during the outset of the season, coaches should have players begin the process from the kneeling position. Not only will this technique help players concentrate on proper mechanics, but it provides the coaching staff with an opportunity to facilitate effective fundamentals to the entire team. Coaches should help players maintain a release point with the elbow above the shoulder, proper follow-through, and four-seam grip on every throw.

When throwing from the standing position, players should be 10 to 15 feet apart while maintaining the mechanics from the previous activity. As their arms loosen, players should move further apart to stretch out the muscles and tendons. During this process, players should not strain or overthrow, but rather strive to effortlessly hit their target with each throw. Players receiving incoming throws should have their hands and arms raised above their heads to provide a clear, effective target. Accordingly, receivers should be in an athletic stance with their feet shoulder-width apart and the knees slightly flexed ready to move in any direction for an errant throw.

Administrative Time-Out

As discussed previously, to maintain healthy arms players may perform therapeutic band and other rotator cuff exercises. These drills can be completed individually or in an organized team set-up. Players can use their fielding gloves, light dumbbells, or tennis ball cans filled with sand as weights. Partner arm stretching and these preventative maintenance exercises can be performed immediately after the dynamic warm-up routine. On game days, coaches may choose not to have players complete these or plyometric training drills to save time and energy.

How far apart should players be during their throwing routine?

One technique for monitoring the distance that players throw is to place several cones on the ground 15 feet apart up to 150 feet as guidelines for players. Coaches can direct players to each cone as they see fit. This approach also creates a uniform throwing length for the entire team. Though different players will have varied levels of arm strength, coaches can allow these players to long toss during position specialization workout sessions or at the end of practice.

Partner Throwing Drills

After completing a daily throwing routine, players can work on position-specific drills with their partner. These drills should be performed from 10 to 15 feet apart and reinforce proper basic fundamentals. Infielders can roll each other balls that require certain footwork on backhand and glove side plays. A variety of flips can be rehearsed as well as pivoting. Outfielders should practice mechanics on ground balls for different game situations (see Chapter 6). Pop-ups from 10 feet away can be provided that require each outfielder to run at various angles and utilize specific footwork techniques. Similarly, this is an opportunity for catchers and pitchers to get repetitions on drills specific to their positions. Teams that possess an extensive coaching staff have the benefit of assigning a coach to each position's players to monitor the drills and fundamentals performed.

Topic of Debate: Assigning Throwing Partners

Some coaches mandate that throwing partners pair up based on position and arm strength. In this system, catchers throw to catchers, middle infielders throw to middle infielders, outfielders to outfielders, and so on. Proponents of this regiment believe that when players from similar positions work together, it is beneficial for discussing mechanical throwing techniques or basic footwork. For example, outfielders may work on a completely overhand arm slot and crow hop, while infielders are focused on a three-quarter arm angle and a shuffle step. In turn, if coaches choose to have players complete partner skill drills as a follow-up to the throwing routine, these player pairs will remain intact and not have to be reconfigured. Other coaches prefer not to be as structured in assigning specific throwing pairs.

Evaluating Players

An important skill for coaches to develop is acquiring an eye for talent. Not only should coaches be able to recognize a skilled player and envision how he can fit into the team concept, but also sense potential in a player. During initial workouts or practices, many athletes do not always stand out, even though they possess tremendous upside. It is the responsibility of a coach to survey talent and figure out how he can get the most out of athletes for the team's purpose. An unskilled player that arrives as a strong-armed right fielder may ultimately fill the role as the team's closer or back-up catcher. While it would be ideal to have *five-tool players* on the team roster, the reality is that few players possess exceptional skills in all aspects of the game. Consequently, coaches must be open-minded and creative thinkers when evaluating player talent.

Assessing Player Ability

During player workouts or tryout periods, coaches can utilize the traditional five tools for assessing baseball talent. These "tools" of baseball include: hitting ability, arm strength, running speed, fielding skill, and hitting power. Coaches may consider other intangible factors such as player hustle, baseball instinct, and willingness to learn when filling in the team roster. Within team tryouts, coaches should develop a *cutting criteria* for making team roster selections that players and parents clearly understand. The criteria for making team cuts should rely largely on the five tools as well as intangibles that the coach deems relevant to team success.

 ## Conference Time

Coaches who manage teams with a limited roster usually have the unpleasant task of cutting players. In cases where a coach has worked with an athlete for several months or years, the task of informing him that he is not part of the team is difficult. Coaches may suggest that players not selected for the team try to find other teams to join. Sometimes, players can be put on a list or "taxi squad" in case active team members are injured or are removed from the team for academic or disciplinary reasons. Coaches may also inform players on which skills they need to improve before participating in another competitive, team tryout.

Typical One-Day Showcase/Open Tryout Activities

- Timed 60-yard dash in the outfield grass
- Throw from right field to third base
- Field ground balls from shortstop area and throw to first base
- *Catcher:* Pop time on throws from home plate to second base
- *Pitcher:* 15 to 20 pitches bullpen throwing session
- Full-field batting practice and/or five-inning scrimmage game

Note: Major League–affiliated organizations and other pro teams hold "invitation only" and "open" tryouts similar to this format. In many cases, as evaluators have dozens of players to assess, players can expect to wait for up to several hours before performing.

Major League Connection

Unlike high school and college tryouts, Major League spring training tryouts can last several weeks. In addition, professional coaches/officials have an opportunity to assess player abilities in numerous outdoor game settings. Despite this arrangement, pro organizations can struggle when making their final roster decisions.

 Administrative Time-Out

Regardless of a coach's criteria for the team selection process, he must be able support his decisions with clear, objective data for parents and administrators. Designing a scoring scale for players to be ranked throughout the tryout process is helpful. Scoring scales of 1 to 5 or 20 to 80 are common assessment ranges for grading player tools. In order to maintain objectivity, coaches can collect running speed times, line drive frequency rates during batting practice, and pop times on throws. Clipboards with charts of this data will aid coaches in logging information to make their decisions. If possible, coaches should videotape and bring qualified coaches to observe and provide feedback during tryouts.

 Topic of Debate: Communication With Players During Tryouts

Opinions vary on the best manner for coaches to announce which players have made the final team roster. Many coaches post a list of player names on the locker room door or bulletin board, while other coaches feel this method is too impersonal. Although it makes it easier for a coach to not have to face each player that he is not keeping on the team, the players do not receive any feedback as to why they have not made the cut. When extensive tryouts have been conducted where players invest physical and emotional energy to make the team, coaches may offer face-to-face meetings to provide detailed explanations.

 Conference Time

After selecting the team, coaches' evaluation duties are not complete. Players must continue to be assessed for playing time and effectiveness in specific roles. Coaches can meet with players soon after tryouts to review where they fit on the *depth chart* at their particular position. Frequently, players will have a different view of their role and proficiency than the coaching staff. As a result, coaches can continue to videotape practices and keep a scorebook to gather data during inter-squad practice games. This process will also assist when parents or school officials request a meeting to discuss an individual's playing time. Coaches can also create a depth chart, detailing player strengths and weaknesses for players to get signed by parents so roles are made clear as soon as the team has been selected.

How do tryouts and roster selections affect team morale?

After the tryout process, coaches must be cognizant of player attitudes. In some cases, players may be disappointed or disagree with a coach's roster decisions, especially if a friend is not selected. On another level, players may relax or lose their intensity after earning a team uniform. Coaches can explain that tryouts are a continual process that spans throughout the entire season. Otherwise, after the selection process certain players may become content or complacent.

Team Drills

When the daily warm-up, throwing routine, and position-specific drills have been completed, players are properly prepared to engage in full-team practice. Depending on the duration of specialized position drills, team-oriented activities can be focused on for the bulk of practice time. Team drills incorporate individual fundamentals and interaction with other players in a group setting. Many team drills deal with in-game strategies and proper communication for reacting to opponents' actions or other developments on the field.

Four-Man Square Drill

As an alternative or extension of partner throwing drills, coaches can assemble players in groups of four to work on various defensive skills (Figure 8-18). The mechanics focused on and players assigned should be organized according to position. Coaches can use their discretion as to which fundamentals to practice within the square configuration. Outfielders can perform crow hops and various ground ball situational strategies. Blocking, rolled out bunts, and throwing inside/outside with communication are activities a catcher can concentrate on. Pictured and described in Table 8-4 are a number of infield skills that all position players can practice in the four-man set-up.

Figure 8-18. Four-man square drill

Four-Man Drill Activity	Application to Game Situation	Points of Emphasis
Crow hop and throw	Infield/outfield footwork on throws	Compact, controlled, and balanced
Reverse pivot and throw	Infielders, pitcher pickoff at second base	Turn glove side on 180-degree turn.
Underhand toss	Double play, squeeze bunt at pitcher	Follow throw toward partner.
Backhand flip	Double play, fielded bunt play	Gain ground with the throwing-side leg.
Throwing from a knee	Double play turn at second base	Controlled, visible throw from ear
Run down toss	Run downs (one or more men on base)	Show ball; stay under control.
Bobble drill	Knocked down or misplayed balls	Quickly find the ball and four-seam grip.
Throwing on the run	Infield ground ball in the hole	Utilize legs to boost arm strength.

Table 8-4. Four-man drill activities

Cut Drill

To build communication and quickness during cutoff plays, coaches can set players up in lines of four 20 to 50 feet apart depending on the age of the players. Players will practice making rapid, accurate throws up and down the line. When receiving, players should have their arms raised and turn toward their glove side as they catch and release the ball (see the Cutoff Plays section in Chapter 5). Coaches can put catchers and outfielders on the ends of each line, as they will only be throwing the ball to a cutoff man as they would in a game. Infielders should be placed in the middle of each line of four to work on a quick release and proper footwork. Coaches can make this drill into a competition in which the losing teams of four do push-ups or crunches after finishing slower than the winning team.

 ### In-Game Strategy: Fielders' Glove Sizes

Middle infielders customarily use smaller fielder's gloves so that they can get the ball out of their mitts as quickly as possible. Cutoffs and double plays require exceptional precision for optimum results. Infielders cannot afford the time to grasp for the ball in an oversized glove. The compact structure of a catcher's mitt reflects this point, as he must get the ball as fast as he can to throw out base stealers. First basemen and outfielders, on the other hand, use as large a mitt as allowed to maximize their chances of catching the ball. For these players, the speed of release is not as critical on most of their chances in the field.

Communication Drill

An excellent activity to foster positive communication and competency with fly ball defense is the communication drill. In setting up this drill, coaches should arrange the field or any playing area so that three outfielders and four infielders are ranging for pop-up fly balls. Coaches will need to be able to hit fly balls that land in between the infielders and outfielders. Doing so requires a soft touch by coaches, as they must find the proper loft and distance when hitting these fungos. When performing this drill, players will be able to practice priority and verbal commands.

At most levels of play, the centerfielder and shortstop have top priority on balls that two or more players call for. Outfielders who are running in on balls should have priority over infielders who are backpedaling or turning their back to run down a fly ball. When devising commands, players can use "Ball," "Mine, mine, mine," "Me, me, me," or whatever the team determines as their communication preference. Regardless of the command, when calling for fly balls, players must be loud and assertive. Furthermore, the timing of the verbal command is critical, as players should do their best to communicate early enough for other players to clear away.

Administrative Time-Out

Even though the communication drill is effective at preparing players for game situations, injuries can occur. Until the team learns how to work together on this important skill, collisions between players may happen. Another common occurrence is players acting tentatively for fear of colliding with teammates. As a result, fly balls may fall directly in between players as they each expect someone else to take charge. Conversely, coaches may need to speak with specific players who are overly aggressive on these plays.

Infield/Outfield Drill

At most levels of play, teams perform infield/outfield, or an *I/O*, for 10 to 20 minutes prior to the start of a game. This drill involves coaches hitting balls to players who must throw to specific bases as directed by their teammates. Infield/outfield provides players with an opportunity to learn the field conditions, strength and direction of the wind and sun, and other field dimensions. Additionally, defensive players are able to loosen up while also practicing verbal communications with their teammates. Many coaches hit a daily infield outfield at practice so that players can learn the pre-game routine and be conditioned to represent the team better on game day. Table 8-5 lists typical activities performed during an infield/outfield routine in sequential order.

How can coaches complete all of these I/O activities in 10 to 15 minutes?

Before starting the infield/outfield session, coaches must gauge several factors. Depending on the strictness of umpires and arrival time to the field, coaches may have more than 10 minutes for I/O. If 10 minutes is all that is permitted, coaches may elect to put only starting players on the field. Other options include not hitting as many balls or omitting some of the activities. Lastly, coaches must develop a fast pace for hitting fungos with a catcher quickly feeding them the balls.

Infield/Outfield Activity	Position(s) Involved	Point(s) of Emphasis
Outfielders field ground balls or fly balls and throw to second base.	LF, CF, RF, 2B, SS	Middle infielders line each other up for possible cutoffs.
Outfielders field ground balls or fly balls and throw to third base.	LF, CF, RF, 3B, SS, 2B	Third baseman lines up middle infielders for cutoffs.
Outfielders field ground balls or fly balls and throw to home plate.	LF, CF, RF, 3B, 1B, C	Catcher lines up third baseman and first baseman on throws.
Infield Star Drill: Infielders throw ball(s) in star-shaped configuration.	C, SS, 1B, 3B, 2B	Infielders practice quick release and shuffle step.
Pop-ups on infield	C, SS, 1B, 3B, 2B, P (option)	Verbal communication and learn wind/sun, priority system
Field ground ball, and throw to catcher.	3B, SS, 2B, 1B, C	Catcher works on force/ tag play.
Field slow roller, and throw to first base.	3B, SS, 2B, 1B (throw to 3B)	Practice throwing on the run.
Field up on grass, and throw to catcher.	3B, SS, 2B, 1B, C	Infield in situation, quickness
Groundball double plays	3B, SS, 2B, 1B, C	Make sure of getting first out.
Field backhand deep on infield dirt.	3B, SS, 2B, 1B	Set feet, make strong throw
Field, throw to first base, and cover the base.	3B, SS, 2B, 1B, C	Catcher throws down to bases.
Field (3) ground balls; throw (1) to catcher, (2) to 1B, and (3) to catcher.	3B, SS, 2B, 1B, C	First base throws (2) ball to 3B; catcher rolls out (3) ball.

Table 8-5. Infield/outfield format

 Administrative Time-Out

Throughout the outfield portion of I/O (throws to second and third base), coaches can have catchers and first basemen work on *roll-outs* (bunt and dropped third-strike plays) fielded by the catcher and thrown to first base. Coaches can hit ground balls or throw scoop plays for first basemen as well. During infield, a reliable coach or pitcher should provide outfielders with fly balls from the outfield line. Routinely, the starting pitcher warms up in the bullpen with a catcher, while another catcher runs the on-field I/O. Catchers are the team leaders and communicators during the I/O.

Batting Practice and Situational Hitting Drills

When devising a batting practice, coaches must consider how to make the activity energetic and productive. Too often, batting practice involves a coach throwing to one hitter with 15 or more players standing around watching. To avoid this downtime, coaches should prepare an organized, rotating system where players perform a number of drills aside from hitting in the batter's box. Assistant coaches or pitchers can aid in this process by hitting fungos to fielders in between pitches to the batter.

Coaches can design batting practice with a one-man rotating system or in hitting groups of three to four players. In either case, hitters should be required to do more than simply swing. Different bunts should be properly executed along with a hit-and-run. Hitters should also attempt to move a runner over from second to third base by hitting a ground ball to the right side. With a runner on third base, coaches can have hitters execute either a sacrifice fly or suicide squeeze bunt to score the runner. After completing these tasks, if time permits, hitters can take several free swings.

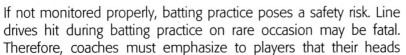 **Administrative Time-Out**

If not monitored properly, batting practice poses a safety risk. Line drives hit during batting practice on rare occasion may be fatal. Therefore, coaches must emphasize to players that their heads should be *on a swivel* at all times and to never turn their back on the hitter at home plate. Although coaches may fungo balls in between pitches, players must refocus on the batter as the pitch crosses the plate. Habitually, players will mistakenly take their eyes off the batter to chat with other teammates. Safety screens are costly and cumbersome, but provide protection to the batting practice pitcher and other players performing drills.

Teaching Tip

After players complete their round of hitting, they should run the bases and react to the next hitter's batted balls. This technique helps players work on realistic baserunning reactions to game situations, while hitters also attempt to execute their task with a runner(s) on base. Furthermore, defensive players get many opportunities during batting practice from balls off the bat of hitters and fungos hit by coaches. The repetitions off hitters' bats are the most similar to live game action and greatly help build defensive effectiveness.

The sample batting practice in Figure 8-19 is designed so that all of the 18 players rotate after each hitter takes his swings. Coaches may select two or three players to rotate in as catcher for six to eight batters. Screens are set up so that fungos can be hit to infielders in between pitches and players can safely make throws to a protected first baseman. Oversized nets protect players when playing pepper and performing soft toss. Two players rotate to "shag man" (#9 and #10 in Figure 8-19), where each will help a coach who is throwing batting practice or hitting fly balls to outfielders. In both cases, the player will feed or

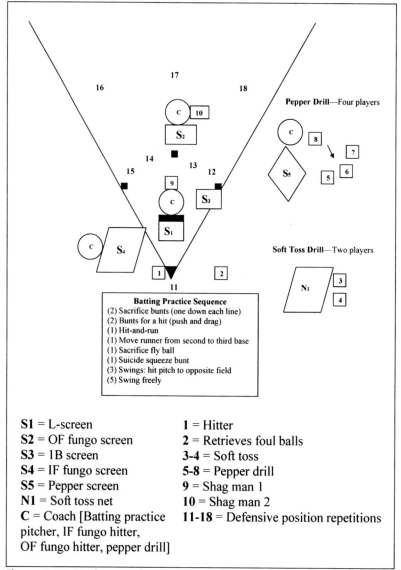

Figure 8-19. Batting practice sequence

flip balls to the coach and have a bucket for balls thrown in from the fielders. Players in this role must always be safely behind the protective screens.

Double Cut Drill

Fly balls that are hit to the deepest parts of the field require more than one cutoff man to be retrieved and thrown back to the infield. Teams should practice the player positioning and movements for dealing with this important situation. Coaches can design fun competitions, where a ball bucket or bag is placed on each outfield foul line or in the gaps. Upon hearing a coach's command or whistle, players will sprint to the bucket and throw a ball to the cutoff man, who throws it to the second cutoff man before it is delivered to home plate. This drill requires two catchers, one for *lining up* or directing infielders on each side of the field. The group of players that retrieves the ball and gets it to their catcher fastest wins the competition. Figure 8-20 shows how the drill is set up.

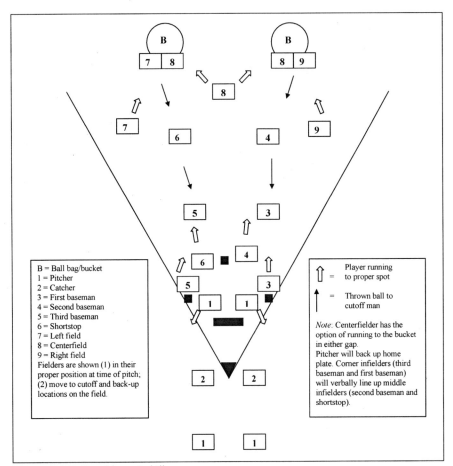

Figure 8-20. Double cut drill

Teaching Tip

In the double cut drill, pitchers should be taught to back up home plate for throws that get by the catcher. However, on double cut or single cut plays during games, throws may be directed to third base or home plate. As a result, pitchers need to run to a spot in between these two areas (in front of dugout steps) and react as the play develops to either base location. Pitchers should be instructed to get as close to the fence, backstop, or dugout as possible so they can get the optimum angle when backing up overthrown cutoff throws.

In-Game Strategy: Double Cut Plays to Third Base and Home Plate

Unlike the double cut drill, balls hit to the deepest parts of the outfield during a game will be on only one side of the outfield: the right field line or gap, or the left field line or gap. As a result, only certain players will be involved in executing the double cut, while the others can cover vacant bases. Specifically, on many well-hit balls, it is unclear whether the play will be to third base or home plate. Initially, catchers may direct the throw to home plate, but can quickly redirect to third base.

Defensive Situation Drills

An excellent activity for improving players' ability to anticipate developing plays, proper on-field positioning, and defensive skills is *situations*. Especially at younger levels, when players are first learning the various responsibilities at each position, defensive situations are valuable in preparing players for the realities of live game action. Coaches can set up this drill by placing nine players in the field and assigning several players to be the base runners. As the pitcher throws a pitch toward the catcher, the coach hits a ball in a random, yet calculated location to test the players' ability to handle the situation. With runners attempting to score on base hits, advance extra bases when possible, or steal bases, the defense is tested to communicate, back-up plays, implement cutoffs, and execute all facets of the game.

 Teaching Tip

Even though defensive situations are conducted in a full-team practice format, individual skills and repetitions are provided at each position. For example, this is an ideal time for pitchers to get their work off the game mound. On days in which certain pitchers are throwing bullpens, they can throw 15 to 20 pitches during these situations. Base runners can put pressure on the defense, practice recognition of signals, and learn their limits on the bases. Most of all, situations provide catchers with a unique opportunity to improve their decision-making and leadership skills.

Signals and Nonverbal Communication

Coaches must allocate a certain amount of practice time to rehearse signals with players. While signals may appear to be a minor or somewhat trivial aspect of team activities, these nonverbal communications are essential for synchronizing offensive and defensive strategies. These signals should not be introduced all at one time, but rather when appropriate activities are performed that coordinate with them. Moreover, a coach must make sound decisions when selecting which player(s) will relay his defensive signals to the other players.

Offensive Signals

 The signals that most players learn at an early age are basic offensive signals or *signs*. These signals are delivered faster and in a more complex fashion as players move up through various levels of baseball. Initially, players are provided elementary signals such as a touch of the sleeve for steal or a touch of the belt for a bunt. But, as players get older and opponents attempt to steal signs, coaches must devise more deceptive components for their signal system. This system can center on a certain number of touches to a specific body part, an *open* or *live (indicator)* signal with a closing *(confirmation)* signal, and an erasure or *wipe-off* system. Other more sophisticated techniques include assigning one hand/side of the body for fake or *dead* signals or creating a different, personalized indicator code for each player on the roster. The goal is for coaches to design a system that is easy for players to understand, relatively quick in delivery from the coaching box, and not easily detected by opponents.

Three Steps to Success ──────────────────────────────

1. Develop a signal system that is easy for players to remember and understand.
2. Make sure the signals can be delivered in an expedited manner (less than 10 seconds).
3. Incorporate spontaneous variations so that opponents cannot steal the signals.

Major League Connection ─────────────────────────────

In professional baseball, managers relay signals from the dugout to the third base coach (an assistant coach), who delivers them to the hitters. This approach is different from the high school level and below, where the head coach stands in the third base coaching box as the sole provider of offensive signals.

 Conference Time

Several players on the team may have learning disabilities, which can create difficulties for them to follow a complex signal system. Coaches should be aware of these players' limitations and make adjustments so that they can effectively *read the signs*. A one-on-one meeting with each player who struggles with team signals may be required to find out the specific issue a player may have with these communications. Captains or players who are proficient with team signals can be called upon to hold after-practice rehearsal sessions for struggling players.

Defensive Signals

During each game various scenarios arise that require teams to use a signal system on defense. Whether it is a bunt situation or when runners are on first and third base, coaches and players must communicate which tactics will be utilized to defend the play. Many teams have the catcher stand in front of home plate and go through a series of signals to alert the team which orchestrated play is planned. In some cases, the third baseman or shortstop delivers the signals. Given that the catcher is closest to the coach and faces all eight defensive players, it is logical for him to handle as much of these duties as possible. Catchers will randomly touch various pieces of their body or equipment several times to signal for a specific strategy in a given situation. Listed in this section are several scenarios in which the defense coordinates a rehearsed play.

Runners on First and Third Base

With runners on first and third base, defenses must strategize for an attempted steal of second base. At the professional level, the catchers and middle infielders possess arms that are strong enough so runners cannot easily advance on a catcher throw to second base. At lower levels of play, offenses can create overthrows, balks, errors, and more by stealing second base with a runner on third.

In-Game Strategy: First and Third Situations

One tactic that catchers will use in a first and third scenario is a fake throw to second base with the hope of nabbing the runner off third. Offensive teams may implement an *early break* or *extended lead play*, where the runner on first base will try to draw a throw from the pitcher to score the runner from third base. Another strategy for getting a run home is to have the base runner on first base steal but stop 10 to 15 feet before second base to draw a throw. These plays are tactically used with two outs and/or two strikes on a weak hitter. In all cases, defenses must practice defending these offensive strategies with *walk-through* sessions (Table 8-6).

Strategy of the Defense	Reasoning Behind the Play
Catcher throws straight through to second base.	Team is several runs ahead, and the run is not important; slow runner at first base and/or catcher possesses strong throwing arm.
Catcher throws toward second base; shortstop cuts the ball off on the infield grass.	Close game; try to cut down runner on third base; fast runner on first base; doubtful throw out at second base.
Catcher throws directly to third base.	Close game; runner on third base is overly aggressive; low chance of throwing out runner at second base.
Catcher throws to the pitcher.	Close game; low chance of throwing out runner at second base; pitcher may nab runner off third base.
Catcher does not throw (eats ball).	Close game; no risk taken.
Catcher throws to second base; shortstop fakes cutting off the ball on the infield grass.	Keep runner on third base at bay; high chance of throwing runner out.

Table 8-6. First and third defensive strategies

Runner(s) on First Base and/or Second Base (No Outs)

With no outs and men on first and/or second base in a close game, offensive teams will routinely sacrifice bunt. These *bunt situations* must be practiced by teams so that they can effectively defend the bunt, especially in pressure games. Many players tense up, fumble the bunt, or make an errant throw. By preparing a game plan for handling these situations, players will demonstrate more poise and confidence in combating the offensive team's tactics.

Conference Time

Coaches should review with catchers when to direct the infielders to throw to a particular base. First base represents a safety valve in case the play at the lead base is too challenging. Factors that should be considered by the catcher include the speed of the lead runner, effectiveness of the bunt, throwing arm of the fielder, and the specific game situation. Practice time and game experience will help catchers gain proper instincts and decision-making on these pivotal, game-changing bunt plays.

Strategy of the Defense	Reasoning Behind the Play
Infielders hold their position.	Team is several runs ahead; getting any out is the strategy.
Infielders rotate in wheel or scissors motion play tactic.	Close game; attempt to cut down or hold the lead runner.
Infielders fake rotating, and pitcher throws pickoff to first or second base.	Cut down the runner who is expecting infielders to rotate.
Infielders hold position; first baseman or third baseman charges; pitcher covers first or third baseline.	Infielders lack speed or struggle executing wheel play; athletic pitcher and corner infielders.

Table 8-7. Wheel play strategies

Which bunt defense strategy should coaches implement?

In determining whether to utilize the wheel rotation play (Figure 8-21) or a less complex strategy (Figure 8-22), coaches must consider the athletic abilities of their infielders. Nimble, quick players can execute the wheel play much more adeptly than slower, less responsive fielders. Accordingly, if pitchers and first basemen are trained to be aggressive in charging bunts, defensive teams can adequately stifle an opponent's bunting game without rehearsing infield rotations or other movements.

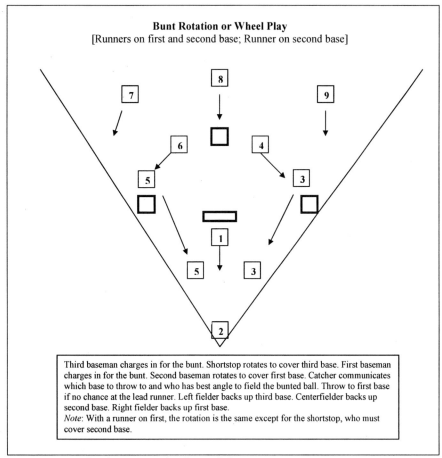

Figure 8-21. Wheel rotation play bunt defense

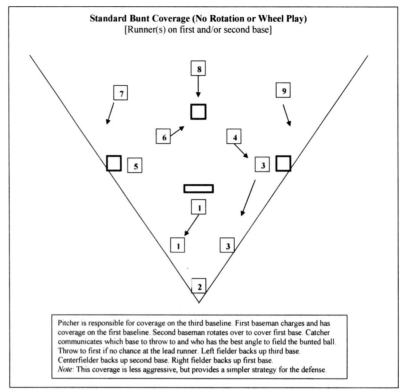

Figure 8-22. Standard bunt defense

Pickoff Throws to Second Base

When pitchers and defensive teams implement a pickoff to second base, three basic methods are used for relaying signals to all fielders involved in the play. Most commonly, the shortstop or second baseman will extend his arm out to signal that the pitcher should turn and fire a pickoff throw to second base (Figure 8-23). This play is coordinated by the pitcher and middle infielders only. In other cases, the catcher may signal for a pickoff throw to second base by putting down a sign or touching a part of his body/equipment as the pitcher comes to the set position. In this case, the catcher synchronizes the timing of the pickoff throw to the base by squeezing his glove closed or dropping his glove hand down. A final method is for the shortstop to go through a sequence of signals before each pitch to alert infielders of not only pickoffs, but also bunt coverage plays as well. Primarily, the coach relays these signals from the dugout to the catcher or shortstop.

Topic of Debate: Calling Pickoff Plays

As with many coaching decisions, views differ on how much autonomy coaches should give their players in making on-field decisions. By calling pickoff plays (and bunt defense coverage) from the dugout, coaches can control the game. Some coaches believe that players should have more freedom in coordinating pickoff plays on their own. These coaches do not try to micromanage the game and trust their players to make responsible judgments; however, the shortstop or catcher may get overzealous and put on too many pickoff plays, which can lead to overthrows or disturb the pitcher's rhythm.

Figure 8-23. Shortstop signals for a pickoff to second base

Pitch Signals

Catcher signals at the youth level consist of showing one, two, or three fingers from the signal stance, squatting position. But, as the player's level increases, catching signals become more complex. For instance, catchers will flash up to five signals, not including location or pickoffs/pitchouts. Furthermore, with base runners on second base, catchers use a variety of sequences to make their signals more deceptive so that the runner on second base cannot steal the pitches and relay them to the batter.

At the high school, college, and professional levels, many coaches relay pitch selections to the catcher from the dugout area. These signals are usually comprised of touches to the nose, chin, ears, or other facial areas to specify a pitch and location (Figure 8-24). Recently, some coaches have started to use wrist or forearm bands with typed numbers as seen on NFL quarterbacks. These bands enable a coach to call out or signal a series of numbers, which correspond to a particular pitch and location for the catcher to relay on to the pitcher.

Figure 8-24. Relaying signals

Table 8-8 shows some typical signals that catchers flash pitchers. It should be noted that with men on base, after communicating with the pitcher regarding which one is live, catchers may flash a series of signals. For example, the second signal in a series of five that are displayed may be the live one. Also, catchers may set up a fake signal for the pitcher to shake off or switch pitches to outthink the hitter. Recently, many professional teams are implementing a hold signal whereby the pitcher holds the stretch position until the batter calls timeout to disturb the baserunner(s) and hitter's timing.

Catcher Signal/Movement	Pitch or Command to Pitcher
One finger straight down	Fastball (pitcher or catcher may signal for two- or four-seam)
Two fingers straight down	Curveball, slider, or other breaking pitch
Three fingers straight down	Third pitch (split finger, knuckle ball, sinker, etc.)
Four fingers straight or wiggling	Change-up
Thumb extended out	Pickoff to first base
Pinkie extended out	Pickoff to first base or location
Five fingers	Pickoff to second base
Clenched fist	Pitchout
Clenched fist and shake of head	Shake off signal ("No") and hold the stretch position
Touch or tap right leg	Location: outside (right-handed batter)
Touch or tap left leg	Location: inside (right-handed batter)
Point down or touch dirt	Location: down in zone or in dirt
Circular motion with finger	Location: up in zone
Touch mask, chest, or knees	Location
Extend both hands toward the pitcher	Step off the pitching rubber
Both arms extended to the side	Throwing down to second base (in between innings)

Table 8-8. Catcher signals

Miscellaneous Signals

Players may use nonverbal, universal baseball signals to signify defensive alignment, number of outs, and other rehearsed plays. While each team has its own personalized signs, many signals are commonly used by players and coaches throughout the game. In some cases, verbal commands are used to signal for a synchronized trick play. For example, a coach may yell "Guard the lines" or "Good wheels on base," which may call for the team to use their hidden ball trick play on the runner at third base. Even though these verbal cues are infrequent, coaches should be aware that these less-subtle directives may signal that a pickoff play is coming. Table 8-9 provides some examples of nonverbal signals used by players and coaches during games.

Signal/Movement	Command
Fingers extended above the head.	Number of outs in the inning
Pitcher points to the shortstop or second baseman.	Throwing to second base on come-backer
Pitcher points to the backstop.	Location of wild pitch/passed ball
Pitcher points upward in the air.	Location of pop-up on infield
Pitcher shakes his head.	Wants a different pitch selection
Catcher picks up or throws a handful of dirt.	Throwing behind the runner on base
Second baseman closes his lips/mouth.	Second baseman covers base on a steal.
Second baseman opens his lips/mouth.	Shortstop will cover base on a steal.
Third base coach points to the dirt, moving fingers.	Base runners read a ball in the dirt.
Third base coach moves hands horizontally.	Base runners must freeze on line drives.
Third base coach raises both hands upward.	Stand up; do not slide.
Third base coach waves both hands to the ground.	Slide; get down.
Third base coach waves arm in a circular motion.	Round the base; keep running.
Base coach points to the base.	Stay on the base.
Bullpen coach lifts hat off his head.	Relief pitcher is warm/ready to pitch.
Coach points at ground/toward the sky.	Fielder(s) move in/back.

Table 8-9. Nonverbal signals

Fielder Positioning/Movements

On every pitch of the game, all nine defensive players should be moving. Whether it is reading the location of a pitch, bat angle of the hitter, or flight of the ball off the bat, every defensive player should react as each pitch crosses the plate. In turn, as plays on the bases develop, fielders must be in motion backing up throws and teammates. Various situations in games require specific player movements and back up duties. Table 8-10 shows each position's back-up responsibilities.

Teaching Tip

When helping players understand their responsibilities for backing up bases and throws, coaches must stress anticipation. If players can envision how each game situation quickly turns into another, based on where and how the batter hits the ball or runner(s) run, then they will be more prepared to be in the proper back-up location. Moreover, by

Position of Player	Back-Up Responsibilities/Positioning
Pitcher	Outfielder and cutoff throws to home plate and third base; cover home plate on wild pitch/passed ball with runner on third base.
Catcher	Throws to first base on infield ground balls; outfielder throws to first base on force outs; right fielder to first base.
First baseman	Outfielder throws to second base; throws from third baseman to pitcher with men on base.
Second baseman	Throws from catcher to shortstop on stolen base attempts; throws from catcher to pitcher with men on base after each pitch.
Shortstop	Throws from catcher to second baseman on stolen-base attempts; throws from catcher to pitcher with men on base after each pitch.
Third baseman	Throws from right fielder to second base; throws from first baseman to pitcher with men on.
Left fielder	All plays at third base; fly balls and ground balls to centerfielder.
Centerfielder	All plays at second base, including pickoffs/stolen-base attempts; fly balls and ground balls to corner outfielders.
Right fielder	All plays at first base, including pickoffs/throws from catcher and third baseman; fly balls and ground balls to centerfielder.

Table 8-10. Back-up responsibilities

teaching these anticipation skills, players will be always moving and more active throughout the game. This approach will help younger players who may find the pace of baseball overly slow or boring at times.

When considering all of the coaching duties that must be fulfilled in managing a team, it is important for head coaches to acquire reliable assistant coaches. At the youth level, most coaches are parents volunteering their time to help their children. The baseball background of assistant coaches will inevitably vary, but if the head coach provides guidance and feedback to these assistant coaches, consequently he can groom them effectively. By providing these "assistants" with helpful baseball resources and directing the proper manner with which to teach athletes, coaches will be able to share the coaching experience with peers. Ultimately by delegating numerous responsibilities to qualified assistant coaches, head coaches can maximize time and develop a comprehensive approach to running practice.

As mentioned, baseball coaches must find the proper balance between teaching basic fundamentals, preparing in-game strategies, and providing players with an adequate number of skill repetitions. The challenge is to keep this balance while also maintaining high energy and interest among players. Building various skill-based competitions into the daily practice routine will help keep team members focused. Although it would be ideal if all players possessed an intrinsic motivation to play baseball, the reality is that many talented athletes (especially at the youth level) are more attracted to faster paced sports, such as basketball, football, and soccer. Hopefully, as coaches become more innovative in their approach to designing baseball practices and team philosophy, the finest athletes will be lured to the sport.

Sources/Further Reading

[1]Thinkexist.com; 1999-2010. February 12, 2010.

Winkin, J. (1995). *Maximizing Baseball Practice*. Champaign, IL: Human Kinetics.

ATHLETIC DEVELOPMENT AND TRAINING

You gotta be careful with your body.
Your body is like a bar of soap. The more
you use it, the more it wears down.
—Dick Allen[1]

Chapter 9

Arguably, during the past few decades the greatest change in professional baseball is the time contemporary players devote to strength and speed training. Given this fact, viewpoints differ on appropriate training methods for baseball players to improve on-field performance. As a result, a dramatic increase has occurred in the prevalence of literature, retail products, and training facilities with strength coaches for athletes of all sports to utilize. While generalized weight lifting and speed programs have been a part of college and professional players' practice regiment for many years, sport and position specific drills are more widespread than ever. In an attempt to gain an edge on the competition, players and coaches at all levels of play are implementing some form of physical conditioning in combination with baseball-oriented training.

Topic of Debate: Age for Players to Begin Strength Training

Many parents have concerns about their child lifting weights at an early age, which may have harmful effects on body development. While strength coaches universally dismiss the notion of "stunting growth" with adolescent lifting activities, players can try alternatives to traditional weight lifting. By using therapeutic bands for resistance training, plyometric drills for explosive speed enhancement, medicine ball drills, balance focused exercises, and other activities without weights, athletes can train for strength and speed at any age.

When designing strength and conditioning programs for players, several considerations must be taken into account. Much like planning a baseball skill-oriented practice, coaches must consider the time and facilities available to them. In addition, coaches must develop a program that revolves around the schedule of their sport season. By accounting for in-season, out-of-season, and pre-season conditioning workouts based on the calendar year, coaches will need to vary the intensity, duration, and frequency of training activities. During their competitive season, this concept of *periodization* is critical to helping athletes attain peak fitness levels and performance. Furthermore, athletes may get bored or burned out by completing the same workout for too long. Therefore, varying strength and speed drills throughout the year helps keep players refreshed when approaching these activities. While the supervision of training activities is required initially, players will be able to master the proper mechanics and approach to training so that they can perform these activities independently several times weekly when their schedule permits.

Three Steps to Success

1. Design a program that varies based on the sport season and needs of the players.
2. Plan duration and frequency of workouts.
3. Consider issues of overuse with specific muscle groups and mental burnout.

Major League Connection

Although in recent years steroid use and other banned substances have dominated the media coverage of weight training among Major League Baseball players, various legitimate and innovative forms of training have emerged to help boost player performance.

Initial Testing and Evaluation

Before starting any strength, speed, or agility program, coaches should test their players to assess their baseline levels of ability, which may take two to three days depending on the age of players and complexity of the evaluation. For younger athletes, elementary activities such as push-ups, sit-ups, pull-ups, sprints of 60 to 90 feet, and more basic testing can be conducted. As players advance to the high school and college levels, coaches may choose to implement more sophisticated, technical assessments that are highly baseball specific in nature. Frank Spaniol at Texas A&M University has developed a baseball athletic test, shown in Table 9-1, designed to assess various athletic qualities among players.[2]

Baseball Athletic Test (BAT)	
Athletic Quality	*Test*
Body composition	Body fat percentage
Flexibility	Modified sit and reach
Muscular strength (grip strength)	Takai/Jamar grip strength dynamometer
Leg power	Vertical jump/standing broad jump
Rotational power	Rotary medicine ball toss
Agility	T-Test; shuttle run; Pro agility test (5-10-5)
Running speed	60-yard dash
Throwing velocity	(Five throws) MPH; flat ground; stretch position; 5 oz. baseball
Bat speed	(Five swings) MPH; line drives off batting tee; ATEC sport speed trainer
Batted-ball velocity	MPH

Table 9-1. Baseball athletic test

Administrative Time-Out

Regardless of the specific testing procedures that a coach designs, technological devices and equipment will be required. Whether it is a radar gun to check throwing or hitting velocities or a caliper used for body fat readings, coaches should be prepared with the necessary tools to conduct initial evaluations. Additionally, assistant coaches will be helpful in directing one or two of the testing stations to gather data. After gathering various types of data, coaches can assess where the team's weaknesses lie and determine how to focus their strength program. In turn, players and coaches can use these initial testing scores to track the progress and effectiveness of the training.

Multi-Purpose On-Field Training Exercises

For two to three days per week, players of all ages can practice various exercises designed to build strength, speed, and athleticism. A major advantage of these activities is that they can be set up on the outfield grass, a turf field, indoor gymnasium, or any space available, using minimal equipment. When working on these drills, coaches must be diligent to ensure that their players use proper form and mechanics. Otherwise, athletes will not experience the optimal benefits and possibly risk injury. Also, coaches should implement a wide array of drills so that different muscle groups are recruited and players maintain high levels of motivation throughout the workouts. As with any intense activity, players should not perform drills that target similar body parts on consecutive days.

Movement Preparation Exercises

When teams are warming up prior to a daily practice or game, it is common for players to complete some form of warm-up or routine before performance. In Chapter 8, a *warm-up routine* is provided. However, on days when time and/or space are limited, a more contained warm-up regimen may be fitting. In particular, when preparing to workout within a weight room setting, a more stationary or less extensive warm-up is appropriate. L.I.F.T., a progressive athletic development training organization in Rye, New York, lists the following guidelines for performing a movement preparation program[4]:

- Movement preparation (MP) should precede any and all activities.
- MP routines should be approximately 5 to 10 minutes long.
- Each exercise should be performed for 10 to 15 yards (or 10 to 15 reps each side).
- Progression is key: always start with less demanding exercises (e.g., walks) to more demanding coordination exercises (e.g., skips, runs, and shuffles).
- Most MP exercise progressions should work up the kinetic chain (ankle → knee → hip → torso → upper-body extremities → neck).
- Do exercises in all planes and directions.

Figures 9-1 through 9-10 illustrate 10 traditional movement preparation exercises, which can be performed in a single set at a distance of 10 yards or stationary.

Figure 9-1. Cocky walk

Figure 9-2. Calf stretch

Figure 9-3. Hand walk

Figure 9-4. Tin soldier

Figure 9-5. Lateral lunge

Figure 9-6. Spiderman

Figure 9-7. Wood choppers

Figure 9-8. Split squat with a twist

Figure 9-9. Sumo squat

Figure 9-10. Sumo squat to stand

Preventative Maintenance Exercises

After completing a warm-up, players should perform a variety of drills that are aimed at preventing injury, known as prehab, which targets both the upper and lower extremities before intense strength training or on-field performance occurs. Each exercise should be performed for 30 seconds continuously with no rest in between exercises. Players must understand that the quality of each exercise is more important than the quantity completed. For the upper body, players should begin by using a light weight and progress. A dumbbell ranging from two to five pounds can be incorporated for high school players, while younger athletes can complete these exercises with no weight.

Lower Body Prehab Exercises

Six lower extremity activities are provided in Figures 9-11 through 9-16 for players to implement several days per week. These exercises focus on walking with a band attached just above the ankle area. The three elastic band exercises should be performed in two sets for each activity at a distance of 10 yards. By focusing on the hips and buttocks, these drills target the major baseball-specific, muscle areas. After completing the first three lower-body exercises, players can complete three sets of a leg circuit with a 90-second rest in between each set. The leg circuit is comprised of 18 two-foot hurdle hop repetitions, 10 lateral box jumps, and 12 lunge jumps.

Figure 9-11. Lateral band walk

Figure 9-12. Forward band walk

Figure 9-13. Backward band walk

Figure 9-14. Micro hurdle hops

Figure 9-15. Lateral box/hurdle jump

Figure 9-16. Lunge jumps

Upper Body Prehab Exercises

Figures 9-17 through 9-28 illustrate 12 shoulder-specific prehab exercises for players to perform before weight training or a baseball-based practice when time permits. These shoulder drills should take a total of six minutes to complete with 30 seconds spent on each exercise. Given the time constraints in season, coaches will have to implement lower and upper body prehab drills on an intermittent basis. Coaches may require players to carry a light dumbbell or tennis can filled with sand in their equipment bag for performing these shoulder-focused, injury-prevention drills.

Figure 9-17. Shoulder shrugs

Figure 9-18. Front raise

Figure 9-19. Side lateral raise

Figure 9-20. V-raise

Figure 9-21. Front raise (fly)

Figure 9-22. Shoulder rotation 90 degrees

Figure 9-23. Palms (down/down)

Figure 9-24. Palms (down/up)

Figure 9-25. Palms (up/down)

Figure 9-26. Shrug with retraction

Figure 9-27. Side rotation

Figure 9-28. Triceps press

Medicine Ball Drills

Medicine balls are available in different weights so that coaches can use training balls that are age-appropriate. Even among athletes of similar ages, it is advisable for coaches to acquire balls of varied weights for certain drills that may incorporate more major muscle groups as opposed to drills that isolate smaller muscles. During in-season practices, station drills are opportune times to work on medicine ball drills. A major advantage of medicine balls is that baseball-specific motions can be performed while building strength. For example, a number of drills utilize the hips through swinging and throwing actions with the arms which enable players to use a full range of motion with the medicine ball, unlike many other weight room based or strength activities.

Overhead Throw (Figure 9-29)

Points of Emphasis:
- Utilize the hips as if throwing a baseball.
- Stride into a lunge power position.
- Drive off the back leg.
- Get over the front leg when releasing ball.

Figure 9-29. Overhead throw

Rotational Throw (Figure 9-30)

Points of Emphasis:
- Keep the knees bent.
- Twist straight across (do not drop the arms).
- Maintain arms parallel to the ground.

Figure 9-30. Rotational throw

Seated Throw (Physio/Swiss Ball) (Figure 9-31)

Points of Emphasis:
- Keep the feet planted on the ground.
- Maintain arms parallel to the ground when throwing.

Figure 9-31. Seated throw (physio/Swiss ball)

V-Sitting Position (Figure 9-32)

Points of Emphasis:
- Twist while keeping the legs still.
- Maintain tight abdominals.
- Be quick.
- Use a medicine ball or a weight/dumbbell.

Figure 9-32. V-sitting position

Explosive Power Drills

Baseball is a sport where players utilize ground forces to create explosiveness. Whether hitting, throwing, or performing most all on-field activities, players want to be as explosive as possible. In particular, players must derive this force from their hips. Exercises such as the squat jump and split squat jump help develop explosiveness in the hip regions of the body.

Squat Jumps (Figure 9-33)

Points of Emphasis:

- Use arms to trigger the drill.
- Swing arms up and down.
- Be explosive.

Figure 9-33. Squat jumps

Split Squat Jumps (Figure 9-34)

Points of Emphasis:

- Explode up with the arms.
- Land in a controlled, balanced position.
- Jump off the front leg.

Figure 9-34. Split squat jumps

Rapid Response Speed Drills

In addition to team-oriented plyometric drills, players can perform other quickness-based exercises to develop fast twitch muscle fiber. By enhancing these muscle fibers, players will improve their reactive ability and speed on the field.

Line Jumps (Forward/Back) (Figure 9-35)

Points of Emphasis:
- Keep the feet hip-width apart.
- Jump; do not shuffle.
- Keep the weight on the toes.

Figure 9-35. Line jumps (forward/back)

Hip Twists (Figure 9-36)

Points of Emphasis:
- Rotate the hips.
- Do not run in place.

Figure 9-36. Hip twists

Line Jumps (Lateral) (Figure 9-37)

Points of Emphasis:
- Keep the feet hip-width apart.
- Jump; do not shuffle.
- Weight stays on the toes.

Figure 9-37. Line jumps (lateral)

Balance Training Drills

A number of balance centered drills, including the single-leg squat and single-leg squat jump, improve player balance and *proprioceptive* ability, the body's unconscious perception of movement and spatial awareness. Hitting, pitching, running, and various baseball skills require effective balance. Moreover, these drills have an additional benefit of strengthening the ankle and knee joints while also preventing injury.

Single-Leg Medicine Ball Catch (Figure 9-38)

Points of Emphasis:
- Stay balanced on a wobble board or mat.
- Do not lean or fall off to one side.
- Maintain an upright position with a slight bend in the knee.

Figure 9-38. Single-leg medicine ball catch

Single-Leg Squat Jumps (Figure 9-39)

Points of Emphasis:
- Drive/jump off the toes.
- Use the arms.

Figure 9-39. Single-leg squat jumps

Hurdle Drill (Flexion-Extension) (Figure 9-40)

Points of Emphasis:
- Stay upright with the upper body.
- Point the knee away from the body with the hurdle leg.
- Rotate the hip.

Figure 9-40. Hurdle drill (flexion-extension)

Hurdle Drill (Adduction-Abduction) (Figure 9-41)

Points of Emphasis:
- Stand tall.
- Do not lean over.
- Pump arms throughout the drill.

Figure 9-41. Hurdle drill (adduction-abduction)

Innovative Speed Training Exercises

A major flaw in baseball speed training is the linear nature of the workouts. Considering that base runners make rounding turns when running the bases, not enough speed training involves the *turning the corner* mechanics required on a baseball diamond. Ryan Crotin from the University at Buffalo has devised a number of curvilinear acceleration drills that focus on athletes running in a circular or snow cone–shaped configuration. According to Crotin, during game activity baseball players never attain maximal running speed velocity because athletes cannot reach peak running speed until 102 to 197 feet and baseball distances of 90 feet or less do not allow for such.[3] Given this data, alternative speed training activities that incorporate circular or turning actions better simulate on-field explosive sprinting.

Speed drills can be designed that require athletes to run in a circular direction. These curvilinear activities will prepare players for rounding bases and taking turns on base paths. By using cones in a gym or field area, coaches can stress the importance of learning proper body lean and beneficial mechanics for running on a curved angle in their baseball training (Figure 9-42).

Figure 9-42. Curvilinear speed drill

In addition to preparing players for the conditions of running the bases, coaches should devise workouts that foster acceleration. These acceleration training drills involve players quickly sprinting from a static position or a change of direction (Figure 9-43). For instance, players can start from a face down or kneeling position before getting up and sprinting to a line on the field. Change-of-direction drills are comprised of sprinting forward after jogging backwards or moving laterally in one direction just prior to the explosive action. Other acceleration drills involve a slow to fast motion. Before the athlete sprints to a designated location, these exercises may be initiated with a walk or jog.

Figure 9-43. Acceleration speed drill

Baseball players should perform explosive drills that train them to reach top running speed as quickly as possible (Table 9-2). By practicing proper footwork, pivoting, and powerful arm action in their speed training, players can enhance quickness. Likewise, players will view these drills as more game applicable than traditional running.

Speed Training Activity	Application to Baseball Game Activity
Curvilinear running drill(s)	Base runners rounding bases; pitchers covering first base; fielders taking curved routes to balls for optimal throwing angle
Sprinting from static position (kneeling/face down, etc.)	Hitters sprinting out of the batter's box; fielders reacting to batted balls; base runners advancing after diving or sliding into a base; fielders running down an overthrow when backing up a throw
Change-of-direction drill(s)	Fielders misreading a ball off the bat and changing their route/angle to the ball; base runners trapped in a run down situation; base runners getting back to a base on a line drive or tag-up situation
Slow to fast motion drill(s)	Stealing bases from a walking lead; fielders getting a jump on batted balls; base runners accelerating from a secondary lead

Table 9-2. Speed training drills

Weight Room: Lifts and Exercises

For high school, college, and professional players, the weight room provides an opportunity to build various baseball-specific muscle groups. Focusing on lifting exercises that simulate movements performed in a game will help players transfer the strength, balance, and physical coordination to the baseball field. Weight room training sessions may be limited to 45 minutes daily and four times weekly. By carefully monitoring the duration of these activities, coaches can guard against burnout and overuse injuries. Furthermore, by remembering to vary the workout routine every four to six weeks, to alter the number repetitions required for each exercise, and to keep periodization in mind, coaches can effectively design a 12-month strength program.

Lower Body Exercises

Sumo Dead Lift (Figure 9-44)

Mechanics to Focus On:
- Keep feet wide.
- Hold the bar close to the shins.
- Keep weight on the heels.
- Place hands inside the knees.
- Use an over/under grip on the bar.

Common Mistakes:
- Lifting the hips first
- Weight coming forward on toes
- Feet angling outward

Figure 9-44. Sumo dead lift

Hang Clean (Figure 9-45)

Mechanics to Focus On:
- Drive with the hips.
- Jump and squat.
- Shrug the shoulders.

- Get underneath the bar.
- Point elbows in the catch position.

Common Mistakes:
- Swinging the bar during the start
- Inducing a forward jump
- Leaning back

Figure 9-45. Hang clean

Back Squat (Figure 9-46)

Mechanics to Focus On:
- Keep the bar across the trapezoids.
- Keep weight on the heels.
- Maintain a deep sitting position.
- Keep the chest up.
- Look up at the ceiling.

Common Mistakes:
- Weight comes forward on toes
- Lifting the hips first
- Looking down
- Bar sitting on the neck
- Feet angling outward

Figure 9-46. Back squat

Romanian Dead Lift (Figure 9-47)

Mechanics to Focus On:
- Drop the hips back to the lower bar.
- Keep the bar tight to the body.
- Keep the knees slightly bent.

Common Mistakes:
- Rounding the shoulders
- Lifting with the back

Figure 9-47. Romanian dead lift

Lunges (Dumbbells) (Figure 9-48)

Mechanics to Focus On:
- Keep the shoulders back.
- Keep the chest up.
- Drop the back knee when stepping.
- Push off with the front heel.

Common Mistakes:
- Stride too short
- Too much weight on the front toes
- Leaning forward too much

Figure 9-48. Lunges (dumbbells)

Pitcher Squat (Figure 9-49)

Mechanics to Focus On:
- Keep the shoulders back.
- Keep the chest up.
- Drop the back knee straight down.

Common Mistakes:
- Letting weight go forward
- Pushing with the front toes

Figure 9-49. Pitcher squat

Leg Curls (Physio Ball) (Figure 9-50)

Mechanics to Focus On:
- Keep the hips up.
- Pull the ball in with the heels.
- Pull the ball in as far as possible.

Common Mistakes:
- Not lifting hips
- Not pulling ball in all the way

Figure 9-50. Leg curls (physio ball)

Step-Ups (Dumbbells) (Figure 9-51)

Mechanics to Focus On:
- Press up with the heels.
- Look up.
- Keep the chest up.
- Get the leg straight at the top of the step.
- Focus on the hips.

Common Mistakes:
- Pushing with toes
- Not getting the entire foot on the bench during the step up

Figure 9-51. Step-ups (dumbbells)

Calf Raises (Figure 9-52)

Mechanics to Focus On:
- Use the full range of motion.
- Get deep during each repetition.

Common Mistakes:
- Bending the knees

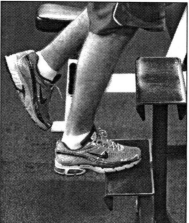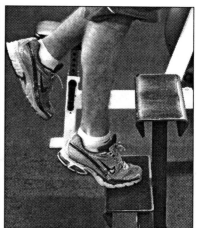

Figure 9-52. Calf raises

Teaching Tip

Important Tips for Spotting a Weight-Lifting Partner

- When using dumbbells, spot partner at the wrist or dumbbell (not at the elbows).
- When squatting, spotter should perform full squat behind with his hands at the partner's chest.
- Do not spot during cleans (let the partner drop the weight and fall back, if needed).
- Pay close attention, and be ready to provide immediate assistance.
- Communicate regarding proper/improper lifting form.

Upper Body Exercises

Dumbbell Push Press (Figure 9-53)

Mechanics to Focus On:
- Drop under the weight in a squat position.
- Get the arms straight at the top of the press/lift.

Common Mistakes:
- Feet get too wide in squat position
- Pushing with the arms first

Figure 9-53. Dumbbell push press

Dumbbell Bench Press (Figure 9-54)

Mechanics to Focus On:
- Flare elbows out to the side (not inward).
- Use the full range of motion when coming down.
- Get the arms extended on the way up.

Common Mistakes:
- Not using the full range of motion
- Short repetitions

Figure 9-54. Dumbbell bench press

Incline Press (Dumbbell) (Figure 9-55)

Mechanics to Focus On:
- Set the bench at a 30 degree angle.
- Use the full range of motion.
- Complete lift all the way to the top.

Common Mistakes:
- Not using full range of motion
- Short repetitions

Figure 9-55. Incline press (dumbbell)

One-Hand Snatch (Figure 9-56)

Mechanics to Focus On:
- Start with the dumbbell in between the knees.
- Keep the knees bent.
- Keep the chest over the dumbbell.
- Drive with the hips.
- Jump, and shrug the shoulders.
- Drop underneath the dumbbell.

Common Mistakes:
- Pulling with the arm
- Not dropping underneath

Figure 9-56. One-hand snatch

One-Arm Row (Figure 9-57)

Mechanics to Focus On:
- Keep the back flat.
- Pull up so the elbow comes above the back.

Common Mistakes:
- Dipping the shoulder
- Lowering the shoulder
- Twisting at the top

Figure 9-57. One-arm row

Pull-Ups (Figure 9-58)

Mechanics to Focus On:
- Maintain tight abdominal muscles.
- Use an overhand grip on the bar.

Common Mistakes:
- Swinging the legs

Figure 9-58. Pull-ups

Curl and Press (Figure 9-59)

Mechanics to Focus On:
- Curl up with the dumbbell facing inwards.
- Press up with the dumbbell facing away.

Common Mistakes:
- Swinging the dumbbell
- Not pressing all the way up to the top

Figure 9-59. Curl and press

Shoulder Raise (Front) (Figure 9-60)

Mechanics to Focus On:
- Keep the arms parallel to the floor.
- Keep the thumbs up.

Common Mistakes:
- Not getting dumbbell high enough

Figure 9-60. Shoulder raise (front)

Side Lateral Raise (Figure 9-61)

Mechanics to Focus On:
- Keep the palms down.
- Maintain a slight bend in the elbows.

Common Mistakes:
- Letting elbows drop
- Swinging arms to get weight up

Figure 9-61. Side lateral raise

External Rotation (Figure 9-62)

Mechanics to Focus On:
- Maintain a 90-degree angle with the elbows.
- Keep the elbows in one spot.

Common Mistakes:
- Not maintaining a 90-degree angle

Figure 9-62. External rotation

One-Hand Cable Pull (Figure 9-63)

Mechanics to Focus On:
- Make two distinct motions.
- Keep the arm parallel/level to the floor.

Common Mistakes:
- Making only one motion
- Pulling upward with cable

Figure 9-63. One-hand cable pull

Dumbbell Wrist Flexion/Extension (Figure 9-64)

Mechanics to Focus On:
- Use the full range of motion.
- Keep the forearms on the bench to stabilize and isolate the exercise.

Common Mistakes:
- Not utilizing a full range of motion

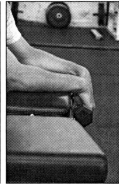

Figure 9-64. Dumbbell wrist flexion/extension

 Topic of Debate: Shoulders and Weight Lifting

Many coaches and players are hesitant to perform weight-training exercises where the lifts involve raising weight above shoulder height for fear of risking throwing arm injuries in the shoulder area. Nonetheless, most strength coaches are strong advocates of using weights above the shoulder level. Keeping lifts in front of the head and limiting the amount of weight may influence concerned coaches to consider above-the-shoulder weight training.

Core Training

All comprehensive sports fitness programs incorporate a segment for the core, or abdominal, pelvic, and hip regions of the body. In completing a *core workout*, players can perform specific strengthening exercises during practice time or on their own.

Athletes most commonly exercise two types of abdominal muscles in core training: the rectus abdominus and the transverse abdominus. While the rectus abdominus muscles look attractive when toned into a "six pack," they are not as crucial in athletic competition as the transverse abdominus. Culturally, the rectus abdominus have garnered the reputation to indicate physical fitness. Body builders helped promote this notion by displaying their clearly defined abdominal muscles during competitions and photo shoots. Yet, the transverse abdominus are the innermost flat muscles of the abdomen and more central to the performance of athletes.

Functional Push-Ups (Figures 9-65 and 9-66)

Typically, although push-ups are associated with upper body strength, functional push-ups are a useful activity for focusing on the transverse abdominus. Players will perform a traditional push-up while maintaining a flat back and balanced base position (first photos in Figures 9-65 and 9-66). As the athlete moves into the up position of the push-up, he takes his hand off the ground and utilizes a lateral rotation with the arm. The lateral rotation should be completed in alternating repetitions with each arm, which enables the abdominals to be targeted or *recruited*. Players should focus on rotating wide with the hand and keeping their feet close together (second photos in Figures 9-65 and 9-66). As the athlete develops body control with this exercise, the workout can implement a dumbbell. As with all strengthening drills, players must mentally focus to isolate the specific muscles that are being emphasized.

Figure 9-65. Functional push-ups (side)

Figure 9-66. Functional push-ups (front)

Pelvic Tilts

Pelvis tilts help strengthen the muscles in the abdominal region as well as the lower back. This exercise can be performed standing with the back against a wall or while lying on the floor. The most important aspect of this workout is that the player's back remains flat against whichever surface is being utilized. Athletes will rock their hips back so that the lower back presses against the surface of the floor or the wall. In essence, players should try to flatten their back and repress the natural curve of the spine. If standing, players will need to move their bodies down the wall. If lying down, the buttocks will not actually lift off the floor. Players should perform 10 to 12 repetitions while holding each for several seconds.

Front Planks

Players will get into the push-up position and put all of their weight on their forearms. It is important to keep the back straight and the buttocks down and level with the back. The plank position can be held for 30-second increments or more depending on the athlete's ability level (Figure 9-67).

Figure 9-67. Front planks

Side Planks

Players can also rotate the plank position to their side for a twisting core exercise (Figure 9-68). Much like the front plank, the side plank is an isometric drill for strengthening the abdominals, back, and shoulders. Isometric workouts require athletes to hold the same position without moving. Players should contract their abdominals and remember to breathe when performing any variation of planks.

Figure 9-68. Side planks

 When a player claims that he is too tired or sore to complete a conditioning workout, what should the coach do?

Coaches must be careful when conditioning their players. Safety must be the number-one priority. Many tragic incidents have occurred because athletes were overly exhausted or not in the proper physical shape to handle team fitness drills. Coaches have to use their judgment as to whether the player is sincere in his communication. If the coach has doubts, the player can complete the drills that he missed before or after the next day's practice.

Crunches

When working the abdominal muscles, players can do a variety of drills from the sit-up position. It is important for coaches to monitor these activities to ensure that proper form is used and players are being rigorously tested. The hands can be kept on the sides, behind the head, or crossed in the chest area. Players should not pull on their head. To increase the effectiveness of the crunch (Figure 9-69), players can push their chest and head up toward the sky. Players must not rush *the negative*, the motion back down toward the ground when fighting the pull of gravity. As with any workout, coaches should be creative in keeping these exercises challenging and fresh.

Figure 9-69. Crunches

Superman Abdominal Exercise

Doubling as a lower back and abdominal workout, Supermans require players to lie in a face down, reverse "V" position with their back (Figure 9-70). The torso, pelvis, and abdominal region are the only parts of the body touching the ground. Players must make sure not to roll their feet up or allow the hands to come back too far during the exercise.

Figure 9-70. Superman

Six Inches

A team-oriented, isometric exercise that tests abdominal strength is known as six inches. Players must lie flat on their back with legs extended and hands behind the head or under the buttocks. On a coach's command, they will lift their legs six inches off the ground and hold the position without dropping their legs (Figures 9-71 and 9-72). Coaches can have players go through a variety of motions with their feet, such as mini-circles, a flutter kick, or scissors to enhance the workout. This exercise can be used for three sets in 30- to 60-second intervals.

Figure 9-71. Six inches (side)

Figure 9-72. Six inches (front)

Designing a Training Schedule

When developing a four-day weekly training schedule, coaches should alternate between lower and upper-body muscles as well as linear core abdominal drills and twisting core abdominal drills (Table 9-3). This alternating daily routine will prevent overuse injuries and provide players with variety in their workouts. Each workout should consist of at least one "big lift," such as the dead lift, hang clean, back squat, or bench press. In addition, a *superset* that ordinarily contains three different lifting exercises and allows players to alternate lifting exercises can be part of each day's workout. In completing the workout, players should target their core strength by performing various activities focusing on the abdominal region of the body. An additional training component consists of speed and conditioning drills performed in a gym, track, or field area.

Conference Time

Coaches should meet with players to review guidelines for strength training. Given that players do not always lift weights in an organized team setting, several points must be emphasized before players enter the weight room. It is important for players to thoroughly warm up with some form of movement prep and prehab drills prior to starting the workout. Coaches must stress to players that this training is for baseball purposes, not body building. A strategy for highlighting this point is for players to perform dry hitting and pitching drills during or after the workout.

A diverse, controlled four-day speed and conditioning program is provided in Table 9-4 for coaches and players to implement within any season of their training program.[4]

Cool-Down (Static Stretching)

After completing their workout, players should perform a *cool-down*. This cool-down consists of stretching exercises in which the athlete holds each *static stretch* for 20 seconds. These stretches should be repeated three times on each side before switching to stretch the opposite side. Player movements should be slow and controlled. Traditionally, this static stretching was performed

Day 1 Schedule: Lower Body and Core Strength

Lifting Exercise	Sets	Repetitions
Sumo dead lift	3	6-8
Lunges	3	10-12
Leg curl	3	10-12
Pitcher squat	3	10-12
Calf raises	3	10-12
Front planks	3	30-50 seconds
Crunches	3	20-40
Supermans	3	30 seconds

Day 2 Schedule: Upper Body and Core Strength

Lifting Exercise	Sets	Repetitions
Dumbbell push press	3	6-8
Dumbbell bench press	3	10-12
Pull-ups (body weight)	3	10-12
Front raises	3	10-12
Side lateral raises	3	10-12
External rotation	3	10-12
One-hand cable pull	3	10-12
Side planks	3	30-50 seconds
Medicine ball rotation	3	25
Functional push-ups	3	12-15

Day 3 Schedule: Lower Body and Core Strength

Lifting Exercise	Sets	Repetitions
Hang clean	3	6-8
Back squat	3	8-10
Romanian dead lift	3	8-10
Step-ups	3	10-12
Front planks	3	30-50 seconds
Sit-ups	3	20-40
Six inches drill	3	20-30 seconds

Day 4 Schedule: Uper Body and Core Strength

Lifting Exercise	Sets	Repetitions
One-hand snatch	3	6-8
Incline dumbbell press	3	10-12
One-arm row	3	10-12
Curl and press	3	10-12
Dumbbell ext./flexion	3	10-12
Side planks	3	30-50 seconds
Medicine ball rotation	3	25
Functional push-ups	3	12-15

Table 9-3. Four-day weekly training program

Day 1

Speed (focus on run mechanic)	Sets	Recovery	Reps
10-yard sprints	1	10-yard walk	8
20-yard sprints	1	20-yard walk	6
40-yard tempo run *Increase speed every 10 yards, last 10 yards at 100%*	1	40-yard jog	4
Conditioning	**Sets**	**Recovery**	**Reps**
Shuttle run (6 x 25 yards)	1	90 seconds	3-4

Day 2

Conditioning	Sets	Sprint	Jog
100-meter sprints	5 or 6	100 meters	300 meters

Day 3

Speed (focus on run mechanic)	Sets	Recovery	Reps
10-yard sprints	1	10-yard walk	8
20-yard sprints	1	20-yard walk	6
40-yard tempo run *Increase speed every 10 yards, last 10 yards at 100%*	1	40-yard jog	4
Conditioning	**Sets**	**Recovery**	**Reps**
Ladder x 120 yards (0-10-20-30)	1	90 seconds	3-4

Day 4

Conditioning	Sets	Sprint	Jog
200-meter sprint	3 or 4	200 meters	200 meters

Table 9-4. Four-day speed and conditioning program

before a workout, but has since been replaced with a comprehensive warm-up, movement prep, or some other routine that fosters blood flow to muscles. Coaches must persist in requiring players to take the time to perform a cool-down since it is less exciting and takes place at the end of the workout. Ultimately, static stretching will increase muscular flexibility and reduce injury occurrence. Figures 9-73 through 9-80 illustrate eight stretches for players to perform after each workout session.

Figure 9-73. Lying hamstring

Figure 9-74. Lying figure four

Figure 9-75. Seated knee hug

Figure 9-76. Seated crossover

Figure 9-77. Standing groin

Figure 9-78. Standing biceps

Figure 9-79. Standing heel grab

Figure 9-80. Standing shoulder

Weighted Implement Training

By using precisely designed weighted bats and baseballs, players can train their bodies in a non-traditional manner. This activity is known as overload and underload resistance training. In theory, the goal of varied resistance training is to improve speed strength or power development. Research studies have shown that the variations in weight of the training implements should range from 5 to 20 percent lighter and heavier than the standard implements, baseballs, and bats. Lastly, a 2:1 frequency ratio of heavy or light implements to the standard implement should be implemented.

Coaches can have pitchers throw with balls that vary from the standard five-ounce regulation baseball. Consequently, staying within a twenty percent variance guideline, pitchers can train with baseballs weighing four or six ounces. In terms of hitting, players can utilize donut rings, metal bats that are underloaded/overloaded, weighted sleeves for the bat barrel, and other training devices to practice with a bat that provides overload resistance and a different weight than their game bat. Studies suggest that swinging overweighted or underweighted bats 240 to 600 times weekly for 6 to 12 weeks with an organized, well-designed plan increases bat swing velocity.[5]

It is imperative that coaches properly design and carefully monitor any activities with weighted implements. Otherwise, the training may be counterproductive and cause undue strain on players' bodies. In analyzing the results of dozens of studies involving pitching and hitting training with weighted implements, it is evident that over 90 percent of players demonstrate an increase in velocities.[5] It can be concluded that these improvements are the result of the weighted implement training or simply the inherent benefits gained from investing extra time to practicing and rehearsing effective pitching and hitting mechanics.

 ## Topic of Debate: Weighted Implement Training

Some coaches fear that pitchers using weighted balls may develop arm injuries. Also, a number of baseball experts claim that players change their mechanics when using a non-standard weighted bat or ball. For instance, swinging a lead pipe or throwing a 20-ounce baseball while maintaining proper fundamentals will be difficult. Proponents of weighted implement training claim that when used correctly and performed in a controlled setting, these instruments will not hamper player mechanics or harm athletes.

Seven research studies on weighted baseball throwing reported no arm injuries. Fleisig et al found no difference in the throwing mechanics among pitchers and also concluded that throwing with lighter, four-ounce baseballs reduced the risk of overuse injuries. DeRenne et al found no throwing injuries among 45 high school and 180 college pitchers who used weighted implements.[5]

Teaching Tip

Dr. John Bagonzi, a proponent of overload training with pitchers, believes that during the off-season weighted balls can be thrown every other day. He also advises throwing a regulation five-ounce baseball at least 20 times before starting overload drills. Bagonzi strongly advocates only using weighted balls with players involved in a regular throwing program. He also believes that using weighted balls as a form of overload training is effective when implemented in conjunction with resistance tubing drills and a systematic throwing program.[6]

Sources/Further Reading

[1]Dickson, P. (1992). *Baseball's Greatest Quotations*. New York: Harper Perennial. P. 9.

[2]Spaniol, F. (2009). "Baseball Athletic Test: A Baseball-Specific Test Battery." NSCA *Strength and Conditioning Journal*. 31(2). Pp. 26-29.

[3]Crotin, R. (2009). "Game Speed Training in Baseball." NSCA *Strength and Conditioning Journal*. 31(2). Pp. 13-25.

[4]L.I.F.T. *Athletic Development: Building the Complete Athlete*; Rye, NY. (Go2lift. com)

[5]DeRenne, C. & Szymanski, D. "Effects of Weighted Implement Training: A Brief Review." NSCA *Strength and Conditioning Journal*. 31(2). Pp. 30-37.

[6]Bagonzi, J. (2005). "Overload Training." *Collegiate Baseball*. 48(1). Pp. 6-7.

Feldenkrais, M. (1977). "Awareness Through Movement." www.feldenkrais. com

Santana, J.C. (2003). "Sport Specific Conditioning: The Serape Effect—A Kinesiology Model for Core Training." National Strength & Conditioning Association. Volume 25, Number 2, pages 73-74.

Santana, J.C. (2009). "Perform Better." www.performbetter.com.

PROGRAM CONSTRUCTION AND DEVELOPMENT

chapter 10

*Well, there are three things that the average man
thinks he can do better than anybody else. Build a
fire, run a hotel, and manage a baseball team.
I hope the average man is right in his thinking.
But I'm not cocky about my job.*

−Rocky Bridges[1]

Upon building a comprehensive baseball program, coaches must possess a clear vision of what they want to accomplish. This vision should center on how each coach defines success. Typically, winning championships has been the focus for many coaches. However, the vision of some coaches extends to teaching values and ethics to their players, fostering community awareness, or other off-the-field initiatives. Most coaches feel pressure to pursue success on the field before branching out in to other areas of emphasis. Regardless of the focus, coaches must hold a vision of what is important to them and where they are steering their program.

Goal Setting

When pursuing their vision, coaches should set short-term, intermediate, and long-term goals. These goals can be quantitative, such as attaining a specific number of victories, team grade point average, or amount of money fundraised. Qualitative goals may also be set to measure the program's accomplishments in underlying values. For example, improvements in team hustle and concentration at practice may comprise these types of goals. Coaches can collaborate with their assistant coaches and, in some cases, veteran players to establish the goals for the program. Nevertheless, it is the head coach who must tap into his own passion and vision to ultimately devise the goals for the program. Listed in Table 10-1 are several examples of goals for a baseball program.

Short-Term Goals (3-6 months)	Intermediate Goals (6 months to 1 year)	Long-Term Goals (1-3 years)
Win enough games to qualify for the playoffs.	Establish off-season athletic development program.	Win league championship. Advance to state tournament.
Implement throwing routine	Fundraise for an infield tarp.	Get a scoreboard (donation).
Maintain a team GPA of 3.0 or higher.	Plan a spring training trip.	Create a local baseball camp.

Table 10-1. Sample goal setting form

Although these goals may or may not be reached, performance and achievement are likely to rise in the pursuit of them. The estimated time period to reach benchmark levels of achievement can be extended if those accomplishments are not attained within a certain time frame (e.g., win a league title or entice local sponsors to donate a scoreboard within three years). Therefore, if coaches plan and strive to reach specific goals, the program is, at minimum, headed in a focused direction.

Positive Verbal Communication

Coaches should harness the skill of maintaining positive language and an upbeat persona with their players. Although a disappointing loss or lackluster team effort at practice may elicit negative comments and emotions in any coach, it is crucial to keep a positive outlook with young players. By consistently encouraging and highlighting player efforts, coaches will foster an enjoyable atmosphere for team members. *Coaches should try to be as optimistic as possible while also remaining realistic about team and player expectations.* The timeless expression "You can catch more flies with honey than vinegar," certainly applies to baseball players who prefer praise over criticism.

In particular, during a team losing streak or an individual player's batting slump, coaches should keep a positive approach. Recognizing all of the players' hard work and previous accomplishments can provide a boost during inevitable in-season low points. Too often when a team is struggling, a frustrated coach will angrily berate players who already feel poorly about their performance. Instead of simply venting, coaches should process their negative feelings with peers, and then approach their team in a more composed manner. They may even have to become "actors" by putting on different faces to motivate, re-energize, and maintain team spirit.

Topic of Debate: Yelling

Parents of players at the youth level may not approve of a baseball coach who yells at their child. While getting angry at a team a couple of times per season is commonplace, it may not benefit a coach to yell on a regular basis; otherwise, players will tune out the yelling and become desensitized to the coach's behavior. As opposed to emphatically stressing a point, yelling is a form of frustration, suggesting a lack of coaching skills. In louder, faster sports, such as football and basketball, yelling is more appropriate.

Parent Communication

Although many coaches dislike, or in some cases dread, communicating with players' parents, it is a part of the job. Maintaining a trust and strong rapport with parents can play an important role in players *buying in* or believing and supporting the program. Furthermore, fundraising efforts can be positively impacted by the efforts and generosity of families. At youth levels, parents are pivotal in contributing with transportation, team gatherings, field permits and maintenance, and as assistant coaches.

Administrative Time-Out

Coaches should hold a pre-season parent meeting to set a protocol for appropriate communications with the coaching staff via email, phone, and in-person interactions. This gathering provides coaches with an opportunity to review their own philosophy of coaching baseball and what parents can expect from them. In addition, it is essential for coaches to inform parents of acceptable ways they can express their unhappiness with a specific aspect of the program. This parent meeting is also essential for reviewing guidelines of proper game/practice behavior and conduct.

While it would be ideal if all parents and fans were able to keep their emotions under control and set a good example for the players, it is not always the case. Public cursing, fighting, and verbal hostilities are ugly occurrences within youth baseball that must be addressed. As players move on to higher levels of play, many coaches discourage in-game player communication with parents or fans. Even an innocuous act, such as dropping off a piece of equipment or sports drink during a game, may be deemed unacceptable by coaches. In turn, it is imperative that coaches inform parents and players of their expectations so that they do not overstep these boundaries. *Coaches must be cognizant of and make a strong effort to objectively judge each player based on merit and not the positive or negative behavior that his parents display.*

 Is a coach required to respond to parent phone calls, emails, and questions?

At the high school level and below an expectation exists that coaches will return parent phone calls. Given that at these levels players still live at home as dependents, coaches should communicate with parents. Even so, coaches can set guidelines for the appropriate time, place, and topics that they are willing to discuss. For example, the discussion of playing time or the abilities of other team members may be determined as off-limits.

Equipment

During the pre-season and post-season, coaches should take a detailed inventory of team equipment. Notes should be compiled regarding quantity, size, and condition of team items. Baseballs comprise the largest component of any program's annual equipment budget. While certain items tend to be purchased and need to be replaced every few years, practice and game baseballs are an expensive entity purchased annually. For other more durable items, such as uniforms, field tools, and screens or nets, coaches may want to gradually acquire these pieces. Ultimately, coaches should create two lists: one detailing immediate needs, and one describing long-term wants. Much like goal setting, coaches must view acquiring equipment in terms of priority and time frame.

In some cases, equipment can be secured through *bootstrapping* or obtained free of cost from teams at higher levels. College teams may have an old set of catcher's gear or an L-screen that they plan to discard. Many local sports stores may be willing to provide teams with discounts on gear or possibly make a donation of equipment with the hope of attracting future team business. Some large chain stores are unwilling to participate in such a program; however, smaller community-based retail shops are more likely to help local teams.

Promoting Your Program

An important off-the-field component of successful baseball programs is an effective marketing plan. Similar to any business that promotes itself through a website, bumper stickers, and flyers, coaches should develop a game plan for creating awareness of their program. This awareness will help with fundraising efforts and direct positive attention to the team. An assistant coach or teacher in the school may be willing to take control of this necessary component. Specifically, high school marketing or entrepreneurship teachers may be willing to incorporate this task as part of a class or individual project. In conjunction with this effort, a photographic *booster yearbook*, calendar, or media guide filled with local advertisements is a terrific vehicle for promoting the team while also raising money.

In addition, coaches should establish relationships with local newspaper and television stations. Not only will this publicity help players gain better exposure, but these media sources will be instrumental in promoting philanthropic and fundraising events. Similarly, coaches can connect within the school system by creating public address announcements and posters to increase game attendance and team events. Furthermore, this connection will build a sense of pride among team members knowing that game highlights and progress are relayed to their schoolmates. The physical education department within schools is a great venue for coaches to network. These teachers can recruit talented players for the program as well as speak to students about baseball team events.

Coaching Your Coaches

A head coach must be mindful of managing and providing clear roles and responsibilities for assistant coaches. By making copies of the daily practice plan and assigning coaching duties, assistants will be better prepared to succeed. During the pre-season, coaches can hand out a duties and responsibilities form to their assistants, which details expectations (Table 10-2). Head coaches must also lead the coaching staff as role models by dressing appropriately, arriving in a punctual manner for all team events, not cursing or using tobacco products, and displaying behavioral traits they deem important.

At the college and professional levels, field managers frequently have their assistant coaches run practice so that they can effectively observe baseball activities. Practices that are structured in this manner free up head coaches to study the finer points within the team, including player mechanics, attitude, and overall approach to the game. Such a practice format also enables head coaches to encourage their assistants to be more assertive and better prepares them to learn the role of head coach, which they may aspire to attain in the future. This practice arrangement also allows head coaches to provide assistant coaches with feedback on the strengths and weaknesses of their coaching methods. Regardless of the practice set-up before and after practices or games, head coaches should hold short meetings with their assistant coaches to review the goals for the day.

 Administrative Time-Out

Aside from organizing local coaching clinics within their community several times a year, many coaches attend professional clinics to observe clinicians speak about proper mechanics, effective drills, and other coaching ideas. These clinics provide an opportunity for assistant coaches to learn details regarding the specialty area that they teach daily. Given

---

Sample Assistant Coach Responsibilities/Duties Form

Junior Varsity Coach

Job Description

- To be responsible to the head coach only.
- To develop junior varsity players and get them ready to be called up to the varsity, if needed.
- To attend all coaches meetings.
- To work closely with the varsity coach on all program-wide planning.
- To attend and provide instruction at fall/winter baseball clinics.
- To attend/instruct early morning workouts in March from 6 a.m. to 7:30 a.m.
- To maintain the safety of players at all times.
- To obtain medical documentation that officially clears each player for athletic activity.
- To have knowledge and certification in CPR and first aid.
- To keep current with players' academic standing and eligibility.
- To maintain control and discipline of players (on the bus, field, etc.).
- To organize structured practice plans that focus on skills development.
- To foster a sense of good sportsmanship among team players.
- To ride with the team on the bus to all practices and games.
- To maintain strong parent-athlete relations (i.e., team dinners, fundraisers, etc.).
- To keep accurate statistics for each game and provide them to the varsity coach when needed.
- To arrange permits and scheduling for facility/field usage.
- To distribute and keep inventory of all team uniforms/equipment.
- To read and implement contents of the baseball program philosophy and guidelines.
- To make suggestions for the betterment of the program when necessary.

Table 10-2. Sample coaching responsibilities form

that most clinics will have speakers on various topics scheduled simultaneously, coaches should split up their staff to take notes on topics that apply to their coaching role. After the clinic, coaches may want to review their notes and share the information they gathered.

Conference Time

Head coaches need to be able to trust their assistant coaches. This trust extends to feeling confident that assistants will keep information and discussions about individual players confidential. Communications with parents and opposing coaches should be professional and appropriate. At higher levels, many assistant coaches are suspected of angling for the head coach's job. This suspicion can create tension and mistrust among the entire staff. One-on-one meetings with assistant coaches are beneficial to providing coaching feedback and establishing consistency throughout the program. Coaches must realize that assistant coaches are peers who may be sensitive to any constructive criticism that they provide.

Academics

Baseball coaches who work with players of varied ages should emphasize the importance of education as part of their program. Being part of a school team can motivate marginal, "at risk" students to apply themselves in the classroom. For younger players who may not see the value of academic performance, coaches should discuss eligibility issues that are prevalent at the high school and college level. Players and their families often overlook the fact that the term "student-athlete" refers to "student" first and "athlete" second. Furthermore, many coaches claim a strong correlation between students who perform well in the classroom and players who are enjoyable to coach. Skills such as *listening* to a coach, *concentrating* on a drill, and *thinking quickly* are strengths transferable to the classroom. At a minimum, educational achievement teaches discipline that players will find valuable as athletes and in their professional lives.

 Teaching Tip

Coaches can help players understand the impact of their academic performance by teaching about college baseball eligibility and scholarship monies directed toward high achieving students. Head coaches may assign an assistant coach to act as an academic overseer who distributes weekly progress reports for players' teachers to complete. Some coaches require that their players sit in the first few rows of every class and hold study sessions before practice. These sessions enable coaches and teammates to help players who are struggling in a particular class.

Nutrition and Lifestyle

Though most young people do not focus on their eating habits, coaches should review energy-producing food groups with players. Players usually eat lunch during their school day from 11:00 a.m. to noon, even though game competition does not occur until late afternoon. As a result, in the final innings of games around dusk when players must perform at the highest level, they commonly lack proper nutrition and energy. To compensate, some players will rely on Gatorade or an energy bar to get them through the competition. But, if coaches educate players on the types of foods that they should eat prior to athletic activity and how to effectively space meals throughout the day, then elevated energy levels will improve or enhance player performance.

Given that adolescents rarely handle the grocery shopping in households, coaches should discuss the importance of nutrition with parents. Handouts and suggestions for player eating habits are worthwhile resources to distribute. Coaches can access a wide array of informational texts and magazines that are devoted to nutrition for athletes. In devising a guideline for a well-balanced diet that includes each of the major food groups, coaches may design a structured plan that players may follow. The sample meals in Table 10-3 demonstrate how foods should be broken down by carbohydrates, fats, and proteins.[2]

	Meal One	Meal Two	Meal Three
Grain **Dairy** **Fruit/Vegetable** **Protein**	Bran cereal/oatmeal Low-fat milk Banana (Milk)	Corn muffin Yogurt Orange Peanut butter	Pizza crust Cheese Tomato sauce

Table 10-3. Sample daily meals

Aside from nutrition, coaches should advise players to lead a healthy lifestyle. Developing a seven to nine hour sleep schedule is essential. Breaking from a regular sleep pattern and staying up late at night will not only affect athletic performance the next day, but also the following day. Additionally, vitamins and proper hydration throughout the day are advocated by athletic performance trainers. Although young athletes will inevitably engage in various athletic activities, it is important that they have an opportunity to get adequate rest. Coaches can also discuss more risky activities, such as extreme games and motor sports that have a greater chance of leading to season-ending injuries. Hopefully, players will cherish the opportunity to be part of a unique baseball program, which will provide the self-motivation to live a healthy and more disciplined lifestyle.

Fundraising and Philanthropy

A challenging, yet necessary component within a baseball program is fundraising. A variety of methods can be used for raising money, which are largely based on the ages of the players involved. Selling raffle tickets, booster/bumper stickers, baseball bracelets, team hats, holding car washes, and other typical fundraising events will generate a base level of money. Several more lucrative methods include selling tickets to a dinner banquet with a guest professional player, organizing a baseball memorabilia auction, running local baseball clinics for elementary students, and playing a 40-inning game with players acquiring sponsorships for each inning of play. Regardless of which events are more applicable to the community or player age group, coaches should fundraise intermittently throughout the year and try various methods to determine which are the most successful.

Besides fundraising, some teams perform philanthropy and community outreach events. In these cases, a coach or player sometimes supports a particular cause that has personal relevance to their experiences. Charitable events focusing on breast cancer, diabetes, muscular dystrophy can be bonding experiences for players. Furthermore, these philanthropic activities make players think about life's challenging issues and the needs of others before their own. Teams may opt to center on more local issues, such as involvement with soup kitchens, Habitat for Humanity, homeless shelters, and other nearby organizations. Regardless of the humanitarian cause, gathering players to help the disadvantaged is a positive learning experience.

Guest Speakers

During the course of each season, coaches can organize a diverse group of guests to speak on various relevant topics. This event provides a change of pace from the weekly routine and also enables players to listen to experts in a particular field on issues central to their development. During the early season, prior to the first game, coaches should have an experienced umpire call pitches at a practice and speak to their team. This visit is an opportunity for players to hear about specific rules of emphasis, changes in rules, proper player demeanor, and pose any questions that they may have. Umpires usually enjoy visiting a team practice as it allows them to get their eye behind the plate several days before games. Additionally, it is a chance to teach the umpire's vantage point of baseball, which is not feasible within the context of game competition.

Coaches should also bring in a scout or coach from the next level of play. High school varsity head coaches, college coaches, and professional scouts or coaches are excellent candidates for guest speakers. Ideally, these coaches are not only experienced and full of interesting stories, but also possess a proven track record. Given that these individuals are coaches, they should be engaging and dynamic as public speakers. Their goal in speaking should be to inform players of what to expect and how to prepare for the next level. Inevitably, attitude, work ethic, and academics will be a significant part of their focus. While their talk may reiterate elements that coaches stress on a daily basis, it is important for players to hear about these issues from other, credible and objective sources.

High school guidance counselors are an excellent resource for coaches. These speakers can address eligibility standards at the high school level, while also discussing NCAA Clearinghouse requirements for college baseball. Counselors will be able to handle scholarship questions, especially regarding academic monies that colleges may be able to provide prospective student-athletes. By bringing academic advisers to practice, coaches are underlining the importance of academics in players' lives. Specifically, at the high school and college levels, coaches may establish a study skills counselor/adviser for players who are struggling in their classes and may risk eligibility.

Miscellaneous speakers can be recruited to meet with players based on the individual or group needs of the team. Table 10-4 displays a wide variety of guests that coaches may select to educate their players on a specific topic.

Teambuilding

Aside from fundraisers and charitable efforts, coaches can plan teambuilding activities outside of scheduled baseball events. During the early season after the team roster has been established, teams can travel on day or overnight camping trips, watch a Minor League Baseball game, play paint ball, or get involved in some other fun-filled activity. While away, coaches should design games and activities that foster positive team spirit. If these out of area trips

Guest Speaker	Topic(s) Discussed
High school guidance counselor	• Academic eligibility • NCAA Clearinghouse • Academic scholarships
Veteran umpire	• Rules changes • Rules of emphasis • On-field demeanor
Pro scout/college coach	• Expectations at next level • Recruiting process
Social worker/sports medicine doctor	• Steroid, substance, domestic abuse
Strength and conditioning coach	• Fitness training • Injury prevention
Baseball team alumni	• Lessons learned • Career opportunities
Summer baseball coach	• Summer baseball options

Table 10-4. Sample guest speaker program schedule

are not logistically feasible, local events are suitable alternatives. Attending high school basketball or hockey games as a team, especially if a baseball team member is participating, are excellent bonding experiences for players. Even though these efforts may seem extraneous or unnecessary, they play a pivotal role in strengthening player commitment and fulfillment as a member of the team. Wilderdom.com provides detailed instructions and offers kits for the teambuilding activities listed in Table 10-5 (http://wilderdom.com/games/InitiativeGames.html).[3]

Promoting Your Players

Although some people may not feel that it is a priority or responsibility, coaches should promote their players. Doing so will reflect positively on the program as players advance to the next level of play. For high school coaches, this promotion means contacting colleges or scouts to alert them about a player. While it is important for coaches to help their players in this capacity, they must also be honest, objective, and accurate in their evaluation of a player's ability; otherwise, they will lose credibility with a school or garner a reputation as an unreliable source for evaluating talent.

Coaches should encourage players to create a baseball profile, which is comprised of an athletic resume, letters of recommendation, a cover letter, and other materials such as a personalized action video or DVD. With YouTube® and other websites enabling users to upload their videos to the Internet, players can post footage of themselves online to attract college recruiters. Each of these profile components must be designed and composed in a professional manner to be effective. Ideally, high school coaches will familiarize their players with the recruiting process, NCAA academic requirements, and establishing realistic expectations for higher levels of play. It is important for players, not

Toxic Waste	A popular, engaging small-group activity. Equipped with a bungee cord and rope, a group must work out how to transport a bucket of "toxic waste" and tip it into the neutralization bucket. This exercise can be used to highlight almost any aspect of teamwork or leadership.
Mine Field	Objects are scattered in an indoor or outdoor place. In pairs, one person verbally guides a blindfolded partner through the minefield.
Keypunch	A powerful teambuilding exercise for medium sized groups. Participants must touch randomly placed numbers, in sequence, within a given time frame in multiple attempts.
Balloon Activities	Group activities that can be done with balloons. Promotes gentle, fun physical movement, people getting to know one another, trust, and working together.
Multi-Way Tug-of-War	Fun, physically demanding, competitive team activity. Several teams pull against each other, requiring communication and tactics as well as strength to outmaneuver and win.
All Aboard	A classic teambuilding activity in which a group is challenged to physically support one another in an endeavor to occupy diminishing space.
Survival Scenarios	"Your plane crashed. Your group needs to choose the 12 most useful items to survive."
Great Egg Drop	Small groups design an egg package to save an egg from breaking when dropped. Groups also create a 30-second jingle to sell their package. Followed by the "Great Egg Drop-Off."
Amoeba Race	A simple, close physical contact group cooperation activity. The group forms the three parts of an amoeba: protoplasm, cell wall, and nucleus. Then, the group travels, splits into two amoebas, and the amoeba have a race.
Zoom	A group tries to create a unified story from a set of sequential pictures. The pictures are randomly ordered and handed out. Each person has a picture but cannot show it to others. This activity requires patience, communication, and trying to understand from another's point of view in order to recreate the story's sequence.
Pipeline/ Gutter Ball	A fast-paced activity that can be modified to suit age and setting. Each participant gets one gutter or half pipe tubing. The object is to move a marble or assorted sized balls using lengths of guttering from point A to point B without dropping them.
Source: Wilderdom (http://wilderdom.com/games/InitiativeGames.html). License: Creative Commons Attribution 3.0 (http://creativecommons.org/licenses/by/3.0/).	

Table 10-5. Descriptions of teambuilding activities

parents, to be the active participants in the promotional process. Too frequently, parents are more passionate than their child for playing college sports, which overwhelms the athlete or turns him away from the opportunity.

Topic of Debate: College Showcases

To showcase their talents to college coaches, dozens of events are offered to high school players for exposure. These showcases can be expensive and difficult to judge in terms of credibility. Parents should establish a budget and register for showcases in the geographic vicinity of where the player is interested in applying to college. While large organizations, such as Perfect Game USA and TPX Top96 attract college coaches, players may focus on smaller, weekend showcases held by a college of interest or a nearby location where the college coach will be attending.

Should players join a local summer team or play travel baseball?

Players may have to choose between playing for their local community summer baseball team or a more selective, travel team. Even though travel baseball can provide more exposure and higher levels of competition, the time commitment and cost can be significant. Moreover, joining an elite summer team may limit playing time and opportunities to practice secondary positions. Players must consider whether the level of play and quality of coaching in the local area will enable them to improve as players. It is also important for coaches to establish a clear protocol for enabling players to practice/play games for a summer team before their spring season is fully completed.

Conference Time

When meeting with a player to discuss his baseball future, coaches should be mindful of the setting, their tone, and body language. Adolescents may be nervous in speaking face-to-face with an adult, especially when it involves their athletic capabilities. It is advantageous to maintain an optimistic and encouraging, yet realistic outlook for the player's chances of playing at the next level. The player should feel as though the coach is rooting for him and believes in his ability. Highlighting a player's work ethic, positive attitude, and innate skills are effective techniques.

Devising Motivational Speeches

Unlike football and basketball which are high emotion sports associated with inspirational coaching talks, baseball has a different vibe. Nonetheless, baseball coaches must be able to deliver an effective speech. Unlike a football team that comes out of a locker room pre-game speech charged up and ready to smash heads, baseball players should enter game action with a relaxed, focused demeanor. Therefore, baseball coaches' inspirational speeches can be geared to promote concentration, execution of rehearsed team plays, and reaching peak performance. These speeches should be given on practice days, on the bus to a game, or any venue where the team needs to be refocused.

Administrative Time-Out

Coaches can watch video of proven dynamic speakers to pinpoint techniques and traits that are worth emulating. Pat Riley, Martin Luther King, Jr., Vince Lombardi, Barack Obama, and other gifted speakers utilize a number of vocal devices and content arrangements that attract audiences. Various books and resources are available that will help coaches refine their speech writing skills and delivery techniques. Coaches can also hang up inspirational quotes on signs in the locker room or field bulletin boards that provide motivation for players. In some instances, a motivational film or speech may be needed to players rile up. Articles in a sports magazine or local paper about a person who overcame obstacles to achieve success can be distributed for all players to read.

In-Game Strategy: Mid-Game Speeches

Unlike other major sports, baseball does not have team time-outs and halftime periods to discuss the game. Baseball coaches can use the time in between innings as players come off the field to address their team. Between innings is also an opportune time to communicate with individual players. For the most part, speeches are not given during a game. Many coaches hold the view that game day is for the players to enjoy and shine. As a result, coaches should remain upbeat while reserving practice time for more firm and stern talks.

Observing Others

In developing a multi-pronged coaching framework, coaches should make an effort to watch other coaches in action. By attending a practice or studying game activity, coaches can learn a great deal from colleagues. Game day visits can be particularly valuable to a coach as the pre-game warm-up, infield/outfield routine, and in-game strategy are observable. Furthermore, visiting college teams' fields provides an opportunity to view what drills, workouts, and methods of communication take place at the next level. Coaches can email or call coaches before visiting their field so no misinterpretation regarding the visit is inferred. This visit is also a chance for coaches to network within the baseball community, which can benefit various aspects of their program.

Aside from attending clinics and watching coaches perform their craft on the field, reading baseball books, magazines, and watching DVDs are valuable resources for coaches. Many new drills, strategies, and teaching fundamentals are discovered through these materials. While an entire book or DVD is not always useful, it may include several worthwhile coaching points. It is important for coaches to stay current with contemporary training techniques. Even though baseball may not change rapidly, over time, learning new drills and strategies will help keep coaches excited to run their team.

Teaching Tip

When attending clinics or watching instructional DVDs, coaches should first pinpoint the needs of their team. By reflecting on the holes within coaching methods and drills, coaches can focus on which areas require immediate attention. Moreover, targeting the specific strengths/weaknesses of player personnel will also dictate how the teaching of certain fundamentals should change. For example, if a team has an underachieving pitching staff, then using coaching resources to bolster pitching mechanics and drills is necessary.

Implementing Alternative Approaches

As with many sports, baseball during the past few years has witnessed players experiment with a variety of nontraditional approaches for improving productivity. Mental imagery and positive visualization techniques are strategies that many athletes have found useful. Timothy Gallwey's timeless work *The Inner Game of Tennis* discusses how players can find the mental state that enables them to experience peak levels of performance. By quieting the mind, Gallwey claims, "A player is on his game, he's not thinking about how, when, or even where to hit the ball....The ball seems to get hit through an automatic process which doesn't require thought." [4]

In *Peak Performance*, Charles Garfield directs athletes to develop a rhythmic relaxation routine prior to competition. Baseball players can benefit from calming down in pressure situations and executing the "big" pitch, bunt, or defensive play. In developing athletic poise, Garfield describes the ability to "recognize and maintain a particular state of psychological readiness (a mental preparedness)." He further describes eight peak performance feelings that athletes exhibit when they are doing their tasks extraordinarily well: [5]

- Mentally relaxed
- Physically relaxed
- Confident and optimistic, with a positive outlook
- Focused on the present
- Highly energized
- Extraordinary awareness
- In control
- In the "cocoon" (insulated from anxiety/fear)

With the goal of improving breathing, flexibility, and balance, a number of players have enrolled in yoga, Pilates, and ballet classes. Several college coaches in various sports have urged their players to enroll in these courses to enhance muscular control, bodily relaxation, and core strength. As a result of these activities, many players describe attaining a positive mental state and report an increased protection from muscle tears.

In a 1975 study published in the *Journal of Sports Medicine*, the strenuous demands of ballet were ranked ahead of 60 other physical activities, including football. The *American Journal of Sports Medicine* in 2003 found that a diverse training regimen of Pilates, weight lifting, floor exercises, and swimming greatly reduced the occurrence of injuries. These cross-training activities along with a proper cool-down are essential components to an injury prevention routine.[6]

Building Personal Time

During a season, coaches sometimes overlook building in time for themselves. Thinking over lineups, practice plans, upcoming opponents, player issues, and other responsibilities take up all of their time. As a result, coaches must remember to build in time for family, friends, and other activities that get them away from the game. Exercise, in particular, is especially important in relieving stress, stimulating the mind, and keeping coaches fit as role models for their players. Many coaches visit the zoo, movies, or a local park as an escape from obsessive thoughts about their team.

Developing Perseverance

Throughout a season or string of seasons, coaches will inevitably endure tough losses, criticism from fans or parents, complaints from players, and the list goes on. While a coach's ability to be self-reflective and sensitive to flaws in his coaching style is important, he must also have a thick skin. Coaching can be a thankless and frustrating endeavor; therefore, riding out low points and trusting that better times eventually unfold is pivotal in surviving the difficult periods of coaching. In his book, *The Coaches*, Bill Libby describes the challenging role of the coach at the college level[7]:

> "He's called a coach, and it's a different job. There is no clear way to succeed. One cannot copy another who's a winner, for there seems to be some subtle secret chemistry of personality that enables a person to lead successfully and no one knows what it is really is….He is out in the open, being judged publicly for six or seven months out of the year by those who may or may not be qualified to judge him….He cannot satisfy everyone, seldom can he even satisfy very many, and rarely does he even satisfy himself. If he wins once, he must win the next time also. They plot victories, they suffer defeats; they endure criticism from within and from without; they neglect their families, they travel endlessly, and they live alone in the spotlight surrounded by others. Theirs may be the worst profession in the world. It's unreasonably demanding, poor pay, insecure, full of unrelenting pressures, and I ask myself: Why do coaches put up with it? Why do they do it?"

Becoming a Diversified Coach

Baseball coaches that run a comprehensive program perform a wide array of roles. As a marketing director, player psychologist, academic overseer, parent liaison, equipment manager, field maintenance supervisor, and fundraising executive, coaches are the CEO of their program. In some cases, coaches can delegate these various responsibilities to other staff members. Regardless, the effective functioning of these diverse program elements rests on their shoulders. Some of the personality traits and interests that a coach possesses may not mesh with certain tasks of running a program. Nonetheless, coaches must become more open-minded to new techniques and duties to successfully perform their role.

 Can a coach be successful without being diversified in his skill set?

Coaches can have a winning season and even win a championship without developing a diversified coaching foundation. Even so, players will not be provided with the optimal experience unless their coach possesses a multi-faceted vision. If winning is the sole priority of a coach, then he may feel he has attained success. Yet, if his players miss out on many aspects of the baseball experience that a well-rounded baseball program includes, he is not entirely successful.

In order to assess their effectiveness, coaches should continually reflect on their practices and game decisions. Baseball coaches cannot view their role as that of an administrator that writes a lineup and hands out baseballs. Sports, such as golf and tennis, where coaches have limited interaction with players on game day, are more of an administrative position. Baseball coaches are constantly interacting with and teaching players, especially on game day. Videotaping practices and games will help a coach learn a great deal about his players, coaches, and his own on-field actions. Table 10-6 is a self-evaluation test to assess coaching strengths, weaknesses, and skills that are or are not currently being implemented in a coaching system.

Upon completing the coaching self-assessment diagnostic, tabulate the areas of focus that are currently being utilized by you and your staff. Next, determine the elements of your coaching that are not emphasized or present at this time. For organizing this self-reflection exercise, refer to the *coaching skill set* categories of administrative, interpersonal, in-game strategy, and teaching skills as a guide (Table 10-7). Tabulate your score for the categories by looking at your ratings for each of the letters in the four columns. Add up your score for each column and check how it measures against the benchmark score for the category.

At this point, it should be evident which coaching elements you've incorporated in your system and skill set. In order to be a more diversified coach, use this diagnostic test to develop a sense of which of the four skill sets are being overlooked or neglected at this time. Perhaps certain personality traits play a role here. For example, if a person avoids potentially confrontational situations, then skill set II (Interpersonal) may be lacking. Likewise, if organizational duties are a weakness, then skill set I (Administrative) will have missing elements. Other factors may play a role, such as player commitment to the program, budget constraints, field availability, or personal circumstances. Nonetheless, these criteria should enable you to evaluate your current systems and make adjustments in order to become a well-rounded, more visionary leader for your program. As a competent and caring coach, be sure to have all your bases covered.

Coaching Self-Assessment Diagnostic Select the number (1-4) that best represents your implementation of coaching skill(s) 1 = Rarely, if ever 2 = Sometimes 3 = Frequently 4 = Always 5 = N/A (Not Applicable)	
Rating 1-4	**Coaching Skill/Responsibility/Technique**
	A. Creating (typed) detailed practice plans for assistant coaches and/or players to view before practice
	B. Communicating with players about how each practice drill or activity will specifically help the team win/play better
	C. Thoughtfully crafting a pre-game speech for motivating team before each game and/or designing a positive address after a difficult loss or successful victory
	D. Holding one-on-one conferences with each team member to discuss individual roles and build overall rapport with players
	E. Attending coaching clinics, reading articles, and viewing videos/DVDs dealing with skills, drills, and strategies for improving team performance
	F. Establishing clearly set team rules and consequences for players breaking rules; consistent enforcement of rules through disciplinary action
	G. Obtaining and reviewing scouting report of opponents at practice before game day
	H. Refining the skill of helping players (pitchers, hitters, etc.) get back on track; by using video analysis, confidence building, visualization, breathing, or other techniques
	I. Holding parent meeting(s) to discuss appropriate behavior at the field and proper communication with coaches
	J. Devising fundraising plans for monies needed for the baseball team/program
	K. Developing an objective system for evaluating talent, determining lineups, setting pitching rotation, making pitching changes, player substitutions, and in-game management; coinciding with accurate statistics and recordkeeping
	L. Monitoring player grades and overall academic/behavior in classes; following up with players and teachers on performance and eligibility issues
	M. Creating a strength training and conditioning program for in/out of season
	N. Holding meetings with assistant coaches and coaches at lower levels to maintain consistency of teaching skills and concepts throughout all program levels
	O. Ordering and keeping inventory of all team/program equipment
	P. Charting opposing hitters for batting tendencies on a spray chart, as well as other data (e.g., charting pitcher and hitter tendencies, speeds, etc.)
	Q. Setting a plan for media relations by players and coaching staff, including team website, communication with newspapers/television, etc.
	R. Teaching a field maintenance system for all players and coaches on team; individuals have understanding how to perform their duty
	S. Establishing a line of communication with coaches at next level of play (e.g., college, high school, summer travel teams, etc.) and helping place players in these programs with written recommendations and other criteria
	T. Developing team signals for offensive and defensive strategies that will be rehearsed in practice and executed successfully in game situations
	U. Planning a trip to work on teambuilding activities, humanitarian efforts (food drive, Habitat for Humanity, etc..), or some bonding experience
	V. Analyzing the positives and negatives of team performance in game(s) and reviewing the details with the players for improvement in future games
	W. Building relationships with umpires and opposing coaches so as to network within the baseball community
	X. Maintain personal physique for carrying out active aspects of coaching (hitting fungos, throwing batting practice, etc.) and looking the part of a coach; dressing in a professional manner for practice and games
	Y. Keeping up to date on CPR/first aid certification and being prepared to respond effectively in an emergency situation
	Z. Implementing a signal or verbal system for positioning and communicating with defensive players (for example, moving an outfielder in 10 feet)

Table 10-6. Coaching self-assessment diagnostic exam

Coaching Skill Set			
Administrative Benchmark = 25	**Interpersonal** Benchmark = 30	**In-Game Strategy** Benchmark = 25	**Teaching Skills** Benchmark = 27
A F I J L N O Q R Y	C D F H I X L N Q S U W	B C E G H K P T V Z	A B E H M N Q R T U V

Note: Letters correspond to Coaching Self-Assessment Diagnostic (Table 10-6).

Table 10-7. Coaching self-assessment scoring guide

Sources/Further Reading

[1]Dickson, P. (1992). *Baseball's Greatest Quotations*. New York: Harper Perennial. P. 59.

[2]Clark, N. (1990). *Sports Nutrition Guidebook*. Champaign, IL: Leisure Press. P. 23.

[3]The Wilderdom Store: Gear for Adventurous Learning; www.wilderdom.com. December 12, 2009.

[4]Gallwey, T. (1974). *The Inner Game of Tennis*. New York: Bantam Books. P. 21.

[5]Garfield, C. (1984). *Peak Performance*. New York: Warner Books. Pp. 158-160.

[6]Heffley, L. (2006). "Relief in a World of Hurt." *Los Angeles Times*. April 23, 2006.

[7]Libby, B. (1972). *The Coaches*. Chicago, IL: Regnery.

Westrum, Wes, 8
wheel play, 130, 132, 223-224
Wiffle ball drills, 84-85
Wilcox, F.B., 93
wild pitches, 189-190
Williams, Ted, 66, 67, 83-84, 85, 88
Wills, Maury, 123
Windup, 29, 110
Winfield, Dave, 64
work down, 49
wrap the bat, 69
wrapping the ball, 28

Z drill, 171
Zingbat, 84

Darren Gurney has been coaching baseball at the collegiate and high school level since 1992. Since receiving his first coaching position, Gurney has coached over 20 players who were selected in the MLB Draft or who have gone on to play professional baseball.

Gurney was the field manager for the Metro New York Cadets (ACBL) from 2005 through 2007. The Cadets was a team comprised of premier college baseball players from top Division I baseball programs, including Vanderbilt, St. John's, Fordham, Stonybrook, Florida State, Yale, Princeton, and more. Gurney was named field manager for the 2006 ACBL All-Star Game in Lafayette, Pennsylvania.

Gurney was an assistant coach at Iona College from 2005 through 2007. His responsibilities included coaching first base and working with outfielders, catchers, and base runners. In addition, Gurney compiled practice plans, scouting of opponents, statistical analysis, and handled the recruiting of high school and junior college players.

Gurney is the founder and director of a college preparatory baseball program for players ages 17-18 at Ultimate College Prep. UCP's comprehensive workouts help market and prepare players for the college baseball experience.

During his tenure as head varsity coach at New Rochelle High School (1997-2005), Gurney compiled a 124-67 record and captured league titles in 2000, 2004, and 2005. In addition, he was voted Section 1 Coach of the Year in 2001 and League Coach of the Year in 1999, 2001, and 2004.

As director of Rising Star Baseball Camp, the largest baseball camp in Westchester County, Gurney develops the daily curriculum, staffing, and player evaluation criteria for campers ages 7 to 15.

Gurney is the chief video analyst for the progressive, online base[ball] instruction website: TheBaseballDoctor.com. By providing mechanical an[d] and feedback through Internet-based instruction, he has assisted a[thletes] around the world.

As a four-year varsity letterman at Washington University, Gurney [compiled] a .389 batting average and a .542 on-base percentage in conferen[ce] competition. He realized his dream when he was signed by the [(Austria) of the European Professional Baseball League in March continued his career for the next 11 years with the Pleasantville [centerfielder and was inducted into the Hall of Fame in November

Gurney is recognized among the elite economics instructors in t[In 2004, he was selected by NASDAQ as one of the top 10 educators in the USA. For the past three years, his students have sc[the highest percentile in the US on the annual AP Macroeconomi[received his B.A. in history from Washington University and his Mas[studies education from Teachers College at Columbia University in

Gurney resides in Westchester County, New York, with his w[his son, Nolan.